Headquarters-subsidiary relationship governance in emerging markets of Central Eastern Europe

A study in Poland

J.S. Hendriks-Guść

Promotor:

Prof. dr. S.W.F. Omta
Hoogleraar Bedrijfskunde
Wageningen Universiteit

Co-promotor:

Dr. H.J. Bremmers
Universitair Hoofddocent, Leerstoelgroep Bedrijfskunde
Wageningen Universiteit

Promotiecommissie:

Prof. dr. W.J.M. Heijman (Wageningen Universiteit)
Prof. dr. J.P. Bahlmann (Universiteit Utrecht)
Prof. dr. T. Elfring (Vrije Universiteit Amsterdam)
Prof. dr. E. Majewski (Agricultural University Warsaw)

Dit onderzoek is uitgevoerd binnen de onderzoekschool
Mansholt Graduate School of Social Sciences

Headquarters-subsidiary relationship governance in emerging markets of Central Eastern Europe

A study in Poland

Joanna Sylwia Hendriks-Guść

Proefschrift
ter verkrijging van de graad van doctor
op gezag van de rector magnificus
van Wageningen Universiteit,
Prof. dr. M.J. Kropff,
in het openbaar te verdedigen
op maandag 8 oktober 2007
des namiddags te vier uur in de Aula

Hendriks-Guść, J.S. (2007), Headquarters-subsidiary relationship governance in emerging markets of Central Eastern Europe. A study in Poland

Ph.D. Thesis, Wageningen University
With references and summaries in English and Dutch

ISBN: 978-90-8504-758-2
ISBN: 978-90-8686-049-4

Table of contents

Acknowledgements

'(...)Your life is going to change, in some very important ways. So is the life of everyone else. All of life is changing, everywhere on the planet. You cannot have missed this. It is happening on every level: political, geophysical, economical, theological, psychological and philosophical. And with understanding the meaning of Life, without holding the key to the Universe, without possessing the Tools with which to fashion your dreams you likely be at the effect of all these changes, rather than the cause of them.(...)'

Neale Donald Walsch, 1995

I strongly believe that my life is an outcome of a creation process. That is why I always search for new challenges. Stepping into the scientific world from business was a big change, sometimes hard, but certainly extremely fruitful. The result is this thesis and lots of knowledge, skills and experiences. By doing research on the management of the multinational enterprises I tried to developed instruments that would allow managers to improve the organisation of their international operations.

Doing a PhD research is basically a management process involving many actors. This thesis would have never been accomplished without the help of many people and without an environment that constantly provided me with new and challenging opportunities. I vividly remember the first meeting I had a few years ago at Wageningen University with Paul van Beek and Onno Omta, who decided to give me a challenge and appointed me on this project.

Onno Omta together with Harry Bremmers became my thesis advisors, I am grateful for their patience and knowledge in guiding me through the world of science and shaping me towards an independent researcher. I would like to thank the members of Business Administration Group for their support in development of ideas, solving methodological issues and critical discussions during the group presentations.

The data collection process for this thesis was supported by Netherlands Organisation for Scientific Research (NWO) and was conducted in cooperation with the Centre for Economic Information (CIG) in Warsaw and the Faculty of Agricultural Economics at Warsaw Agricultural University in Poland. I would like to thank Professor Wojciech Ziętara, Sławek Jarka and Michał Pietrzak for their support and organizing my stay at the University as well as the secretaries of the group who patiently collected my survey mails.

My appreciation goes to companies participating in the research for their willingness to share their information with me, as well as to the Mandersloot family for their active participation in the pilot study.

During my project I always enjoyed working with students on their Master theses. My special appreciation goes to Joanna Żuraw, Gautier Mulliez and Wieteke Kamps, whose projects' imprints are present in this thesis.

Dziękuję mojej rodzinie za stawianie mojego doktoratu w perspektywie życia i nieustanną wiarę w moje możliwości.

My friends: Ada, Ewa, Christa, Marysia, Iman and Mark; thank you for releasing the stress and showing me the pleasures of life. Finally, Joanna and Elena, next to your friendship, thank you for solving the technical bottlenecks of finishing my Ph.D.

Finally, I dedicate this work to my love – Henk. We have found each other so far away, but it feels like we have never existed without one another.

Joanna Hendriks-Guść

Scherpenzeel, August 2007

Chapter 1. Introduction

'Whenever an individual or a business decides that success has been attained, progress stops

Thomas J. Watson Jr

Since the expansion of the EU by ten Central Eastern European Countries (CEECs) in 2004, it has become more attractive for Western multinational enterprises (MNEs) to invest in the emerging economies of e.g. Poland, Hungary, Slovenia and the Czech Republic. Emerging economies are characterized by a (relatively) low income, rapid growth, and they use economic liberalization as their primary engine of growth (Hoskisson *et al.*, 2000). The opening of markets in these countries, cheap labour, the availability of raw materials and not forgetting a favourable geographical location are stimulating factors for multinationals to invest and expand towards Central Eastern Europe. However, multinational expansion is a challenging move for enterprises and their management, since it calls for the exploration and comprehension of new environments to overcome the liability of foreignness (Andersen, 1993). The liability of foreignness, caused by environmental and political turbulence, requires special arrangements: reviewing existing corporate strategies and a redesign of governance mechanisms. In the present study, we explore these governance challenges in one of the emerging economies of Central Eastern Europe, namely Poland. We will elaborate on the MNE expansion in CEECs in general, and in Poland in particular in Section 1.2.

Many companies think that once they have entered a new market the most difficult task is behind them, but that is the moment when the real task begins! Many questions need to be asked, such as how adequate the management processes for the new foreign operations are. What are the managerial implications of the entry into a new market for the MNE as a whole? How is it possible to avoid information chaos and still have a real-time view on the actual status of the different foreign outlets? How to maintain control over subsidiary operations while at the same time not de-motivating its managers? How should the power be distributed between headquarters and its subsidiary? Can cultural differences hamper the management process and in what way? And finally, how should a company react to changing pressures in the business environment?

Not answering these questions, in the pre-entry stage or in due course, will most likely lead to unfavourable organisational outcomes and financial distress. The whole MNE might even be in danger, if a foreign subsidiary is ill-governed. Recent research by Gomez and Werner (2004) provided evidence for the importance of well-structured and organised governance for the performance and sustainable development of the whole MNE, not only the subsidiary itself. Management of foreign outlets not only includes setting up production processes, marketing and logistics, but also information processing, and again, last but not least, governance mechanisms.

By governance mechanisms we mean: the provision and application of instruments to keep companies within the boundaries of a strategy. In this way, the governance mechanisms spell out the rules and procedures for making decisions. They also provide the structure upon which the company objectives are set especially with regard to MNEs' foreign operations, as well as the means of attaining and monitoring MNEs' and subsidiaries' performances. These governance mechanisms are applied to the relationship between headquarters (HQ) and their subsidiaries (S). In fact, the quality of the governance of the HQ-S relationship, measured as the effectiveness and efficiency, is a key success factor for foreign entries. Our research explores some of the intriguing questions we have put forward above. It attempts to give an answer on how to design effective governance mechanisms of the relationship between an investing company – headquarters (HQ) and the receiver of the investment – the subsidiary (S).

Managerial efforts in this respect serve three goals:
- first, bridging the gap between the developed economy of the headquarters' country and the emerging economy of a subsidiary;
- second, developing instruments to cope with turbulence and dynamism;
- finally, pursuing strategy choices.

Managerial efforts to bridge the gap...

The 'gap' we refer to is not only economic (the lagging-behind of the subsidiary economy), but also cultural and relational. For example, in Poland, the over 50-year-old communist regime, which did not allow any transparency, left an imprint not only on the economy but also on people's mentality, which manifested in a tendency to withdraw from decision making, and the habit of collective sharing of responsibilities inhibiting individual initiatives (Mikułowski-Pomorski 2001). The bureaucratic communist system left little space for developing reliable long-term relationships between business actors. The 'static and atomistic mindset' of managers makes bridging the gap between two cultures of key importance to business success. Furthermore, weak property rights' protection and a lack of incentives inherited from communist times (especially from the 70s, through to the beginning of the 90's) caused a stagnation of research and development activities. This was also the main cause of out-dated technology in production, especially in the early stage of the transformations (Borsos-Torstila, 1997). Next to these economic and societal factors, cultural specificities are of key importance for understanding business relationships; and these differences may seriously hamper business performance, as Hofstede (2001) argued. For the economic exchange to take place, a solid foundation of interpersonal understanding and meaningfulness has to be built.

Managerial efforts to cope with turbulence and dynamism...

The transitional character of the CEE markets requires special managerial attention to the environmental forces, during and after the MNE expansion into such a country (Luo and Peng, 1999). McCarthy *et al.* (1993) found that MNEs often seem to be on a 'roller coaster' in these economies, because of the fast changes in the business and political environment. Extreme examples of environmental turbulence are the evacuation of most expatriate personnel in the aftermath of the Tiananmen Square incident in China in 1989, and the panic surrounding the violent coup in Russia in 1991 and 1993 and the Russian economic crisis in 1999. MNEs investing in turbulent markets experience business failures, caused by the high speed of environmental (including institutional) changes and/or the insufficient reliability of local stakeholders. Sometimes their investments quickly end in divestments or buy-outs. There are examples of investors in Poland, who made quick profits from privatising by buying out de-organized formerly state-owned factories or leading 'old' brands during the early state of transformation. A continuously increasing flow of foreign investment to Poland during 1998-2000 contributed to the fact that foreign investors formed the largest group participating in the privatisation of state-owned companies and their share kept growing (e.g. from 19.8% in 1998 to 26.1% in 2001)[1]. In many cases, long-term relationships with subsidiaries were not established. However, there are many examples of investors who managed to cope with the turbulence, especially those with a strategic character in which an investor planned for long-term growth in the market and fostered the relationship with a subsidiary helping to enhance smooth cooperation. In those cases, short-term business failures did not cause investors to withdraw. From the macro perspective, those direct investments were extremely important as they provided mutual profits to both the investor and investment country economy (see more in Section 2.1.2), especially in the case of Greenfield investments which contributed to job creation and infrastructure development. These investments accelerated the transformation from a transition to an emerging economy in Poland.

Pursuing strategy choices...

MNEs investing in CEECs are like any other MNEs in the world, subject to changing pressures in the global economy which makes them rethink their once-developed worldwide strategic approaches. Although traditionally the investments in CEECs were low-cost driven and subsidiaries were only pipelines for implementing HQ orders, nowadays MNEs face much more (often extrapolated) pressures. Therefore, choosing between worldwide standardisation of production (i.e. application of a global strategy) or serving selected multidomestic markets (i.e. application of a multidomestic strategy), or combining elements of both strategies need to be taken into consideration in order to create sustainable profitability of the overall MNE.

1.1 Research area

In general, most research up till now has focused on the exploration of the incentives and factors influencing the entry-mode decision (Anderson and Gatignon, 1986; Agarwal and Ramaswami, 1992; Bell, 1996; Harzing, 2002; Luo, 2002; Werner, 2002; Luo, 2004; Slangen, 2005), and has not included the development of the management processes for subsidiaries.

---

[1] R. Woodward and P. Kozarzewski, 2002, 'Economic efficiency and changes in the ownership structures in enterprises in Poland', publication in Polish language on www.case.com.pl

In fact, just after the entry many MNEs found out that a properly prepared and executed entry into the market did not guarantee the success of the foreign operations. This makes research into the best methods for developing and fostering the governance relationships with the newly set-up or acquired subsidiaries even more important. For that we may expect that MNEs which succeed in creating sustainable relationships with their subsidiaries acquire a stronger competitive position for the whole company in the international markets. Moreover, in the Central Eastern European Countries the study on the multinational companies has been complicated, mostly due to the lack of well-developed structures for sharing information. Therefore, *this research takes the governance of the relationship between headquarters (HQ) and subsidiary (S) in the CEEC as the main study subject.*

Governance serves as a framework for interchanges and relationships, including mobilization of investments, information transfer and most importantly by management itself (Chandler and Mazlish, 2005). In the present study, it is spanned between two companies; headquarters and subsidiary. The dual influence of HQ and S organisational characteristics and the cultural peculiarities both companies have to cope with, add to the governance complexity. Two elements of governance are centrally addressed in the present study: control related to 'power exertion' and coordination focused on 'joint actions' studied respectively from agency and stewardship perspective (see Sections 3.2.2 and 3.2.3 for further explanations). These two elements will form the core dimensions of the governance mechanisms in the HQ-S relationship.

With respect to the distribution of power, McDonald's Chief Executive Officer (CEO) Jim Skinner said in an interview in 2005 on the 50th anniversary of McDonald's Corporation '(...) *the clue of a good life is a balance*'. These words apply to the cross-border governance of MNEs as well. 'Finding a balance' implies empowering a subsidiary and at the same time controlling certain functions to gather essential information about the conditions and processes of foreign operations. For instance, smart integrated planning can reduce total costs by streamlining logistics, and joint marketing campaigns may provide scale economies. Information exchange safeguards against negative surprises and a potential deterioration of a company's reliability when something goes wrong, but may at the same time create a constant feeling of 'being watched'. Malfunctioning information exchange can have dysfunctional effects. The Dutch MNE Ahold, for instance, had a 'hard time' in 2003[2] when the company's annual results were published, showing the consequences of bad information exchange and control over its subsidiaries. In the Ahold case, insufficient information and superficial control of operations in South America, as well as problems with the management of the American US Food Service led to a serious decrease of more than 70%[3] in shareholder value and toppled all values of the related companies on the Amsterdam Stock Exchange in 2003 (9% decrease of AEX-index in

---

[2] More to read in: Smit, J. (2004). Het drama Ahold. Amsterdam, Balans

[3] Source: de Volkskrant, 23.02.2003

two days)[4]. Perhaps this crisis could have been avoided if Ahold had imposed a higher quality governance relationship with its subsidiaries.

1.2 Multinational expansion into CEEC

Multinational expansion into CEECs is a relatively new phenomenon. It developed after a political revolution took place in Poland. The present study focuses on HQ-S relationship governance in Poland. This country's changed political circumstances and a high market potential have created new business opportunities for western companies. With the fall of the Berlin Wall in 1989, most CEECs began a process of establishing democratic governments and market-driven economies. The European Union's strategy of integrating the CEE economies into the Western sphere gave rise to a gradual process of accession. In 1993, the European Council agreed that CEECs with an established association with the European Union (EU) could become members if they demonstrated their ability to meet the political and economic obligations of EU membership. For CEECs, the principal tool of economic renewal was the trade liberalization protocols and the fulfilment of the broader objectives of market reform required for EU membership, which was laid down in the White Paper of the European Commission. As a result of these arrangements, the European Union was enlarged by ten countries in May 2004. Poland was included in the first wave of this EU expansion. Poland's EU membership secured the transformation path towards economic openness and trade liberalization, which in effect attracted many investors from all over the world. Between the years 1992-2004, the investment inflows to Poland showed continuous growth, reaching a value of US$ 84.5 billion in December 2004. This massive inflow of investment contributed to fast economic growth. Indirectly, it enhanced the development of environmental care and improved social living standards.

1.3 Research aim and research questions

Research on the factors that influence the headquarters governance of its subsidiaries in international ventures is a relatively new phenomenon. Although the research on MNEs and their structures and management mechanisms is becoming more popular, only a few studies in international business research explore and describe the characteristics of the relationship between headquarters and their subsidiaries (Doz and Prahalad, 1984; Gates and Egelhoff, 1986; Nohria and Ghoshal, 1994; Rodrigues, 1995; O'Donnell, 2000; Harzing *et al.*, 2001; Harzing, 2002; Gomez and Werner, 2004; Andersson *et al.*, 2005). None of these studies covers CEE countries. Moreover, little is known about the design of the HQ-S governance that would successfully assist in managing complex and competing forces from the external environment (Chenhall, 2003). Consequently, there is a lack of knowledge about the mechanisms and factors that contribute to successful HQ-S relationship governance.

---

[4] Source: de Volkskrant, 26.02.2003

This research aims at understanding the factors that determine successful HQ-S governance mechanisms in Poland. Furthermore, from a practical standpoint, it aims at facilitating the governance of newly established subsidiaries in Central Eastern Europe with a special emphasis on Poland. We expect to explain the differences in the governance mechanisms. In doing so, we hope to contribute to a further understanding of the management challenges of the HQ-S relationship. Ultimately, a positive effect on the profitability and continuity of the MNEs and their subsidiaries is expected. Therefore, we will answer the following research question:

1. *What are the characteristics of the different HQ-S governance mechanisms used by international headquarters in relation to their Polish subsidiaries?*

The dimensions of the HQ-S governance we investigate are coordination and control. Coordination refers to the bilateral horizontal relationships between headquarters and subsidiary managers, the day-to-day company-to-company links which guarantee concerted action and alignment. Control refers to the vertical relationship between the two and to the execution of power (by means of directives and procedures, prescribed information exchange, etc.), which guarantees that the HQ adheres to the overall company goals, policy and processes.

The HQ-S governance is not an independent stand-alone concept but is embedded in the specific business environment of the Polish subsidiary. This environment has a transitional/emerging character and at the same time is part of a large European environment. It is interesting to explore which of the environmental aspects influences the HQ-S governance and how companies deal with these aspects. Therefore, the second research question is:

2. *What is the impact of the Polish business environment on the HQ-S governance mechanisms?*

The way MNEs deal with their external environment is included in the MNEs' strategy. One may expect, for instance, that an MNE establishes a subsidiary in order to produce for the local market exclusively, and then focuses less on winning economies of scale than an MNE investing in a subsidiary for their worldwide production and focusing on serving the global market. This competing strategy is called: global. A third strategy focuses on a combination of global efficiency and multidomestic responsiveness. For each of these three strategies, HQ-S governance may have a different function. For example, a company conducting a strategy with a focus on the local market may give more freedom to the subsidiary, whereas a firm pursuing a global strategy may put strong focus on cost and time efficiencies. Therefore, the third research question arises:

3. *What is the influence of the strategic choices of MNEs on the HQ-S governance mechanisms?*

And finally, once we have determined what factors have an impact on the HQ-S governance, we will establish their relative impact on the organisational outcomes:

4. What is the impact of the different governance mechanisms on the MNE's performance?

In our study, performance includes not only factors related to profitability, but also factors which have a positive impact on the long-term continuity of a company, such as market share, strategic position, consumer satisfaction, etc.

1.4 Theoretical framework and research design

The research questions will be dealt with in three steps: model design, testing and evaluating the results. First, we develop a theoretical framework for describing the HQ-S relationship governance. This theoretical framework rests on 3 pillars:
* agency theory;
* stewardship theory;
* contingency theory.

Agency theory is considered appropriate to situations that have a principal-agent structure. Specifically, the HQ-S relationship governance in MNEs can be considered as such a principal-agent structure, as the headquarters delegates decision-making authority and responsibility to its foreign subsidiaries (Gupta and Govindarajan, 1991; Nohria and Ghoshal, 1994). Behavioural constraints and incentives based on obedience, as well as rewards for fulfilling the principal's goals constitute the basic propositions of the agency theory (Jensen and Meckling, 1976). The linkage between a headquarters and a foreign subsidiary can be appropriately compared to the agency relationships between principal and agent in that the parent company invests funds and resources in the subsidiaries, and the subsidiaries, in turn, are expected to work for the benefit of the parent headquarters (Chang and Taylor, 1999). Although agency costs in MNEs have not been specifically defined, they might include any subsidiary decision undertaken to promote its own interests at the expense of headquarters interests. For reducing the risk of self-serving behaviour by a subsidiary (behaviour that is not in the interests of the principal), agency theory suggests monitoring results and increasing information exchange about the agent's (subsidiary) behaviour (O'Donnell, 2000). In the MNE context, monitoring can be defined as activities or mechanisms used by headquarters to obtain information about the behaviour and decisions of the subsidiary management. The most direct form of monitoring is personal supervision of managers (Ouchi, 1979; Eisenhardt, 1989). However, in the case of MNEs, the absence of proximity makes it difficult for the headquarters to directly supervise the subsidiary's management behaviour. Using expatriates for this purpose has drawbacks and is very expensive (Egelhoff, 1984). Thus, it is likely that mechanisms other than direct supervision will be used to monitor subsidiary management, such as bureaucratic instruments: rules, programs and procedures (Galbraith, 1976). Through monitoring devices headquarters increases the amount of information regarding the actions of the subsidiary management, thus limiting subsidiary-level behaviour that is not congruent with the headquarters' expectations. From agency theory we learn that information processing, incentive schemes and formalisation are key devices for controlling the actions of agents.

Stewardship theory originates from psychology and sociology and stands in contrast to the view of human behaviour that underlies agency theory (Donaldson, 1990; Davis *et al.,* 1997). It postulates that basically there is an alignment of the interests of equity holders and managers (HQ and subsidiaries). Stewardship theory emphasises that pro-organisational and collectivistic behaviour has a higher utility than individualistic, self-serving behaviour (Davis *et al.,* 1997: 24). Here the governance mechanisms based on social interaction and interdependence instead of relying on power or authority, are important in fast-changing environments. Lateral relations that cross the formal lines of the MNE-joint teams, task forces, committees, individual integrators and integrative departments, informal communication channels, informal relations among HQ-managers and subsidiary managers, are important for coping with fast-changing business environments and consumer demands (Martinez and Jarillo, 1989). Stewardship theory can help explain the emergence of the new cross-departmental, informal and subtle mechanisms aimed at building network relationships between the units of MNE to cope with complex environmental conditions. Business relationships are often dependent on social contacts, informality, mutual non-formalised interests, and understanding (Granovetter, 1985). Such relationships between HQ and subsidiaries can also have an important function in bridging the cultural and geographical gap.

Finally, the third pillar of our study includes the contingency theory, which allows for placing the HQ-S governance in an environmental and strategic context.

Contingency Theory was introduced by Lawrence and Lorsch (1967) who pointed at the need for multivariate studies about organisational behaviour. The Contingency model of MNE-organisation relates managerial decision making to a number of constraints. These constraints include: the size of the organisation, how it adapts to its business environment, resources and operations, managerial assumptions about employees, strategies and technologies (Burton and Obel, 2004). The theory is 'contingent" in the sense that it views the functioning of organisations under different conditions, especially the dynamics of business environment. The outside contingencies, i.e. the environment, can be treated as both constraints and opportunities which influence the organisation's internal structures and processes (Lawrence and Lorsch, 1967: 187). In the dynamic contingency theory, flexibility is considered as an organisational potential for maintaining a dynamic fit between the organisation and its environment (Volberda, 1992). A major point in Contingency Theory is that different *external* conditions might require different organisational specifics and behavioural patterns *within* the organisation (Donaldson, 1990).

For the management of MNEs, an integrative contingent approach was proposed by Bartlett and Goshal (1987). They observed that companies with governance mechanisms for competing in either local or global markets experience difficulties in seizing full market capacity or fail to notice emerging market opportunities. A new strategic option for MNEs proposed by Bartlett and Goshal emphasises the importance of the influence of and organisational adjustment to the external environment to simultaneously combine global scale economies and seize local opportunities. The proposed differentiation in the response towards the modalities of a dynamic environment has been included in the contingency view of the organisation's strategy and organisation (Burt *et al.*, 2002; Chenhall, 2003). The present study integrates the three different theoretical viewpoints in a conceptual model for describing and explaining HQ-S relationship governance.

Having developed a theoretical framework, we will collect empirical data by means of a survey research. We will obtain the data by a mail questionnaire in one investment country (Poland) and include a large number of investor countries spread over different cultural clusters. We will complement the data on the investor's company with secondary data sources. To check our results, we will perform multiple in-depth interviews on investor companies in France and in the Netherlands. Then, the conceptual model will be tested empirically. We will adopt a comprehensive perspective by focusing on a broad range of elements in the HQ-S relationship governance, including both parties involved, as well as the environmental context. As a final step, we will present our results, conclusions and formulate managerial recommendations.

1.5 Structure of the thesis

The structure of the thesis is as follows. Firstly, in Chapter 2, we describe the study domain in detail. For a better understanding of the context and origin of the research questions, we briefly present the processes laying at the genesis of the HQ-S governance – that is, the investment flows. It is important to show that our research questions are going to be answered for a specific kind of investment – Foreign Direct Investments (FDIs). The main characteristic of FDIs is that they are performed on a long-term basis. We explain the important contribution of those investments in accelerating the transition process and upgrading both local businesses as well as the local economy, specifically of countries in the CEE region. We take one CEE country – Poland – for an in-depth analysis of these contributions. The reason for choosing Poland is its pioneering role in the political and economic transformations in Central Eastern European and because of the enormous opportunities for MNEs to develop their activities in this country. We complete Chapter 2 with an attempt at forecasting further developments in the Polish economy after the EU accession, as well as pointing out the most important issues on the economic agenda. Secondly, in Chapter 3, we deepen our understanding of the theoretical building blocks by paying extensive attention to the dimensions of the HQ-S relationship governance. We present different theoretical approaches in MNE research and propose a theoretical framework for addressing governance problems in multinational enterprises (MNEs). Chapter 4 presents a logical extension of the previous chapter and illustrates the conceptual framework, operationalisation of the concepts and the description of expected relationships. It includes the theoretical underpinning of the propositions. Next in Chapter 5, the survey and in-depth interview research design are described, together with the study population characteristics and the methods of data analyses. Chapter 6 presents survey results and the data analysis including the concepts' validity and reliability as well as the testing of propositions. Survey data are acquired from 76 questionnaires from Polish manufacturing subsidiaries with foreign capital participation. This chapter begins with the general description of subsidiary and headquarters in the sample. Then it shows interesting bivariate relationships between environment, strategy and governance variables. Finally, these relationships are placed in a conceptual model and simultaneously tested for their significance using the multivariate technique Partial Least Squares (PLS). The findings from Chapter 6 are further elaborated on in Chapter 7, in which the results of the multiple in-depth interviews with headquarters are presented. Finally, in Chapter 8, we draw the conclusions of this study, elaborate on the answers to our research questions, and propose managerial implications and directions for future research.

Chapter 2. Study domain

In this chapter we will elaborate on the study domain that is covered by this thesis. Chapter 2 includes two parts: first we focus on the Foreign Direct Investments (FDIs), which lay at the origin of HQ-S relationships. The second part of this chapter focuses on the actual investment flows.

Section 2.1 describes the emergence of the HQ-S relationship based on FDI multinational expansion. In Section 2.1.1 different entries of FDI streams are presented. Through FDI-flows multinational enterprises (MNEs) have an impact on host and home economies. Some of the possible positive and negative effects of these influences will be described in Section 2.1.2. In the second part of this chapter, we include a general description of worldwide FDI flows in the last decade (Section 2.2) and we shed light on the FDIs to the CEE region (Section 2.3). This is particularly interesting because of the transition stage these countries are in and because of their booming economies. In this part we compare the expected development in the group of CEE countries that joined the EU in 2004 with the long-term developments in Spain, which joined the EU in 1986 (Section 2.3.1). Finally, in Section 2.4 we pay special attention to the transformation processes and FDI flows to Poland.

2.1 FDI at the genesis of Headquarters-Subsidiary (HQ-S) relationship

The central issue addressed in the present study is the governance of the relationship between two companies, in which as a result of an investment flow, one company (headquarters) partially or wholly owns the other (subsidiary), located in a different country.

There are two basic types of international investment flows: foreign direct investments (FDIs) and portfolio investments. Portfolio investments represent passive holdings of foreign stock or of other financial assets, none of which entail active management or control by the securities issued by the investor (Dickinson, 1971). Our study focuses on international investments with a managerial impact, so-called foreign direct investments (FDIs). Management influence is prominently present in the OECD benchmark definition of FDI formulated in 1983, which still represents the most complete delineation of the concept:

> 'FDI reflects the objective of obtaining a lasting interest by a resident entity in one economy ('direct investor') in an entity resident in an economy other than that of the investor ('direct investment enterprise'). The lasting interest implies the existence of a long-term relationship between the direct investor and the enterprise and a significant degree of influence on the management of the enterprise. Direct investment involves both the initial transaction

between the two entities and all subsequent capital transactions between them and among affiliated enterprises, both incorporated and unincorporated'

(OECD, 1996).

As a result of managerial and control inputs as well as the ability to influence management decisions, foreign direct investments are often called entrepreneurial investments (Maffry, 1954). FDIs usually have a more long-term perspective as compared to portfolio investments. Table 2.1 summarises the similarities and differences between these two kinds of investments.

In a portfolio investment, financial investors focus only on short-term performance and income flows. Whereas in the case of FDI the investor uses his ownership stake as a means to foster its strategic interests which may involve securing access to new markets, location of specific resources and low-cost production facilities (Douma *et al.*, 2006). In FDI, the managerial control of the investor over the investment company and its long-term character create a special relationship and requires a tailored governance to facilitate interactions between the investor and the investment companies, for instance by means of:
a) representation in the board of directors;
b) participation in policy-making processes;
c) material inter-company transactions;
d) interchange of managerial personnel;
e) provision of technical information;
f) provision of long-term loans at lower than existing market rates (OECD, 1996).

In FDIs, the quality of the investor-investment company (headquarters-subsidiary) relationship is essential for building and expanding foreign operations, and thus for making profits.

Table 2.1. Comparison of portfolio and foreign direct investments.

	Foreign direct investment	**Portfolio investment**
Ownership of shares/stock	Yes	Yes
Management influence	Yes	No
Character	Build and expand	Purely financial interest
Time range	Long-term or permanent	Short-term or temporary
Engagement/participation	Majority to Full	Minority participation > 25%

2.1.1 (Dis-) advantages of different FDI entry modes

The literature recognizes a number of FDI entry modes. They are ordered along two dimensions: first, a company can engage in an existing enterprise or create a new company from scratch; second, a company can choose among different levels of involvement: from a minority stake to full ownership (Agarwal and Ramaswami, 1992; Root, 1998). In minority participation, the investor company has only partial control and its management influence is affected by one or more other local shareholders. The 50/50 joint venture assumes equal participation of both local and foreign partners in capital, ownership and management. In a majority participation joint venture, the balance of control is pulled, together with the ownership level, to the investor company. Finally, in sole ventures the investor has full ownership and full control over its investment company (Root, 1998). Figure 2.1 shows this control-ownership continuum.

Each investment mode has its particular advantages and disadvantages. Therefore, the investment decision is a difficult and long process. For example, an investment entry with a full ownership of newly established foreign operations such as Greenfield enables a full exploitation of local market advantages and gives full control of a production process. However, at the same time it requires a large capital investment and a vast management involvement since the company is vulnerable to political and business uncertainties. In the case where an investor company chooses the acquisition mode, it acquires immediate access to the market and local knowledge but at the same time should be aware of additional managerial efforts and time needed for restructuring the acquired subsidiary into its own structures. The organisational structure has to be reorganized so as to match the MNE's structure. An overview of the advantages and disadvantages of the two groups of entry modes is presented in Table 2.2.

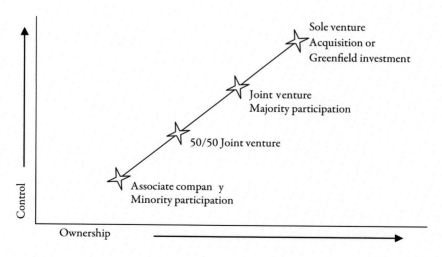

Figure 2.1. Continuum of FDI modes. Adapted from Root (1998).

Table 2.2. Advantages and disadvantages of FDI entry. Based on Root (1998).

Advantages	Disadvantages
Greenfield	
1. Exploiting full advantages of the target market	1. Strong management involvement
2. Full control of production process	2. Due to higher resource commitment – a
3. Better quality assurance	higher exposure to risk
4. Marketing- more opportunities to adjust to	3. Need for a balanced strategic planning
local preferences	4. Greater information requirements
5. Support of target country government (for	
creating new jobs, etc.)	
Acquisition	
1. Faster start in foreign target market (new	1. Constraint in performance due to post-
establishment takes 3-5 years)	acquisition process of adjustment of acquired
2. Shorter payback periods creating immediate	company operations and policies
income for the investor	2. Problems in transferring ownership and
3. It may provide a scarce resource: human skills	control
or license to produce, etc.	3. Different accounting standards, production
	processes and technology advancement

Next to these company aspects which influence the choice of the investment mode and the organisational structure, a number of institutional aspects should be considered, such as government encouragement laws for foreign investors and/or political stability in the investment country. In our research framework, we will have to deal with these factors as well.

2.1.2 The effects of FDI inflow for the recipient's economy

As mentioned in the previous section, the relationship between the investor and investment companies originates from the investment flow. The FDI inflows have been a well-known and booming phenomenon worldwide. The discussion as to whether FDI positively or negatively contributes to the recipient's economy has been on the political agenda for quite some time.

On the one hand FDI-receiving economies benefit and get upgraded as the international cash flows are accompanied by a *knowledge and technology transfer*. Greenfield investments contribute to job creation and together with creation for special economic zones boost the development of often neglected regions. Firms of foreign headquarters are involved in trade and business contacts with local entrepreneurs and their activities indirectly contribute to an upgrade of local business. Also domestic companies are forced to *improve their efficiency* and innovate in order to survive. In some cases, domestic companies copy behaviour of foreign companies. This contributes to innovation which allows them to stay in the market. On the consumer side, the quality and range of products offered increases. In this way investors contribute to the development of the local economy.

On the other hand, opponents believe that FDI distorts the development of a local economy. They lobby for setting up limits for foreign cash flows or ask for strict regulations of the process (Kumar and Pradhan, 2002). The negative effects occur especially when profitable activities stay centralised at the headquarters level and when only older (old-fashioned, sometimes environmentally dangerous) technologies and production lines are moved to the FDI-recipient countries (Lipsey, 2000). The possible harmful effects emanate from the divergent interests between the international companies and the host economies, especially if economic development indexes (such as GDP) between countries are strikingly different (UNCTAD, 2003). For example, an international company may be interested in maximising profits worldwide (i.e. overcoming market imperfections), but the host economy might not be better off. A tax policy stimulating reinvestment of the money withdrawn from closed-down activities into new investment projects in the recipient countries moderates the unfavourable rent-seeking effects of FDI (Kumar and Prakash, 2002). In the case of FDI flows to the CEE region we are dealing with the transition economy, a change from planned to free market economy. According to the World Bank's '10 Years of Transition' report the transition process eliminates the wide dispersion in the productivity of labour and capital across types of enterprises and between old and new sectors which was present at the onset of transition (WorldBank, 2002). According to this definition the eight CEE countries, which joined EU in May 2004, finished the transition process. Therefore we believe that some of the generally known negative effects of FDI such as crowding out[5] of local companies and technological dependence will have no long-term effects in CEECs. The *crowding out* effect appears when FDI harms the development of local entrepreneurship by deterring domestic investors from entering activities dominated by foreign investors. While foreign subsidiaries profit from easy access to the skills, capital, technology and brand names of parent companies, the local companies may not be able to build such capabilities (on-time). Eventually, they are forced to withdraw to less complex activities or those with a lower foreign presence – possibly selling their activities to the foreign investor. This happened, for instance, in the automotive components industry in Brazil (Mortimore, 1998). In the CEECs the entrepreneurship was limited by the political regime, so when the limitations were taken off the development of the domestic companies also sky-rocketed. The *technological dependence* had probably played a role at the beginning of the transition process, just after the markets opened. Since EU expansion, the trend of shifting the R&D centres to CEECs has become more popular. The *relocation ability* of foreign operations in less prosperous times has been a serious negative effect of the transitions in these economies. Foreign investors were more likely to relocate their operations, especially when the divestment costs were low and the political and economic environment were unstable (UNCTAD, 2003: Ch 4). Again in this case, EU membership of

---

[5] Crowding-out effects are described by Buckley (1996) and Mortimore (1998) amongst others.

the CEE countries guarantees political stability and enables free economic exchange. Table 2.3 summarizes the contribution and possible drawbacks of FDI inflow.

Although the above-described threats can cause serious damage to the FDI recipient's country, larger empirical tests do not definitively support the negative effects of FDI. For example, the results of empirical research covering 39 economies over a longer period of time did not prove univocally the crowding-out effect. The effect did not exist in Asia, but was fairly frequent in Latin America (UNCTAD, 1999). A more recent study by Kumar and Pradhan (2002) proved the crowding-out effect in 29 enterprises, but didn't support it in 31 others in developing countries and did not consider Central European Countries at all. In the long term, FDI has a favourable influence on the economy of the receiving country if the gap (technological, infrastructural or societal) between the investor's and the recipient's country is not too large. Generally, an FDI-inflow increase is accompanied by the GDP increase (see data UNCTAD, 2006).

Acquisitions of domestic enterprises are likely to generate less favourable externalities than Greenfield investments, which as investments in new facilities or the expansion of existing facilities create new production capacity and jobs, transfer technology and know-how, and can lead to linkages to the global marketplace. Discouraging experiences with acquisitions of domestic enterprises shift governmental preferences towards Greenfield investments, which appear in the form of, for example, tax exemptions and special economic zones (examples in Lipsey, 2000). To cope with the drawbacks and explore the opportunities the recipient's country offers, Stoever (2001) suggests improving the legal framework, creating transparent regulatory procedures and sustainable rules in both investing and the recipient's countries. Transparent and stable institutional frameworks reduce market distortions and improve competitive conditions. Still, reaching a trade-off between the positive and negative effects of FDI flows forms the most challenging task for many governments (Stoever, 2001). These

Table 2.3. Positive and negative effects of FDI flow.

Positive contributions	Possible threats
+ knowledge transfer	− crowding-out effect
+ positive influence on other domestic companies − crowding-in domestic investments (Kumar and Pradhan 2002)	− local technological dependence
	− relocation ability
+ improved overall efficiency	
+ technology transfer	
+ job creation[1]	

[1] It occurs mostly in Greenfield investments; in acquisitions reduction in employment often occurs.

trade-off decisions, together with economic growth cycles, cause strong dynamics in global investment flows. The next section illustrates this dynamic of FDI flows in the last decade.

2.2 FDIs' development worldwide

The last years of the 20th century were characterised by a very strong dynamic of global FDIs. After two periods of FDI decline (1991-1992), in 1996 a real FDI boom occurred. The number of mergers and acquisitions, joint ventures and other equity and non-equity types of inter-firm agreements was increasing and so was the growth in FDI flows. Corporate restructuring in developed countries aimed at improving efficiency and modernization continued, giving rise to efficiency-seeking investments. However, the global growth-trend continued for a few years after 1996 and came to a halt with the financial crisis in Russia and overall slowdown of the economy after September 11th, 2001 (see Figure 2.2).

In comparison to 2000, in 2001 the value of FDIs dropped by 41% globally, and fell another 13% in 2002 to reach not more than half of the peak value of 2000. The continued decrease in 2002 was different both geographically and between the sectors. The flows into manufacturing and services declined and the inflow into the primary sector increased. The decrease in FDI inflows in the form of mergers and acquisitions was much steeper than Greenfield investment inflows. Both the FDI flows of developed as well as developing countries fell by 22%. Two countries (the United States and the United Kingdom) accounted for half of the decline in FDIs. The very small decrease in Asian countries was only the effect of the enormous increase of FDIs to China, which reached a record inflow of US$53 billion in 2002. In Europe, an increasing trend of FDI inflows occurred in the flashy transforming countries of Central Eastern Europe (CEEC). Detailed CEEC inflows will be elaborated upon in Section 2.3.

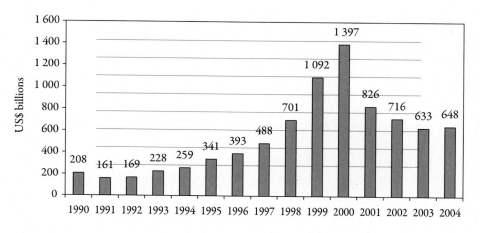

Figure 2.2. Global FDI inflows from 1990 through 2004. Source: UNCTAD (2005).

In 2003, global FDI fell for the third consecutive year in history by 12%. The weak global economic recovery and concerns about international security contributed to this decline (OECD, 2004). For example, the USA had not managed to recover from the 9-11 crash and FDI inflows kept decreasing (-20% in 2003). Only developing countries experienced a slight recovery of 9%, mainly due to the increasing FDI inflow to Asia. In contrast to the USA, China seemed not to suffer at all from the events of 9-11 and maintained growing FDI inflows. Only once, during the period 1981-2004, in 1999 did China register a decrease in FDI inflow, supposedly related to the Russian crisis. In 2003, for the first time in history China managed to attract almost as much (inward) FDI (US$54 billion) as the USA (US$56 billion), which was much more than any other country (except Luxembourg).

According to a worldwide survey performed yearly by the United Nations Conference on Trade and Development (UNCTAD), in 2003 investors were more interested in the emerging markets than in developed economies. Continuous liberalisation of FDI flows was expected to accelerate the recovery. Out of 244 changes in law and regulations concerning FDIs, 220 were directed at liberalisation (UNCTAD, 2004).

For the first time since the slow-down in 2001, the FDI flows increased by 2% in 2004 (see Figure 2.2). While inflows to developing countries surged by 40%, inflows to developed countries decreased by 14%. The latter despite the fact that for the first time the new European Union members were included in the developed countries group, and experienced a strong increase of 50% in their FDI inflows (see Figure 2.3). The continued growth of inward FDIs to developing countries had its explanation in growing competitive pressures forcing companies to invest in emerging developing economies. Higher prices for many commodities have made investments in developing countries that are rich in resources even more attractive.

The prospects for FDI development in the near future are promising. The continued need for firms to improve their competitiveness by expanding into new markets, reducing costs and accessing natural resources and strategic assets abroad, provides strong incentives for further FDI investments in transition countries in particular. Central Eastern European Countries, especially Poland as one of the most promising emerging regions for FDI inflows, will be the geographic domain of our study. Below, we elaborate on the FDI flows to CEECs.

2.3. FDI in Central Eastern European Countries (CEECs)

UNCTAD hosts 19 countries in the CEEC region, including the Balkan states and former Soviet Union republics and the Russian federation. In the description of the FDI inflows we will only cover the group of CEE countries which entered the EU in May 2004: the Czech Republic, Estonia, Hungary, Latvia, Lithuania, Poland, Slovakia, and Slovenia. In these countries, the transformation process that enabled a free flow of FDIs had already begun in the nineties. Based on the data in yearly investments reports from UNCTAD published in 1992-2005, we see that in 1991 the FDI inflows showed a more than 300% increase (see Figure 2.3)

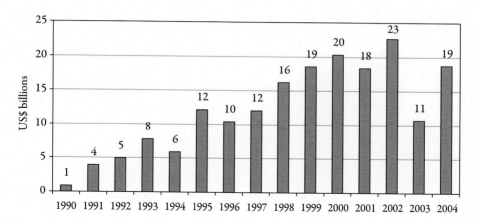

Figure 2.3. FDI inflows to the CEE EU member countries. Source: UNCTAD (2005).

as compared to 1990. Between 1992 and 2004 the average annual change in the FDI inflows was 20% showing a continuous increase. Next to some high peaks in the FDI inflows in 1995, 2002 and 2004, some deep slumps in 1994 and 2003 appeared as well (Figure 2.3).

In 2002, the Central Eastern European region did best compared to the rest of the world, and increased its FDI inflows to a record US$23 billion, compared to US$19 billion in 2001. It seemed that the investment inflows into Central Eastern European Countries did not suffer from the overall slow-down of the economy and continued with a moderated growth-trend in 2002 (UNCTAD, 2003). Unfortunately, the 'global FDI plunge' of 2001 appeared in the CEEC as well, two years later in 2003. The decrease was only temporary and in 2004 the FDI flows to the CEEC recovered and showed a strong increase by 74%. It was the EU accession of these countries that contributed to this increase and a fast recovery (we describe 'the accession effect' in detail in the next section). Throughout the whole period (1991-2004) the region maintained a steady 3% share of the worldwide FDI inflows.

The FDI inflows to the CEEC showed strong differences between countries. In the period 1993-2004 each country experienced at least one year of a slowdown or decrease in FDI inflow. The Czech Republic, Slovakia, Lithuania and Estonia showed the largest amplitudes in the FDI inflows. For example, in 2003 the Czech Republic and Slovakia experienced a decrease in FDI inflows of 85% and 70% respectively. This was partly a result of the one-off effect of large privatisation investment projects in 2002, in the automotive and energy sectors. On the contrary, Poland managed to maintain the rising trend of FDIs through the whole period, with the exception of 2001 and 2002.

The motives for FDIs differed among CEE countries. In the case of Poland, it was the size of the market, and in smaller countries such as the Czech Republic, it was the advance of the privatisation process that stimulated FDIs. Companies investing in those countries gradually depart from activities based on unskilled labour and enter the higher value-adding sectors, taking advantage of the educational level of the local labour force. Traditional investment incentives (cheap labour and availability of raw materials) are being supplemented by new key strategy drivers: being present (first-in) and acquiring a strong position in the emerging markets, as well as serving local markets by a local company. These new factors contribute to a significant change in global allocation of so-called 'first-time' investments. Central Eastern European Countries, together with Asia, accounted for more than 60% of first-time investments in 2002 (see Figure 2.4).

The attractiveness of the CEE countries as an FDI recipient even increased after their accession to the European Community.

2.3.1 The effect of the EU enlargement on the FDI flows

In concordance with the expectations, in 2004, fuelled by the momentum of EU enlargement, all countries experienced higher FDI inflows: an increase of 74% as compared to 2003. Despite the sceptical opinion that the main advantages of the integration with the EU had already been obtained and the scale of additional revenues would therefore have been limited, the EU accession increased investors' confidence in the eight countries of Central and Eastern Europe, mainly because of the unification of legal regulations and the disappearance of national trade barriers. As the results of the AT Kearney Executive Survey of 2004 showed, the legal regulations and unsolved problems of corruption and red tape together with poor infrastructure (ICT, physical and energy) were the most often-mentioned threats to the competitiveness of the CEEC regions in the race to attract more FDIs. Removing these obstacles by creating a uniform market under EU regulation may serve as the catalyst for further FDI inflows. The EU accession helped to overcome the impact of the slowdown of GDP growth (as a late '9-11 effect').

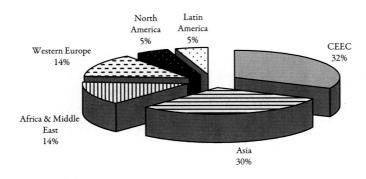

Figure 2.4. Global allocations of first-time investments. Source: AT Kearney (2003).

Experiences from other new member countries, e.g. Spain and Portugal, which joined the EU in 1986, show that accession to the EU boosts the inflow of foreign direct investment and accelerates GDP growth (see Figure 2.5).

In the long run, economists expect a gradual shift of production from the 'EU-15'-countries to the new EU member states, as a result of lower labour costs, a high market potential and relatively small distance-to-market. The hourly wage still remains 5-6 times lower than in the western part of Europe, and the labour force is continuously expanding its skills and qualifications. These factors, together with a willingness to change, make this region very attractive for foreign investors.

From the European Union perspective, the 'old Europe' has experienced a strong economic lift after the accession of the ten new members in May 2004. These countries registered a strong productivity[6] growth (averaging 4.2%) over the last eight years (1996-2004). A broad program of structural reforms in these countries was expected to spur productivity gains. In comparison, the 'old' 15-member European Union showed a productivity growth of only 0.8% in 2003, down from 0.9% in both 2001 and 2002.

The next section describes the development of the FDIs in Poland.

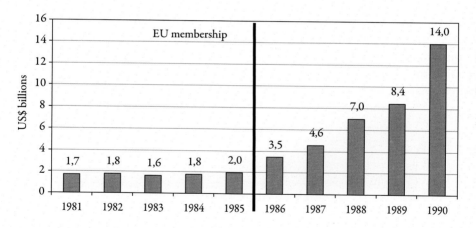

Figure 2.5. FDI inflows to Spain: before and after EU accession. Source: UNCTAD (2006).

---

[6] Labour productivity measures how much output is obtained for each hour of work, and determines a nation's living standards (as measured by per capita income). The more hours people work and the higher the level of productivity, the higher is the per capita income.

2.4 The emergence of HQ-S relationships in Poland

The Polish economy is one of the most attractive economies for foreign investors because of its central geographic position in Europe and the large size of its market. The attraction is the result of the size of the population – some 39 million – and an infrastructure that includes developed road and rail systems, airports, as well as three ports which all enable speedy handling and transport.

Over the last 15 years of economic transformation, inflation rates have decreased (Figure 2.6) and the GDP has grown, but at the same time Polish companies have experienced a strong need for capital to run the restructuring processes and to be able to compete internationally. Similar to other transition economies, a lack of domestic sources of financing and pre-maturity of the banking system hampered the capital flow and its allocation (Durka, 2004). Therefore, Foreign Direct Investments (FDIs) acquired a priority role in the transformation of the Polish economy and was perceived as 'safer' than foreign external financial instruments (i.e. bank-loans).

Until the 90s, Poland was isolated from the free trade and market economies. The opening of the goods and services trade and the liberalisation of the capital markets boosted trade and investment opportunities. In the start–up phase (1990-93) the inflow of foreign investment had an unfavourable impact on domestic companies. Polish enterprises failed to accumulate working capital. With an underdeveloped banking system and hardly any sector-related funding available from the state, many companies collapsed. Huge lay-offs followed which contributed to a very high unemployment rate of 20%. Domestic companies, suddenly placed in the open international arena, appeared to have difficulties in competing with 'experienced' companies from western countries. In 1989, Poland initiated a wide-ranging political and economic transformation which culminated in its entry into the European Union on the 1st of

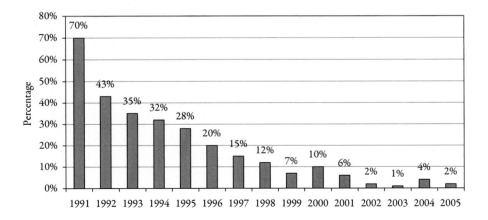

Figure 2.6. Inflation rate in Poland in 1991-2005. Source: Polish Statistical Office (GUS).

May 2004. As a part of the single European market, Poland is still undergoing vast economic and social changes. With a year-on-year economic growth of 3.21% (average of the period 1999-2005), a young, well-educated and ambitious labour force, location at the very heart of the continent, and low corporate income tax (19%-2005), Poland is an interesting place for investors from around the world. The AT Kearney's Foreign Direct Investment Confidence Index (2003) ranked Poland fourth in the world and first in Europe as a potential destination for FDIs. This attractiveness developed during more than a decade of eager transformations.

Foreign investors participate in the Polish market through three basic entry modes:
1. through *privatisation* of a state-owned company,
2. *acquisition* of an existing company,
3. *Greenfield* investment (solely or jointly with a Polish investor)

In the start–up phase of the transformation process the privatisation and acquisition modes prevailed over Greenfield entry modes. Since 2000, the inflow of FDIs in the form of Greenfield investments has been structurally increasing; 37% in 2002; 51% in 2003 and 58% in 2004. The share of FDI inflows in the privatisation of state–owned companies clearly decreased, from 36% in 2002 to 17% in 2004. Figure 2.7 exhibits the share of investment modes in the FDI inflows in 2004.

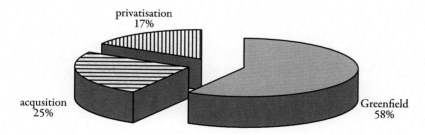

Figure 2.7. Investment entry modes in Poland in 2004. Source: PAIZ (2005).

2.4.1 Privatisation as investment entry mode

Privatisation of state-owned enterprises with the participation of foreign investors has been seen as the most important source of capital, and an important instrument in the restructuring process of the economy. The privatisation is a sale or a lease of an enterprise to the corporate (foreign) investor or a group of investors which may include the employees (so-called employee buy-out) of this state-owned enterprise as well as the Treasury[7]. In some cases the Treasury

---

[7] Treasury is a Ministry of Finance.

first transformed a state-owned enterprise into a joint stock or a limited liability company and held 100% of shares. After that potential investors were invited to participate in public offering or a tender. In a tender, the Treasury sold shares of a company to one of the pre-selected investors. In the invitation, the Treasury specified the number of shares an investor was allowed to buy, the minimum price per share, other social commitments (e.g. concerning lay-off limitations), and the period for which an investor was bound by this offer. Potential investors had to submit information about their organisation and a surety[8]. Based on this information a Tender Commission, appointed by the minister, assessed the quality of the submitted offers and selected the best bidder. If there were more potential investors, negotiations were repeated so that finally only two or three remained for the final mediation. Being successfully applied to several Polish industries (i.e. tire, breweries, detergent plants, pharmaceutical enterprises, the sugar industry, electrical engineering plants and banks), negotiations based on a public invitation became the most popular method of privatisation among foreign investors.

Since the beginning of the transitions in 1990, 66% of 8,441 state-owned companies started the privatisation procedure, of which 72% had completed it by March 2004 (PAIZ, 2005). More than a third of the state-owned companies were terminated after their applications for liquidation as they did not qualify for any kind of privatisation due to poor economic performance without reliable future improvement. The largest capital privatisation in 2002 was the purchase of 85% of the shares in the energy sector companies by German and Dutch investors (Durka, 2004). The companies, privatised in this manner, adapted fast to the market economy, improved economic performance and enhanced investment and innovation activities. Along with the capital flow, modern management skills were introduced, as well as new organisational structures and marketing practises. Polish privatised companies improved their competitive position in the local market and gained access to the foreign markets through the investor's own marketing and distribution channels.

2.4.2 Acquisitions

Acquisitions took place especially with respect to companies with strong Polish brands (for example, in the food sector – Wedel in confectionery and Animex in meat processing). Acquisitions usually go together with reorganisations and increasing efficiency through job reduction. They are difficult to monitor, especially in the dynamic economy of Poland. Industries where the most acquisitions took place were trade and repair, hotels and restaurants, and manufacturing.

High investments and restructuring programs in the acquired companies contributed to their overall better financial performance. Companies with foreign capital base their activity on external capital more often than domestic companies. The share of external capital compared to own capital is large in the acquired companies (Durka, 2004). This greater use of external

---

[8] A pledge, guarantee or bond, to back the performance of a company. (definition: www.investorwords.com)

financing allows for higher investments (GUS, 2004). Companies with foreign participation invest much more in fixed assets than companies with purely domestic participation. In 2001, the investment outlays of companies with foreign participation in manufacturing accounted for 68%, and in transport for 80% of all investments in fixed assets (Durka *et al.*, 2003).

2.4.3 Greenfield investments

Greenfield investments receive priority in Poland as they contribute to job creation and technology and knowledge inflows. This priority is set by the Polish government as Poland's unemployment rate is the highest among all EU countries.[9] To attract foreign investors to build production facilities in Poland, the Polish government proposed a number of encouragement policies. Firstly, in 1992 a special government-funded Investment Agency (PAIZ) was established to promote Poland as an investment country and encourage potential Greenfield investors. PAIZ needed time to develop its capabilities and was strongly criticised by foreign investors in the beginning. Nowadays, it has improved and is the first contact point for companies interested in the development of an activity in Poland[10]. The Agency has built a large database for potential Greenfield locations in Poland, which is freely accessible on the internet. The largest Greenfield investments are awarded prizes during an annual conference for foreign investors organised by PAIZ. In 2005, the first prize went to LG Philips LCD for an investment of 429 million Euros and the creation of more than 3000 jobs.

A second example of a governmental initiative is the establishment of Free Economic Zones in the regions with the highest unemployment level (usually as a result of a terminated state-owned factory). In these zones, companies receive full tax exemption. Special investment treatments are provided if they create jobs and invest with a long-term vision. These zones contribute to the attractiveness of Poland as a location for Greenfield FDIs. Despite EU criticism, the Polish government attempts to continue the development of such zones, as they are essential for fighting unemployment and indirectly (through interconnected business-suppliers, intermediates) accelerate regional economic development. EU authorities see the privileged benefits and tax releases as inhibiting free competition in Europe. Nevertheless, as long as tax inequalities exist among EU countries, the existence of Polish Free Economic Zones is not under threat.

The last example concerns the tax policy. In an attempt to attract companies and reduce unemployment, the Polish government developed a special long-term policy – the Act on Corporate Income Tax (CIT) – concerning the reduction of the main tax rates for companies operating in Poland. The base for taxation is profit taken as a surplus of income over the cost of acquiring it. In 1994, the rate of this tax equalled 40%. In concordance with the above-

---

[9] Averaging almost 18% in the 1st quarter of 2006 according to Polish Statistical Office.

[10] More to find on the website http://www.paiz.pl/index/

mentioned act the percentage has been gradually reduced, and in 2004 it accounted for 19% (see Figure 2.8).

The policy on the gradual decrease of taxes not only encouraged potential investors, but actually resulted in an increase of tax inflow to the state budget.

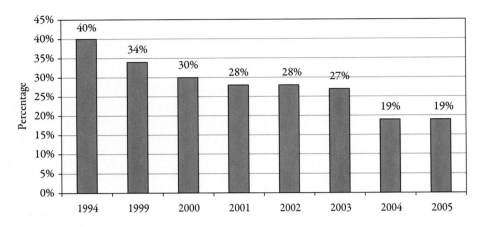

Figure 2.8. Corporate income tax rate in Poland. Source: Polish Statistical Office (GUS).

2.4.4 FDI inflows to Poland

The effects of the government policies became apparent in the amount of FDIs that Poland attracted in the period 1993-2004. The accumulated value of FDI inflow amounted to US$61.6 billion (according to UNCTAD) and to US$78.6 billion according to PAIZ[11]. However, Poland still experienced a decrease in FDI inflows in two consecutive years 2001 and 2002. The growth trend of FDIs in Poland was affected by, among other things, forbearance and delay in restructuring of the economy's tight monetary policy, as well as unfavourable trends in the global economy. In 2001-2002, the Polish economy was growing at the slowest rate of the CEE countries. The GDP increased by 1% in 2001 and by 1.4% in 2002. From 2003 on, the Polish economy began to recover and the GDP rose to 3.7% and continued to grow by 5.5% in 2004. Together with the economic growth the FDI inflows recovered as well (see Figure 2.9).

At the end of 2002, the number of companies with foreign participation registered in REGON (the Polish statistical database) amounted to more than 47 thousand (Durka *et al.*,

---

[11] The difference is due to methodological disparities. They are explained in the Annex to the Report of Foreign Direct Investments in Poland, 2003 published by IKiCHZ (Foreign Trade Research Institute in Warsaw).

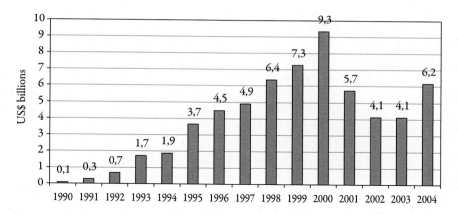

Figure 2.9. FDI inflows to Poland. Source: UNCTAD (2005).

2003). Despite the fact that the share of companies with foreign capital in the total number of companies operating in Poland had decreased since 2000, the number of registered new companies with foreign capital increased, for example, from 1621 in 2003 to 2530 in 2004 (Chojna, 2005). The growing significance of foreign-owned companies in Poland is reflected in the relatively high employment ratio, labour efficiency and revenue generation. With respect to the manufacturing companies, which are the subject of the present study, they represented 23.7% of all companies but employed 32.4% of the total workforce and generated 52.2% of the revenues (Chojna, 2005).

France is the largest investor in Poland, and the USA, Germany and Netherlands share the next three positions (see Table 2.4). Transport and manufacturing sectors received the largest investments in 2002 (PAIZ, 2003).

Table 2.4. FDIs by country. Source: PAIZ (Prachowska, 2005).

Country	Invested capital in US$ billion (rank position)		
	2002	2003	2004
France	12.2	13.9	16.0
Netherlands	5.8 (4)	9.9 (2)	11.2 (2)
USA	8.7 (2)	8.7 (3)	10.2 (3)
Germany	7.8 (3)	8.4 (4)	10.1 (4)

While the inflows of FDI decreased, the estimated composite ratio[12] illustrating the share of foreign companies' activity in the economy, increased from 36% in 2000 to 37% in 2001. In the early nineties the share of companies with foreign participation grew by 5% a year, but since 1998 a slow-down trend has developed (Durka *et al.*, 2003). This trend, together with the decrease in FDI inflows can be explained by the changing nature of the inflow of the FDIs. Instead of a growing number of new investors, an increasing number of mergers and acquisitions, re-investments and large privatisation transactions occurred (as was the case with the national telecom operator in 2000). Despite this trend, companies with foreign capital continue to play a leading role in exports and investments as well as in improving labour productivity (see example of manufacturing companies in Figure 2.10).

In 2004, companies with foreign capital share showed higher gross and net profits as compared to purely domestic companies. Moreover, those companies showed more than three times higher export intensity. However, when we look at the number of companies declaring gross and net profits, we see that domestic companies declared profits more often (see Table 2.5). The explanation for this unexpected finding could lay in the intensive investment activity of foreign-owned companies.

Foreign headquarters also assure wider access to know-how and external financing. Moreover through knowledge flows, they stimulate the restructuring and modernization processes. Research conducted on Polish firms suggests that privatized firms and those with foreign participation have a stronger market orientation and are more likely to build a competitive advantage based on company and brand reputation than state-owned and purely domestic enterprises (Lascu *et al.*, 2006).

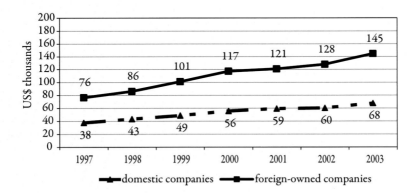

Figure 2.10. Labour productivity per employee in Polish manufacturing companies. Source: Chojna (2005: 106).

---

[12] This ratio has been used by B. Durka and it is the arithmetic mean of the share of companies with foreign participation covered by the financial reporting to the total number of entities submitting their balance-sheet reports. Durka *et al.*, 2003, 'Foreign Investments in Poland' page 17.

Table 2.5. Financial performance of companies in 2004. Calculations based on Zagozdzinska et al. (2005): Table 24.

Financial Indicator	Foreign-owned companies	Domestic companies
Gross financial result (US$ billion)	13.1	10.8
Financial result after taxes (US$ billion)	10.7	8.7
Share of entities reporting gross profit	59%	93%
Share of entities reporting net profit	58%	92%

2.4.5 The effect of the accession to the Euro Zone

In May 2004, after the ratification procedure had been completed, Poland became a full member of the European Community and a new period began, in which Poland pursued a course to adopt the European single currency – the Euro. A decision on admission to the Euro zone was made at the meeting of the European Council in Copenhagen, in June 1993. At that meeting, the conditions for the accession of Central and East European countries to the European Union were established (the 'Copenhagen Criteria'). By entering the European Union, Poland gained the status of a member state with derogation, i.e. a member without full membership rights in the Economic and Monetary Union. Polish economic policy is faced with an obligation to meet the nominal convergence criteria. After meeting the criteria (called the 'Maastricht criteria'), the country is formally ready to adopt the single currency. Although the Treaty does not provide any specific time period for Poland to meet the criteria to adopt the European single currency, today the Polish government faces the challenge to account for the benefits and costs of the adoption and develop a strategy for accession to the Euro zone. The major problem zones for entering the single-currency system are, in general, the budget deficit and the state of public finances. In 2005, Poland still exceeded the permitted 3% limit of the budget deficit. This hinders Poland's participation in the EURO zone (see Figure 2.11).

The convergence program of the Polish government expected the deficit to reach the EU maximum of 3% in 2007, but was not approved by the EU commission as it was assessed to be too optimistic. More reliable prognoses expect Poland to reach the budget deficit limit of 3% by 2011. The EU Committee on Financial and Economic Policy agreed to grant the 'new' EU members more time to restructure their public finances. However, for Poland, there is an advantage in not participating in the Euro zone yet, namely a flexible exchange rate, which gives the Polish government an instrument for stimulating economic development.

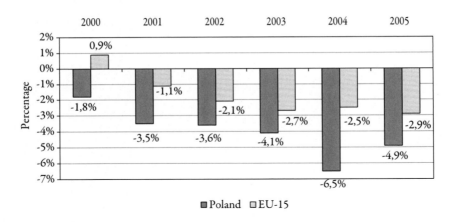

Figure 2.11. Poland's budget deficit compared to EU average. Source: Eurostat (2005).

2.4.6 Future strategy

Stable economic growth and a large unsaturated centrally-located market in Europe are undoubtedly the advantages of Poland in attracting FDIs. The Polish economy seems to have recovered from the slow-down in 2001 and 2002 and registered a 3.2% growth in 2005. Certainly there are still some weaknesses, such as the poor state of public finances and a huge budget deficit. Foreign investors complain about fast-changing legal regulations, unpredictable and still high taxes (VAT) and the slow improvement of the infrastructure. According to a World Bank report from 2005, managers spend more than 10% of their time exploring fast-changing laws. The Report advised the Polish government to review their tax policy (i.e. VAT rate) and to restructure the investment policy (revise ± 50 laws), and in doing so enable easier access to capital. The intention is to reduce corrupt practices, as well as decrease uncertainty about the legal regulations. The high unemployment rate (18% in 2004) worsens the overall economic picture of Poland. At the same time, despite the high unemployment rate, companies are having difficulties acquiring specialised personnel. Since the opening of the EU labour market for Polish employees by some EU countries in 2005, a shortage of qualified blue collar workers arose as an effect of their migration to countries like Great Britain and Ireland.

According to a PAIZ investment report on 2005, none of the macroeconomic factors changed after Poland joined the EU. However, the conditions for doing business in Poland stabilised and companies have easier access to EU funds, for example for building highways. Also stable economic growth increases the purchasing power of customers and creates new market opportunities. The stability of the EU membership enables smaller companies especially, usually less eager to pioneer new markets and more keen to copy their competitors, to undertake investments in Poland. Poland, with its large market, which is far from saturated and with gradually increasing competencies and skills of the labour force, has the potential to attract more FDIs. The small geographical and cultural distance to Western Europe encourages potential investors to choose Poland over alternative locations in Central Eastern Europe or in Asia. Based on this, Poland can develop a unique set of capabilities which will keep on attracting new investments from abroad.

2.5 Concluding remarks

The flows of Foreign Direct Investments (FDIs) lead to the emergence of foreign subsidiaries. In this chapter we have described the effects of different kinds of entry modes, especially acquisitions and Greenfield investments, on the recipient's economy and business environment. Based on this description, we can conclude that although generally both positive and negative effects of FDI may occur, the positive contribution of FDIs to the local business development is very important. Eventually, the economy profits from the presence of foreign capital.

This chapter has described the role of FDIs in a transforming economy, from planned to free market, with hardly any national savings and an under-developed banking system. The fast capital shoot in the form of FDIs enabled and significantly shortened the transition period. Of course there are companies that did not survive in the fast-changing economy and went bankrupt, but if their inefficient operations were supported by the subsidies (instead of foreign capital injection) it would only take more time for them to terminate their operations and eventually a customer would have to pay the costs in the form of higher prices and increased personal taxes. The negative effects of FDI flows into under-developed economies as described in Section 2.1.2 seem not to form a threat to the Polish business environment. The reason lays probably in the dynamic development and the emerging character of the Polish economy. In that case, the differences in the development level between investors' countries and the investment receiver – Poland are less striking and should not hinder the company's growth (Steensma *et al.*, 2005). Poland's business environment profits from the flow of FDIs, therefore it is an important task for the Polish government but also other organisations to make this location attractive for FDIs.

Finally, we have shown that FDI flows have a long-term orientation, which means that it is in the investment companies-headquarters' interest to build HQ-S governance mechanisms that will support long-term development of the whole MNE. In the next chapter, we will build a theoretical framework to explain the governance mechanisms that will emerge. The results of the model will be taken to formulate advice on proper HQ-S governance.

Chapter 3. Theoretical building blocks

As mentioned in the introduction, the present study focuses on the design and governance of a headquarters-subsidiary (HQ-S) relationship. Section 3.1 shows that this relationship emerges when a company goes on the internationalisation path and becomes a multinational enterprise (MNE). As Section 3.2 describes, the governance issues have different characters and therefore form a complex problem which requires a multidisciplinary approach. But at the same time, the complexity of the headquarters-subsidiary relationship creates difficulties in identifying a sound and robust theoretical framework for the analysis (Werner, 2002). Therefore, for the HQ-S governance analysis we propose dividing the theoretical building blocks in two parts: first, including theoretical approaches for internal analysis concerning the basic mechanisms of governance (Section 3.2), and second explaining governance as a function of external factors (Section 3.3). Finally, the contingency-governance fit is described and internal and external perspectives are combined in a general research framework (Figure 3.4) that serves as a departure point for conceptualising it into a detailed research model presented in Chapter 4.

3.1 Multinational enterprise (MNE)

The governance problem in MNEs originates from the emergence of subsidiaries resulting from the internationalisation process of firms in a form of FDI flow (see Chapter 2). A foreign subsidiary is defined as any operational unit controlled by an MNE and situated outside the home country, whereas the unit that controls the subsidiary is defined as the headquarters (Birkinshaw and Morrison, 1995). If an international company has subsidiaries in multiple (at least two) countries, it is referred to as a multinational enterprise (Birkinshaw and Morrison, 1995). MNE can also be characterized as a group of geographically-dispersed and goal-disparate organisations (Bartlett and Goshal, 1987). Physical distance and separate organisational structures call for the design of mechanisms which allow for the achievement of the MNE's strategic and operational goals and are referred to as the governance of the HQ-S relationship. According to Richard Scott (1987), MNE is one of the most influential modern organisational forms which must simultaneously operate in multiple societies and, hence, multiple environments.

Although the first multinational was the Dutch East India Company founded in 1602, the history of research on MNE does not have a long tradition and actually started to develop in the 1960s, while its research accelerated in the 1980s (Wright and Ricks, 1994). This relatively short history of research on MNE makes finding a suitable (comprehensive, and at the same time robust) conceptual framework for the analysis of HQ-S relationships a difficult task. For that reason, the theoretical approaches to the analysis of MNE have been changing over time, both in the level of analysis and in the content (Birkinshaw, 2001).

3.2 Governance of the headquarters-subsidiary relationship

The MNE is an institutional governance structure that serves as a framework for interchanges and relationships, including mobilisation of investments, exports and imports, knowledge, general information transfers and most importantly management itself (Chandler and Mazlish, 2005). It is thus crucial to focus not on a single function such as FDIs, but on how the entire firm operates across the international boundaries developing and managing different relationships over time. There are several possibilities of governance relationships in MNEs (Aoki, 2004):
a. between the firm and its main bank;
b. between a subsidiary and its management /holding company;
c. between an entrepreneurial start-up firm and a venture capital company;
d. between a state-owned enterprise and the government;
e. between banks and a governmental regulatory agency.

Governance of HQ-S relationship (b) has an important function in lubricating the operations of two or more units of MNE. Governance issues have been subsumed within the competence perspective by those researchers who consider good governance – in the form of trustworthy, non-opportunistic management (in the case of MNE-subsidiary's management) – to be a competence in itself, and therefore a potential source of sustained advantage, e.g. (Barney and Hansen, 1994; Davis *et al.*, 2000). However this approach of subsuming governance issues into competence issues runs the risk of tautologically reducing every conceivable inter-firm difference to a competence. As such, it might therefore miss the point that the governance perspective does offer a genuinely different way of thinking about phenomena that leads to different conclusions and predictions (Makadok, 2003). For example, a shift from a uni-dimensional to a multidimensional perspective on the management of the linkages between different parts of a MNE (Werner, 2002).

3.2.1 Governance definition

Governance in a broad sense can be defined as processes and systems by which an organisation operates (Wikipedia, 2005). Remaining at the general abstraction level, Kahler (2003) defines governance as a set of authority relationships. These two are not easily falsified due to their high abstraction level which at the same time decreases the applicability and power in explaining certain i.e. HQ-S relationships. To solve this problem we will present a more detailed definition of governance. To be able to do so, we divide the research on governance in two separate streams: **the structure-oriented and the process-oriented**.

In the **structure-oriented stream,** governance is defined as '*the institutional framework in which the integrity of transaction or set of transactions, is decided*' (Williamson, 1979). In the World Bank's terminology governance is a set of traditions and institutions by which authority in a country is exercised embracing six dimensions: accountability, stability, effectiveness, regulatory quality, rule of law and control of corruption (Kaufmann *et al.,* 2005). In the economic field, this stream focuses on explaining the existence and boundaries of economic institutions, such as firms (Grossman and Hart, 1986). With respect to the MNE, the following governance question is answered: if and to what extent should foreign operations be internalised in the MNE's structure? The question is first posed in the transaction-cost approach to MNE analysis and originates in the early work of Coase (1937), who distinguished two forms of organising a transaction: market and hierarchy. In Coase's view the market mechanism is sometimes more costly than forming an organisation (hierarchy) to perform the transaction. Williamson (1999), building on Coase's work, defined governance as an exercise in assessing the efficacy of alternative modes of organisation. In his view, governance is the effect of the ownership element in an organisation and is as such opposed to the 'nexus of contracts' (Williamson, 1999). In summary, with respect to the MNE, governance is an institutional arrangement that enables transfer of products and/or resources into and from a foreign country.

In the **process-oriented stream**, governance is defined as the *management processes* and *systems* by which an organisation operates and that need to be in place for successful performance. It encompasses exercising power, authority and control, includes managerial incentive schemes, and coping with pressures from institutional investors (Zingales, 1997). Governance research raises theoretical questions about the coordination of complex social systems and the evolving role of different parties (e.g. stakeholders) within that process (Flinders, 2002). Governance as a process can be differently defined depending on the theoretical perspective we use. For example in the *transaction-cost* theory perspective, Hennart (1999) showed how economic institutions use a mix of two mechanisms; price and hierarchy to govern internal processes. Markets are biased towards the use of the price system, and organisations are biased towards the use of hierarchy. These two governance modes are distinguished based on their ability to reduce shirking and cheating costs. For example, in the market, a party might claim a higher quality of the products than they actually have and thus cheat the customer. In the hierarchy, a party (employee) may under-perform and shirk on their employer. The price and hierarchy mechanisms allow for measuring and supervising the quality of received products or monitoring the work of employees. Leiblein (2003) and Geyskens *et al.* (2006) indicate that hierarchical authority structures provide one exchange partner with the ability to develop rules, give instructions, and in effect impose decisions on others.

In the process-oriented stream, the governance issues may be addressed from agency theory, accounting and organisation research perspectives. They are addressed briefly in this chapter.

In the *agency* theory the focus in governance research lies on the safeguarding of parties' interests in the separation of ownership and control. Governance encompasses the methods and ways in which providers of capital to corporations assure themselves of their return on investment (Shleifer and Vishny, 1997). It is referred to as corporate governance and includes all the influences affecting i.e. the appointment of the controllers and/or regulators involved in organising the production and sales of goods or services (Turnbull, 1997). Corporate governance is a set of formal and informal self-enforcing rules that regulate action choices of three strategic players: the managers, the investors, and the workers (Aoki, 2004: 33). In the agency theory, the following definitions of governance are formulated:

> 1. *Governance includes all the influences affecting the institutional processes, including those for appointing the controllers and/or regulators involved in organizing the production and sale of goods or services*
>
> (Turnbull, 1997).

> 2. *Corporate governance is a set of self-enforcing rules (formal and informal) that regulates action choices of three strategic players: the managers, the investors, and the workers, contingent on evolving states*
>
> (Aoki, 2004: 33).

In *accounting* research corporate governance is often limited to the composition, presence and the size of management teams and the ratio of 'outside directors' in the board (Carpenter *et al.*, 2003). In line with this view, Kim *et al.* (2005) define corporate governance as the structure of the board of directors and the compensation systems, which have been recognized as mechanisms geared towards controlling and linking managerial behaviour to achieve desired organisational outcomes. They may concern resource deployment decisions, but also control and ownership (Hennart and Park, 1994: 420). Governance mechanisms refer to:
- a process of supervision and control over company management;
- economic agents giving overall direction to firms;
- the sum of control and co-ordination activities that compose the internal regulation of business in compliance with external obligations;
- the system by which companies are directed and controlled;
- the system of external and internal checks and balances that ensures companies discharge their accountability to stakeholders (Solomon and Solomon, 2004).

Finally, in *organisation* research, governance is defined as an organisational design that incorporates systems of decision making, operational control, and incentives (Yin and Zajac, 2004). This is similar to the definition recently used by Todeva (2005) in the analysis of the transnational corporation. She defined corporate governance as a system/mechanism for the allocation of resources, control and co-ordination of economic activities at the firm level that facilitates strategic direction, accountability, transparency and wealth creation. In the organisation research, *governance is defined as an organisational design that incorporates systems of decision making, operational control, and incentives (Yin and Zajac, 2004).*

Summing up the governance processes from different disciplines, the aims of governance are to:
1. **ensure and control** the **accomplishment** of planned activities and **targets**;

2. **enable and smooth information flow** so that information can quickly flow between the various parts of an MNE and to ensure that both customer needs and the environment in which the organisation operates are effectively factored into decision processes;
3. **align the actions of the individual parts** of the organisation towards aggregate mutual MNE's benefit;
4. **create trust** and transparency in the organisation by providing the means by which each member (in our study subsidiaries and headquarters) of the MNE can trust that the remainder are doing their part for the mutual benefit of the organisation and that none is unfairly gaining at the expense of others. Based on (Mayntz, 2003).

In our view, the three theoretical perspectives of the process-oriented research stream may successfully address the explanation of international HQ-S governance. In this view, governance is the determination of the broad uses to which organisational resources will be deployed and the resolution of conflicts among multiple participants in the MNE organisation (Daily *et al.*, 2003).

We use the elements of those definitions for discerning the governance mechanisms in the present study:

> *Governance is a process which aims at aligning goals and managing MNE subsidiaries while at the same time facilitating the feedback from a subsidiary in the form of personal interaction and information flows.*

Classically, in the international headquarters-subsidiaries relationships in MNEs, the agency theory has been applied for explaining governance mechanisms. But, as agency theory (AT) reveals some shortcomings as discussed in the following Section 3.2.2, we suggest supplementing AT with stewardship theory as described in Section 3.2.3.

3.2.2 Agency approach to governance

Agency theory focuses on problems that arise when the desires of the principal and the agent come into conflict with each other and when it is difficult or expensive for the principal to verify what the agent is actually doing (Eisenhardt, 1989). This allows managers (in this case, subsidiary managers) to pursue their own interests at the expense of shareholders (i.e. owner = headquarters). The agency problem arises from the separation of management and finance (Shleifer and Vishny, 1997). Jensen and Meckling (1976) defined the agency relationship as an interaction mode, in which one party (the principal) delegates work to another (the agent), who performs that work. Agency theory attempts to analyse this relationship, using the metaphor of a contract, which is the main unit of analysis in AT. The agency theory tries to solve the problem of inducing the agent to behave as if he were maximizing the principal's welfare. This problem exists in all organisations, and in all cooperative efforts, at every level of

management in firms (Jensen and Meckling, 1976; 309). The problem area originates from information economics and has three underlying assumptions:
1. Goal divergence between the principal and the agent;
2. Existence of hidden information either before or after contracting, i.e. it is difficult or expensive for the principal to observe the agents action; and
3. The principal and the agent have different risk preferences, which lead to different actions.

There are two kinds of contracts in agency theory: behaviour-based (e.g. use of salaries and hierarchical governance) and outcome-based (e.g. use of commissions, stock options, property rights or market governance). One of the proposed questions is: are the behaviour-based contracts more efficient than outcome-based contracts? Behaviour-based contracts are applied in organisations. For example, Ouchi (1979) used agency theory in the study on organisational control. Ouchi's behavioural control is linked to task programmability and output control with measurable outcomes. Ouchi extended the control framework that originates from Thompson (1967) with clan control as a significant mechanism in structuring organisational behaviour. It was Eisenhardt (1989) who claimed that Ouchi's extension of Thompson's framework (1967) including clan control, is similar to assuming low goal conflict. This is because clan control implicates goal congruence, and therefore a reduced need for monitoring of behaviour or outcome. Motivational issues are therefore not prominent (Eisenhardt, 1989: 64). In fact, agency theory fails to deal with situations of low/no goal conflict, as this questions the basic assumption of this theory. Eisenhardt (1989) argues that agency theory is closely linked to several mainstream organisational perspectives; the classical works of Barnard (1938) on the nature of cooperative behaviour and that of March and Simon (1958), on the behavioural theory of the firm. She claims: *'As in earlier works, the heart of agency theory is the goal conflict inherent when individuals with differing preferences engage in cooperative effort, and the essential metaphor is that of the contract'* (Eisenhardt, 1989: 63).

Agency theory has found application in explaining MNE governance (O'Donnell, 2000; Peng and York, 2001; Makadok, 2003; Schaffer and Riordan, 2003; Kim *et al.,* 2005). In the context of an MNE, headquarters-the principal delegates responsibilities and decision-making authority to the management of a foreign subsidiary – the agent. An agency problem exists if a subsidiary's management makes decisions that are not congruent with those desired by headquarters. This can, for instance, be a result of self-interested behaviour (goal incongruence) of the subsidiary management (O'Donnell, 2000). Relying on goal incongruence and information asymmetry requires monitoring. In that sense agency theory can provide a framework for the analysis of the governance mechanisms leading to the achievement of the first two aims of governance mentioned in the process-oriented stream (Section 3.2.1), namely the control of the accomplishment of planned goals and the information flows through the use of, for example formal, including standardisation, instruments. According to Child (1984) *'Control is essentially concerned with regulating the activities within an organisation so that they are in accord with expectations established in the policies, plans and targets.'* Cray (1984) defined management control as a set of mechanisms that overtly limit behavioural alternatives, so that behaviour is in concordance with the pre-set targets. The *'overt limitation of behavioural alternatives'* includes the use of power. Power usage refers to the limitation of behavioural alternatives despite the resistance of the subject (Weber, 1968). Mintzberg's (1983) managerial control primarily stresses the power element in the HQ-S relationship and concentrates on the assessments of standards and plans. A 'control' relationship, from Mintzberg's perspective, means a formal, hierarchical unbalanced relationship between headquarters and a subsidiary, regulating activities according to the expectations of the headquarters.

Focus on the imbalanced power relationship and behavioural limits in goal incongruence have been the main points of criticism of agency theory, especially in its application to international management. In the real business environment, the assumed static character of the relationship between the principal and the agent is hardly present, many relationships are dynamic and evolving, and the roles of the principal and agent are interchangeable. This relates to the fact that agency theory presents a partial view of the world and ignores the complexity of the organisation (Eisenhardt, 1989), which is one of the main characteristics of the MNE (Birkinshaw, 2001). Additionally, it involves a simplistic view of the relationship, in which agents have only one common interest – self-interest, and all agents are without exception risk-averse and shirking in all possible ways, whereas the principal is risk neutral and strives for nothing but profits (Perrow, 1986: 224).

As a response to the critics of agency theory, Kim *et al.* (2005) showed how the control of managerial behaviours adjusts to the roles foreign subsidiaries fulfil in the MNE network. Some subsidiaries play more sophisticated roles than others. They share goals and work together with the HQ on developing and implementing the strategy (Roth and Morrison, 1992). Moreover, according to Zajac and Westphal (1994), an empowered subsidiary performs better with less supervision and control, which in effect contributes to cost reductions. Also Chenhall (2003) stressed the importance of applying a broad concept of management control, including informal controls and integrative mechanisms, such as socialisation and clan control.

Summing up, relying on agency theory in explaining HQ-S governance would bring us to the classical 'headquarters' hierarchy syndrome', which would indicate a clear superior-subordinate relationship (Bartlett and Ghoshal, 1998). In such a relationship subsidiaries are only implementers of headquarters' decisions and are strictly controlled for their outputs. In such a case the threats to which AT provides solutions, such as goal incongruence and information asymmetry, are most likely to appear and there should be mechanisms to reduce their negative effects. In fact such a situation hardly ever appears in real life. Such an organisation would be doomed to extinction and would disintegrate sooner or later. Therefore, in order to reach the remaining two aims of governance mentioned in Section 3.3.1 of assuring effective information flows and aligning actions of individuals towards aggregate mutual benefit, agency theory should be supplemented with a theory that would accommodate the mechanisms for aligning the interests of different parts of an organisation, and developing and pursuing joint goals based on trust and cooperation.

3.2.3 Stewardship approach to governance

Stewardship theory has its origins in psychology and sociology (Donaldson, 1990; Davis *et al.,* 1997) and in contrast to agency theory, it assumes that managers are stewards of equity holders and that their interests are aligned. The theory was developed as a response to the agency deficiencies in explaining multiple factors that affect managers' decision making (Davis *et al.,* 1997). In the principal-steward relationship managers put the company's interests above their own and see accomplishing their own goals as serving the interests of the organisation. Managers have an intrinsic need to do 'a good job' and therefore governance should be designed so that the manager is able to work efficiently. In the HQ-S relationship the decision-making power would be evenly distributed between HQ and its subsidiaries. In such a relationship the headquarters' function is one of counselling rather controlling. It aims at creating trust and enhancing goal alignment between headquarters and subsidiaries. The purpose of such governance is sharing and enhancing resources, knowledge and experience. This is in line with the network structures in MNEs. In these organisations, relationships between units are more dependent on social contacts and mutual interests, and are less guided by formal structure of authority (Powell, 1990). With a network defined as a set of actors connected by a set of ties, these actors might be persons, teams, or organisations (Borgatti and Foster, 2003). In this approach the subsidiary is no longer a subordinated entity but an equally-powered partner – a node in a network. This new role of a subsidiary requires different governance mechanisms which facilitate information exchange and reciprocal learning. In the literature stewardship mechanisms are related to the integration, harmonisation and linking of different parts of the organisation and are referred as coordination mechanisms. For example, Van de Ven *et al.* (1976: 322) refer to integrating or linking together different parts of an organisation to accomplish a collective set of tasks and goals. Ouchi (1979) describes mechanisms which accentuate the role of groups of people that follow the same rituals, traditions and beliefs in leading to organisational success. This ceremonial form of control concentrates on intrinsically motivational factors. Mintzberg (1983) and Galbraith (1995) described the application of liaison devices such as communication for establishing and maintaining mutual understanding and cooperation. In addition, Mintzberg (1983) pointed at the importance of both lateral and vertical linkages for the management of an organisation, where the lateral linkages rely on mutual adjustment mechanisms. These mechanisms apply to large organisations operating in complex and dynamic environments[13] such as MNEs, as they have to deal with multiple national environments and with transition economies without a continuous need for measuring and evaluating output. In the accounting literature, for example in Anthony and Govindarajan (2001), coordination establishes concerted actions among functional activities or organisational units with the aim of internalisation of norms and beliefs by employees. Stewardship mechanisms include coordination, aiming at the establishment of concerted actions among functional activities and the internalisation of norms and beliefs between organisation members.

---

[13] The effect of the environment on governance is elaborated upon in Section 3.

3.2.4 Comparison of agency and stewardship theories

Different assumptions about human motivation lead to different prescriptions for control of the manager or unit (Tosi *et al.,* 2003). In agency theory, in order to counter the divergence of interests, the principal (HQ) seeks to motivate the agent to act in the principal's interest through monitoring, providing incentives and by controlling the output (Fama and Jensen, 1983). In contrast, in stewardship theory the interests of HQ and subsidiary are aligned to the interests of equity holders and managers. Moreover, the motivation of the steward subsidiary is ordered such that 'pro-organisational, collectivistic behaviours have higher utility than individualistic, self-serving behaviours (Davis *et al.,* 1997: 24). While agency theory suggests a strong focus on control in HQ-S governance, stewardship theory emphasises coordination. In control-oriented approaches, the relationships between headquarters and subsidiaries are generally transactional in nature or based on institutional power[14], whereas in coordination approaches the relationship is based on trust and personal power[15] (Davis *et al.,* 1997). Grounded in these assumptions each approach prescribes certain roles and governance mechanisms. The key assumption in coordination-oriented approaches is that when subordinates are given challenges and responsibility they will develop self-control over their behaviour. The assumptions of agency theory and stewardship theory are compared in Table 3.1. In the management of foreign subsidiaries focusing exclusively on one of these mechanisms may endanger a company's performance as was illustrated in organisational theory by Sundaramurthy and Lewis (2003). For example, a strong focus on a coordination usually grounded in past success may provide seeds for groupthink and strategic persistence. An unquestioned and positive framing of the firm's strategy and operations may foster risk aversion and as a result under-investment in new initiatives. While in low performance periods, the focus on coordination may cause executives to ascribe their failure to external causes beyond their control and so engage in 'wishful thinking', helping manage their personal anxiety and image. Similarly, the overemphasis on control may prove counterproductive, and excessive use of rational controls simultaneously signals and reinforces a growing distrust (Ghoshal and Moran, 1996). This, especially in high performance periods, may suppress managers' aspiration and motives, pushing them either to reduce their organisational commitment or to become increasingly withdrawn and resistant. Sundaramurthy and Lewis (2003) suggest trust and learning to work with constructive conflict as a possible remedy for the failure of both mechanisms. However, they should be balanced so that the trust performs as a lubricant and conflict stimulates critical feedback. The authors propose two means of building shared understanding among managers, directors and executives: 1) cooperative, strategic decision-making; and 2) greater formal and informal interaction. Economic progress requires both kinds of behaviours, not just one or the other (Ghoshal and Moran, 1996).

---

[14] Institutional power is vested in the principal by virtue of his/her position in the organization (Gibson, Ivancevich and Donelly, 1991).

[15] Personal power works through identification of one person with another and is developed over time. It is not based on the formal roles in the organization (Davis *et al.*, 1997).

Table 3.1. Comparison of Agency and Stewardship theory. Adapted from Davis et al., 1997; Sundaramurthy and Lewis, 2003.

	Agency theory (economics and finance)	Stewardship theory (sociology and psychology)
Theoretical basis		
Model of man	Economic man	Self-actualising man
Psychological motivation	Lower order needs (physiological, security, economic)	Higher order needs (growth, achievement, self-actualisation)
	Extrinsic	Intrinsic
Assumptions		
Human tendencies	Individual opportunism	Collectivist cooperation
Behaviour	Self-serving	Collective-serving
Management relations	Goal conflict (risk differential)	Goal alignment (firm identification)
	Distrust	Trust
Situational mechanism		
Management philosophy	Control-oriented	Coordination-oriented
Power	Hierarchy	Partnership
Goal of governance	Discipline and monitor	Service and advice
Subsidiary position	Subordinated entity	Node in a network
Risk orientation	Control mechanism	Trust[1]
Time	Short-term	Long-term
Objectives	Cost control	Performance enhancement

[1] Trust is defined here as a willingness to be vulnerable in the context of the relationship (Mayer et al., 1995).

Agency theorists have increasingly noted the costs and limits of vigilant (watchful) control. Several studies have explored how different control mechanisms may substitute or complement one another (Morck et al., 1989). Likewise stewardship researchers have explored how contextual factors may constrain or enable a coordination approach. For example, Davis et al. (1997) noted psychological, situational, and cultural factors that predispose individuals to stewardship. Based on these findings it is reasonable to think that both theories coexist; managers seem to act as both agents and stewards and studies report mixed results concerning which is the right one (Desai et al., 2003). With respect to the HQ-S governance, it indicates that combining these two theories could enhance the explanatory power of the research framework and allow for the inclusion of a broader range of governance mechanisms. In view of the above, we supplement agency theory with social aspects of stewardship theory for the internal analysis of HQ-S governance in this study.

3.2.5 Integrated view on HQ-S governance

We propose an *integrated view on HQ-S governance*, including mechanisms from agency and stewardship theories: control and coordination. The integrated model allows for avoiding the earlier mentioned 'headquarters hierarchy syndrome'; it does not assume centralisation of decision making at the HQ but the HQ's control of key decisions. This integration may help MNEs to cope with the fast-changing environment and challenges of changing customer needs, while combining global economies of scale with an increase in domestic market share. In such a setting, pure structural formal and control-focused mechanisms fail to respond to the diverse strategic requirements of global strategy and local responsiveness (Martinez and Jarillo, 1989). Successful organisations supplement traditional control, such as international-specific departmentalisation (global matrix), centralised decision-making, highly formalised processes and systems, tight controls and frequent reports with more subtle coordination activities. To conclude, the integrated governance model for HQ-S relationships works towards establishing optimal correspondence between the action, goals and strategies of the subsidiaries (sub-systems of the MNE) and enables effective information flows. In Figure 3.1 moving along the ovals from left to right; the governance changes its function from low-power pro-active coordination-based to high-power reactive control-focused governance.

We will describe the governance mechanisms in more detail in Chapter 4.

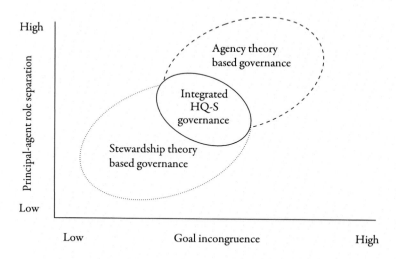

Figure 3.1. HQ-S governance integrated stewardship and agency theory aspects.

3.3 Contingency approach to the HQ-S governance

The contingency approach allows for placing the HQ-S relationship governance in its organisational and environmental context. The term contingency means that something is true only under specified conditions. As such there is no 'contingency theory', rather a variety of theories that explain and predict conditions under which a particular governance mechanism will be associated with enhanced performance. Here Ashby's (1956) law of requisite variety is fundamental: '*the variety of potential actions by the organisation must be as large as the variety of the disturbances in the environment.*' The basis for the contingency model is an information processing perspective (Galbraith, 1976), where the organisation is designed so that the information processing demands are aligned with its information processing capacity. These alignments are strongly embedded in the organisation's volatile and complex task environment and require multivariate studies of organisational behaviours (Lawrence and Lorsch, 1967). The contingency model of HQ-S relationship governance fits it to a number of constraints. These constraints may include: the size, its environment, differences in resources and operations activities, managerial assumptions about employees, and strategies and technologies used (Burton and Obel, 2004). The theory is 'contingent" in the sense that it views the functioning of organisations under different conditions, especially the dynamics of the environment. The outside contingencies, i.e. the business environment, can be treated as both constraints and opportunities, which influence the organisations' internal structures and processes (Lawrence and Lorsch, 1967: 187). In the dynamic contingency theory, flexibility is considered as an organisational potential for maintaining a dynamic fit between the organisation and its environment (Volberda, 1992). A major point in the contingency theory is that different *external* conditions might require different organisational specifics and behavioural patterns *within* the organisation, e.g. specific interpersonal skills (Donaldson, 1990).

3.3.1 External environment

In a formal way, we can define the environment as all the elements that exist outside the boundary of an organisation and have the potential to affect all or part of it (Daft, 1989). There are numbers of environmental elements that have a direct or an indirect impact on the HQ-S governance. Empirical studies have often shown contradictory results of the influence of the business environment caused by the difficulty in specifying the number of dimensions of the environment, measurement issues and the question of whether perceived or objective environmental measures should be used (for an overview, see Burton and Obel, 2004). At the outset, the environment was regarded as a single entity (Daft *et al.,* 1988). Contingency theory researchers mostly used one or two variables to measure environmental influence related to uncertainty. Lawrence and Lorsch's (1967) uncertainty was related to the clarity of available information, causal relationships, and the length of time-spans of feedback. Lawrence (1981) mapped a number of environmental aspects into two dimensions: unpredictability and complexity. Next he reduced them to one aggregate concept of 'uncertainty' (see Figure 3.2).

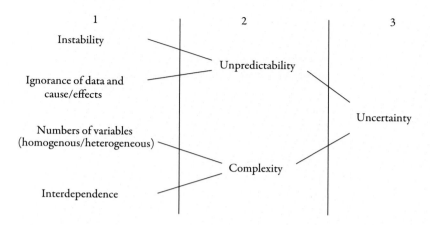

Figure 3.2. Description of the environment. Source: (Lawrence 1981).

In the search for a more robust description of the environment, later studies departed from the single dimension. Basically, the environment was split into two groups: one comprising those factors most closely related to the company itself, usually called micro-environment or task environment; and another which contains the elements affecting all the firms as a whole, also known as the macro-environment or general environment. Dess and Beard (1984) analysed the task environments of companies and provided validated multidimensional concepts for the task environment including a parsimonious set of three key dimensions: munificence, dynamism and complexity. The three dimensions are based on the earlier work of Aldrich (1979) and are conceptually similar to those of Mintzberg (1979) and Child (1984): liberality, variability and complexity. Other dimension of the environment, namely munificence is related to Starbuck's (1976) concept and refers to the extent to which the environment can support sustained growth of a company by for example building in slack (oversized capacity) to continue the growth despite an unfavourable environment. Dynamism, also called instability, refers to the extent to which the environment of the organisation changes conditions in unpredicted directions, e.g. fast-changing customer expectations or volatile supplier network. Complexity is the number of variables in the environment and their interdependence (Burton and Obel, 2004). Interdependence occurs, for example, when a company's prices or sales are dependent on those of competitors, or if the prices depend on more than just demand. According to Dess and Beard (1984), interdependence is explained by geographical concentration and specialisation.

Luo and Peng (1999) related the dimensions of environment to the company's performance in transition economies (see Table 3.2). Environmental hostility defined as the extent to which the environment can have a negative impact on the firm's growth and performance. In hostile environments, e.g. transition countries, institutions are underdeveloped and property rights are weakly protected which results in increased uncertainty of business operations. In

Table 3.2. Environmental factors. Source Luo and Peng (1999).

Environment	Groups: competitors, customers, suppliers, legal administration, socio-cultural groups
Environmental hostility	Importance of the impact for the firm's performance
	Deterrence: threat to the growth of the firm
Environmental dynamism	Predictability of the actions of the groups
	Variability: groups undergo major changes
Environmental complexity	Diversity of external groups (i.e. how many different factors and issues a company has to deal with in each group)
	Heterogeneity of the multiple factors and issues within the same category

such environments organisations find it difficult to pursue a long-term strategy and build relationships with suppliers and customers.

In transition economies, the HQ-S relationship governance is relatively young (as mentioned in Chapter 2, most of the subsidiaries were set up after the political transformation had started) and rapidly developing. This makes them particularly susceptible to environmental hostility. The rapid growth in emerging markets or transition economies induces strong dynamism. Dynamism and complexity are related to each other and have a similar effect on the organisational structure; higher levels require a more decentralised, organic structure (Mintzberg, 1979). In dynamic markets, both HQ and subsidiary managers may lack sufficient information to accurately forecast customer demand, competitor reactions, and market response. As a consequence, it may be difficult to rely on long-term relationships, for example with customers or suppliers. While almost assumed in a developed economy, access to key resources and stakeholders would be expected difficult in a transitional setting (Peng and Heath, 1996). According to Mc Carthy et al. (1993), MNEs often seem to be on the 'roller coaster' in these economies. Taking this into account the environmental dynamism has an important impact on the MNE's performance. Furthermore, strategic planning of organisations must be more short-term in nature, with a large magnitude of flexibility for long-term decisions. In dynamic environments organisations with diversified and longer experience are better able to survive (Luo and Peng, 1999). Complexity determines the diversity of environmental segments and the level of heterogeneity within each segment (Venkatraman and Prescott, 1990). An MNE successfully deals with a complex environment by acquiring experience and utilizing tacit knowledge which facilitates the strategy-environment alignment, improves resource deployment, and enhances the competitive edge of the firm (Miller and Friesen, 1983). Moreover, the impact of the external environment on the HQ-S governance mechanisms and performance changes depending on the phase of the transition process an economy is in at a certain moment (Peng, 2003). For example, in the early transition stages, HQ support and institutional linkages to governmental organisations could be most beneficial (Hoskisson *et al.,* 2000). Failure to appreciate the institutional changes makes the fit between, for example, strategy and environment obsolete under the new circumstances. Luo and Peng (1999) therefore stressed the importance of incorporating environmental forces in the research of venturing into transition economies.

3.3.2 Cultural distance

Cultural distance is defined as the degree to which norms and values or working methods between two companies differ because of their separate national characteristics (Jobber, 2001). The organisation's structure and management are more complex when they cross national borders to culturally distant countries. International management research widely demonstrates the necessity to recognise and manage cultural differences (Hofstede, 1980; Lebas and Weigenstein, 1986; Kogut and Singh, 1988; Hofstede, 1997; Hennart and Larimo, 1998; Hofstede, 2001).

In the HQ-S governance members of at least two[16] cultures have to cooperate. Sometimes, the cultural distance between the countries is so large that this hampers the growth and development of the MNE (Pease *et al.,* 2006). It is claimed that structure should be suited to the national culture and that governance mechanisms working well within one national culture may produce dysfunctional behaviours when transplanted thoughtlessly into a different cultural context. Hofstede (1997) analysed the connotations of two dimensions of the cultural distance: power distance and uncertainty avoidance with the management styles and organisational structures. Power distance, as defined by Hofstede, is the extent to which the less powerful members of institutions and organisations within a country expect and accept that the power is distributed unequally (desirability for centralisation). Uncertainty avoidance is the extent to which the members of a culture feel threatened by uncertain or unknown situations. This is expressed in the need for written and unwritten rules (formalisation). Hofstede links these two dimensions to Mintzberg's (1983) organisation typology and suggests that people with a particular national background will prefer a particular organisational structure. For example, in cultures with a large power distance the hierarchical structure of organisation with minimal lateral relationships based on a system of command and control would perform better than a flat decentralised organisation (which is better suited to small-power-distance cultures). In risk-averse cultures (strong uncertainty avoidance), managers try to avoid uncertain situations by providing greater stability of relations or developing extended normative rules with little tolerance for deviant behaviour to govern organisations (Hofstede, 1980). In Figure 3.3, Hofstede's findings related that these two cultural dimensions are mapped into four governance models by Lebas and Weigenstein (1986).

---

[16] This is the case in major or full ownership by a single investor. If there are more major international investors, multiple cultural influences will have to be accommodated in the HQ-S governance.

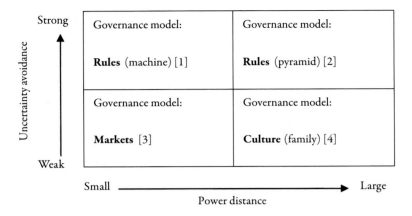

Figure 3.3. Governance models. Adapted from Lebas and Weigenstein (1986).

In strong uncertainty avoidance cultures, governance is based on rules. It couples strong input control (through externally imposed procedures, planning, budgeting, etc.) with strong output control (reporting, monitoring and performance evaluation). In small power distance cultures (quadrant 1), clearly defined and carefully planned procedures are sufficient for the functioning of an organisation. While in large power distance cultures (quadrant 2), these rules are defined within hierarchical structures (the pyramid) and these hierarchies can even twist the rules if needed. The Rules model works best where the casual model (who is the subordinate and who is the principal) is clear and the environment is relatively stable, as behaviour must be prescribed in advance and the time-span for corrective feedback is elongated (Lebas and Weigenstein, 1986).

In weak uncertainty avoidance cultures, governance models are less focused on mitigating uncertainties. The market mechanism (quadrant 3 in Figure 3.3) leaves much freedom to organisation members, relies on mutual adjustment and minimises inequality across MNE subsidiaries. Equality of all members of an organisation is typical for small power distance cultures. External market forces control managerial behaviour and the focus is entirely on outputs, the market will issue a final judgement on the subsidiaries' decisions. In large power distance cultures (quadrant 4) the culture model will be favoured. Culture internalizes common goals and shared expectations about roles and behaviour, thereby reducing perceptual differences among sub-units. It establishes a system of values and informal rules, which are extrapolated quickly for new situations. These rules and norms are personalised in a kind of father-figure who is trusted and followed by the rest of the organisation. Culture models work well in uncertain environments, where the causalities are not clear, communication is difficult and the cycle of action-consequence is compressed. However, the main drawback of this model is that it takes time to build; dynamism in the environment can easily make such a model obsolete.

The MNE needs to learn to cope with different cultural environments, but it is difficult to suggest which model will provide superior performance in an international setting. Hofstede (1997) posited that it is easier for headquarters to organise and manage a subsidiary that is situated in the same or neighbouring quadrant, when companies coincide on at least one cultural dimension. Also a difference in power distance seems to be more manageable than a difference in uncertainty avoidance. Local managers can adopt more authoritative management practices when the subsidiary is established in a country with larger power distance than HQs.

3.3.3 Generic strategy

Miles and Snow (1978) developed the concept of three superior performing generic strategies that companies can follow in the market, depending on the extent of innovativeness of their operations and products. In this view, MNE superiority is derived from the clear and direct match between the organisation's mission/values (its definition), the organisation's strategies (its basic strategy set), and the organisation's functional strategies (characteristics and behaviour). The three strategies (prospector, analyser and defender) show higher than average performance while the fourth strategy – reactor – is unsuccessful and shows lower than average performance.

Prospector companies are pro-active, and pursue an offensive strategy, aggressively seizing new market opportunities no matter what risks it takes. They are characterised by fairly broad product lines that focus on product innovation and new market opportunities. Creativity is more strongly emphasised than efficiency. Defenders are less pro-active, and can be seen as being protection-oriented, seeking stability by maintaining current market positions and defending against encroachment by other firms. Defenders, unlike prospectors, engage in little or no new product or market development. Their strategic actions seek to preserve market share by minimizing the impact of competitor initiatives and focusing on improving the efficiency of their operations. This cost orientation makes them unlikely to innovate in new areas. Analysers, are somewhere between prospectors and defenders, balancing the opportunity-seeking nature of prospectors against the risk aversion of defenders. Analysers seek to maintain their position in the marketplace.

While the strategies of prospectors, defenders, and analysers are all to some extent proactive, the strategies pursued by reactors are inconsistent and reactionary responsive to environmental change. Thus, the reactor strategy is not considered a viable one, and firms pursuing such a strategy would either have to adopt one of the other three types of strategy or face decline.

Under the contingency theory, governance mechanisms are suited to fit the generic business strategy. Shortell and Zajac (1990) call it the administrative domain of business strategy and showed which kind of mechanisms are best suited to the different strategies (see Table 3.3).

Table 3.3. Domains of organisations' strategies. Adjusted from: Simons (1987) and Shortell and Zajac (1990).

Strategy	Entrepreneurial aspects	Administrative mechanisms
Prospector	First in the market	Flexible system, informal, variety of loose mechanisms but also formal planning as a forecasting tool (to improve response to new market opportunities)
Analyser	Relatively stable products and services, selective movement to new areas with demonstrated premise	Formal planning, focus on internal efficiencies, building in some flexibility on project basis
Defender	Defined markets, stable sets of services	Tight control focused on internal efficiencies, cost control, low output monitoring, stable systems
Reactor	No consistent strategy, characteristics of all types at different times	No consistent pattern

The differences in governance mechanisms between prospector and defender strategies are the most evident and significant (Simons, 1987). Prospector firms attach great importance to forecasting and thus the availability (access) to data. Therefore, their focus is on output monitoring in order to prepare precise forecasts of the developments of new initiatives. Since they are continuously searching for new market or products opportunities they allow the organisation's members a large amount of freedom and appreciate bottom-up initiatives. In contrast, the defender's strategy is served by less intense monitoring and emphasizes bonus remuneration based on the achievement of budget targets. It tends to mean few changes to the control systems that are used and there is pressure to secure cost efficiencies (Simons, 1987). Defenders make the least use of formal planning, as compared to analysers and prospectors (Shortell and Zajac, 1990). All three groups of strategies impose different organisational mechanisms with the aim of reaching a so-called 'design parameter fit'. Burton and Obel (1998) proposed that prospector strategy mis-fits with high formalisation and centralisation, whereas a defender and analyser mis-fit with the low complexity of the environment. To sum up, the generic business strategy can be seen as an important contingency in designing governance mechanisms.

3.3.4 International strategy

An international strategy is the way in which a company positions itself in the global business environment and creates and sustains competitive advantage across national boundaries

(Harzing, 1999). However as Table 3.4 exhibits, views on the international strategy have changed over the years.

In general, MNEs have two basic strategic options for competing in the international market: global optimisation or local responsiveness. A **global strategy** gives primary importance to efficiency and builds on the global convergence of customer tastes and the technical possibility of standardized products (Levitt, 1983). A global strategy is characterized by a high level of globalization of competition and a focus on capturing economies of scale, with national products markets being interconnected. Because of the dominant requirement of efficiency in the production of standardized goods, subsidiaries are considered as pipelines for headquarters and are not expected to respond to local market needs (Harzing, 1999). The competitive

Table 3.4. The evolution of international and global strategy (1950–21st century). Source: Stonehouse et al. (2004: 17).

Period	International strategy of the period
1950-60s	Multinational expansion through the establishment of miniature replica subsidiaries abroad. Predominance of multidomestic strategies, with largely autonomous foreign subsidiaries supplying local/regional markets. Limited global co-ordination or integration of geographically dispersed operations.
1970s	Multinationals in retreat: divestments, rationalizations and host country plant closures.
1980s	Shift toward co-ordinated and integrated global strategies by established MNEs; focus on global competitiveness and use of global scope as a competitive weapon in global industries involving plant specialization and national interdependency.
1990s	Transition to global and transnational strategies. Businesses focus on developing core competences with outsourcing of non-core activities. This results in the development of horizontal and vertical global networks and strategic alliances. Increasing emphasis on knowledge as an asset and early forms of learning organisation begin to develop.
2000s	The era of the 'virtual corporation'[1] and the 'intelligent organisation'[2].

[1] A virtual corporation is a firm that outsourced the majority of its functions. A small group of executives will contract out and then coordinate the designing, making, and selling of products or services. Source: www.wikipedia.org.

[2] The intelligent organization is one that adopts a holistic approach to knowledge management that successfully combines tacit, rule-based, and background knowledge at all levels of the organization. Source: 'The Intelligent Organization' by Chun Wei Choo (1998) http://choo.fis.utoronto.ca/FIS/IMIO/IMIO1.html.

advantage of global companies lies in optimizing the upstream value chain activities[17] on a world-wide scale. The automotive and electronic industries are examples of global strategy, e.g. at Matsushita (Bartlett and Ghoshal, 1998). Companies that pursue a global strategy focus on increasing profitability by reaping the cost reductions from experience-curve effects and location economies that arise from performing a value-creation activity in the optimal location for that activity, wherever in the world that might be (transportation costs and trade barriers permitting). For example, the production, marketing, and R&D activities of companies pursuing a global strategy are concentrated in a few favourable locations. Location economies can either lower the costs of value creation and help the company achieve a low-cost position, or enable a company to differentiate its product offering and charge a premium price. Thus, striving to realize location economies is consistent with the generic business-level strategies of low cost and differentiation. Low costs are gained by offering a standardized product worldwide so that MNEs can reap the maximum benefits from economies of scale (if an increase in the number of units produced results in a drop in the average fixed cost of each unit) that underlie the experience curve (the systematic reduction of costs of production, which has been observed to occur over the life of a product). In terms of Porter's (1986) framework, these subsidiaries are governed by a high dispersion of assets and centralized governance. HQ usually find it important to centralize decision-making and consider a subsidiary as the implementer of its decision choices (Rugman and Verbeke, 1992; Birkinshaw and Morrison, 1995). Global strategy makes most sense when there are strong pressures for cost reductions, but minimal demands for local responsiveness. Increasingly, these conditions prevail in many industrial goods industries (Jackson *et al.,* 1997: 120).

Global strategy at General Motors

General Motors' (GM) international expansion has been driven by the belief that emerging markets offer the greatest potential for future demand growth. GM is not alone in this belief. Not only are many other automobile firms pursing a similar expansion strategy, but so are firms from a wide range of industries. Although GM has a long tradition of operations overseas, until the 1990s these operations took a second place in the company's Detroit-centred view of the world. From 1990 on, GM has recognized that to compete successfully in emerging markets, it is no longer enough to transfer outdated technology and designs from Detroit. GM has built a globally integrated corporation that draws on centres of excellence everywhere in the world to engineer global cars and state-of-the-art production systems. For all of its economic benefits, though, the trend toward greater integration causes some worries within GM's units as well. The units fear that an ability to respond to local market needs may be lost in the implementation of a global strategy. Source: Snow *et al.* (1992).

---

[17] Porter's value chain divides a firm's operations into a series of generic value-adding activities: 'primary activities' including inbound logistics, production, outbound logistics, sales and marketing, maintenance; and 'support activities' including administrative infrastructure management, human resources management, R&D, and procurement. The costs and value drivers are identified for each value activity.

A second strategic option is pursuing a **multidomestic strategy** to develop and manufacture products specifically for a particular country market customer needs and conditions (e.g. government regulations). Companies pursuing a multidomestic strategy orient themselves toward achieving maximum local responsiveness. They experience a lower level of global competition and compete mostly on a domestic level by adapting products and policies to local markets. In doing so, they differentiate product offering and marketing strategy from country to country (Harzing, 1999). Multidomestic companies try to accommodate the diverse demands arising from national differences in consumer tastes and preferences, business practices, distribution channels, competitive conditions, and government policies. Because differentiation across countries can involve significant duplication and lack of product standardization, it often raises costs, for it typically creates pressures for the delegation of production and marketing functions to national subsidiaries. The whole value chain of activities is created in each subsidiary's country in order to optimally serve the local market. The downstream activities of the value chain allow for creating competitive advantage as they are closely related to the buyer. Responsiveness to the local markets' requirements leads MNEs to decentralise organisational decision-making and grant a relatively high autonomy to subsidiaries. For example, pharmaceutical companies are subject to local clinical testing, registration procedures, and pricing restrictions, all of which mean that the manufacturing and marketing of a drug has to meet local requirements (Stonehouse *et al.*, 2000).

A multidomestic strategy makes most sense when there are strong pressures for local responsiveness and weak pressures for cost reductions. The high-cost structure associated with the duplication of production facilities makes this strategy inappropriate in industries where cost pressures are intense. Another drawback of this strategy is that many multidomestic companies develop into decentralized federations in which each national subsidiary functions in a largely autonomous manner. As a result, after some time they lack the ability to transfer the skills and products derived from distinctive competencies to their various national subsidiaries around the world.

Freshfields LLP – **a multidomestic law firm**. Quite different from the international firm, the strategies and assets of the multidomestic law firm are located in foreign offices. There is little mention of a home office, and the firm prefers to call itself a truly international organisation. Offices in foreign locations practice international and local law; lawyers are qualified in multiple jurisdictions and speak the local language. Skills become specialized according to country or region, yet there is little concern about merging competencies across regions. The firm's source of knowledge and competencies is the foreign offices. The flow of skills and knowledge is within regions, rarely among regions. Each region's needs are addressed separately, and regional offices are autonomous. Freshfields uses networking to achieve its international objectives, operating in 23 offices in Europe, Asia, and the United States. By not listing the UK office as the home office, Freshfields suggests that its assets are located throughout the three regions. Skills and knowledge are said to flow freely within the three regions, and the European, Asian and U.S. offices provide services unique to the regions' needs. Lawyers are trained in international and local law, are qualified in multiple jurisdictions within the regions, and many speak several languages. Many of Freshfields' Asian lawyers are trained at UK law schools but are then assigned to locations outside of Asia to give them broader world experience. Source: Mears and Sánchez (2001).

Levitt (1983) has argued that consumer demands for local customisation are on the decline worldwide. Modern communication and transport technologies have created the conditions for a worldwide convergence of tastes and preferences of consumers. The result is the emergence of a global market for standardized consumer products. Levitt's argument has been characterized as extreme by many commentators. For example, Bartlett and Ghoshal (1987) and later also Gomez and Werner (2004) have observed that in the consumer electronics industry consumers reacted to an overdose of standardized global products by showing a renewed preference for products that are differentiated to local conditions. However, concentrating on one of these strategies solely may lead to unsatisfactory performance, as both strategies carry some shortcomings, especially in a globalizing world with fast-developing information technology (Jackson *et al.*, 1997). On the one hand, global strategies, in which subsidiaries are dependent on a central headquarters, may be unable to exploit local market opportunities and eventually respond ineffectively to strong national competitors. On the other hand, in the multidomestic strategy, independent subsidiaries of an MNE may lose in the competition with companies pursuing global strategy whose coordinated global approach gives them the strategic advantages of global-scale operations and the ability to cross-subsidize the losses from 'battles' in markets with funds generated in others (Bartlett and Ghoshal, 1998). As a response to these threats and to capture the opportunities from both approaches, a third strategy has been proposed, that combines local responsiveness with global integration – a **transnational strategy**.

Many American companies are typical purely domestic companies with simple organisational structures. Where international activities exist, they are usually only an appendage to the domestic organisation. In contrast, many European companies, because of their relatively small markets, had to adopt an international orientation and build a worldwide organisation earlier, leading to the development of more complex organisational forms. The establishment of a healthy balance between national and international markets contradictory tendencies is one of the most difficult challenges to the organisation in an international company. The classical 'Pyramid Organisation,' where there is only one path for directives with each staff member having only one superior, no longer meets these requirements. This organisation has been replaced by a multidimensional organisational form, where an attempt is made to link and balance the different organisational groups in a meaningful manner. Source: Agthe (1990).

Earlier, global and multidomestic strategies were described in terms of a conflict between forces for local responsiveness and global integration (Doz *et al.*, 1981). Prahalad and Doz

(1987) developed a more sophisticated approach to the integration-responsiveness grid, which showed these two pressures as orthogonal, requiring MNEs to judge the degree of strategic emphasis on both dimensions simultaneously rather than treating them as alternatives. This strategic alternative was discerned by Bartlett and Goshal (1987), who investigated a strategic alternative that benefits both integration and national responsiveness. MNEs following the transnational strategy recognise that they should pay attention to global efficiency, national responsiveness and world-wide learning. The type of organisational structure that fits the transnational strategy is very flexible. It is referred to as an integrated network structure that connects the major sub-units of the company (Bartlett and Ghoshal, 1998). It takes advantage of home- and host-country assets, as well as location-bound and non-location-bound firm resources. A subsidiary can serve as a strategic centre for a particular product-market combination. Competition is now based on the ability to link subsidiaries' activities across geographic locations (Kobrin, 1991; Birkinshaw *et al.*, 1995). Bartlett and Ghoshal (1987) argued that the environmental competitive conditions are so intense that in order to survive in the global marketplace companies must exploit experience-based cost economies and location economies, transfer distinctive competencies within the company, and do all this while paying attention to pressures for local responsiveness. They also noted that in the modern multinational enterprise distinctive competencies do not reside just in the home country but instead may develop in any of the company's worldwide subsidiaries. Thus, they maintain that the flow of skills and product offerings should not be all one way, from headquarters to subsidiary, as is the case of companies pursuing a global or multidomestic strategy. Rather, the flow should also be from foreign subsidiary to HQs, and from foreign subsidiary to another foreign subsidiary – a process they refer to as global learning. Companies that pursue a transnational strategy are trying simultaneously to achieve low-cost and differentiation advantages. This makes the strategy difficult to pursue as pressures for local responsiveness and cost reductions place conflicting demands on an MNE.

Caterpillar is a **transnational** company. The need to compete with low-cost competitors such as Komatsu of Japan has forced Caterpillar to look for greater cost economies. At the same time, variations in construction practices and government regulations across countries mean that Caterpillar has to be responsive to local demands. To deal with cost pressures, Caterpillar redesigned its products to use many identical components and invested in a few large-scale component manufacturing facilities, sited at favourable locations, to fill global demand and realize scale economies. At the same time, the company augments the centralized manufacturing of components with assembly plants in each of its major global markets. At these plants, Caterpillar adds local product features, tailoring the finished product to local needs. Thus Caterpillar is able to realize many of the benefits of global manufacturing while showing local responsiveness by differentiating its products among national markets. Source: Jackson *et al.* (1997).

Although it was expected that MNEs would slowly emerge from multidomestic or global into the transnational strategy, the study by Harzing (1999) showed that younger MNEs and subsidiaries were more likely to adopt the characteristics of transnational strategies than older ones.

Variations in the strategic roles of foreign subsidiaries pose different HQ-S relationship contexts (Kim *et al.*, 2005). Calori *et al.* (2000) showed how these strategies relate to the coordination and company processes of an MNE. Global companies tightly control their international activities, e.g. Nike and Mars, whereas differentiation or low-cost expansion i.e. multidomestic moderately coordinated their subsidiaries, e.g. Timberland and Ferrero. For the transnational strategy, a transnational cross-border form of organisation was suggested combining elements of global and local strategy (e.g. Nestle) implying that a combination of tight and loose coordination would be characteristic for that type of strategy.

3.4 The contingency-governance fit

The contingency model of organisation claims that the firm's environmental, technological, strategic, and management situations should be aligned so as to create a 'contingency fit' (Pfeffer and Salancik, 1978). The 'contingency fit' is the degree of the precision with which the organisational design and contingency factors such as size, strategy, innovation and external uncertainty are adjusted to each other (Donaldson, 2001). Performance is often the final dependent construct in strategic management models (Venaik *et al.*, 2005). A mis-fit between the strategy and the organisation and environmental factors may diminish performance. The contingency theory argues that the contingency change leads to adaptive structural change, because organisations suffer performance loss while in misfit (Donaldson, 2005: a,b). The contingency fit is relatively easy to achieve if the number of contingencies is limited. The situation becomes more complicated when an organisation tries to adjust to multiple contingencies. Furthermore, some of these multiple fits can be contradictory, i.e. if the environment of an organisation is both uncertain and dynamic, the fit to the uncertain environment would work out better with centralised governance, whereas the dynamism would require a decentralised structure. In such environments the challenge arises of designing systems that retain sufficient unity and coherence to operate as a common enterprise and, at the same time, to allow sufficient latitude and flexibility to adapt to greatly varying circumstances (Scott, 1987). Successful firms develop new processes in two categories: locally leveraged and globally linked (Bartlett and Goshal, 1987: p. 133), that is simultaneously reaching multiple fits. The first capitalizes on the resources and entrepreneurship of local business units and leverages them to create innovations for exploitation on a worldwide basis. The second links the resources and capabilities of diverse worldwide units in the company, at both headquarters and subsidiary level, to create and implement innovations on a joint basis. In this process, each unit contributes its unique resources to develop a corporate-wide response to worldwide opportunity. The challenge is to develop an organisation that has a definitive focus on either of the two, or facilitates both processes simultaneously, creates multiple fits and maintains flexibility. Applying multi-contingency fit allows for comparing the actual effectiveness of different governance-strategy-environment configurations across subsidiaries. The fit is based on the concept of equifinality[18], which underlines its emergent and multidimensional character. The emergent character of the fit means that the combinations of strategy and governance provide better performance only for a limited time period. Therefore, the analysis of fit focuses on the investigation into whether certain configurations are related to higher performance at a given moment and whether they can be sustained for longer periods of time. Multi-contingency fit of those [which??] factors and subjecting them to periodical evaluation with the aim of creating a knowledge base has a positive effect on performance (Donaldson, 1990; Donaldson, 2005). As some of the contingencies are likely to change in time, the design is an ongoing dynamic process. The multidimensionality of this fit makes the final fit difficult to estimate. For example, the strategy of the MNE should be organised around the variables of multinational integration, internationalisation through innovation and national responsiveness (Sullivan, 1994) in Harzing (1999). To a large degree, the global business landscape is shaped by macroeconomic, social, environmental, and business trends. Correctly anticipating their future impact on global business and on the profitability of individual companies can enable companies to succeed '*by riding the currents rather than swimming against them*' (Davis and Stephenson, 2006). For the present study we suggest exploring which factors of the triangle 'strategy-environment-governance' do have a significant influence on performance.

3.5 Summary and concluding remarks

In this chapter, we have reviewed different theories with the goal of defining a theoretical research framework for the analysis of HQ-S governance.

Multiple theoretical perspectives are applied in the research on governance, of which none is universally correct (Kim *et al.*, 2005). It seems that the simultaneous consideration of multiple perspectives in the context of foreign subsidiary governance, in conjunction with MNE strategic needs, other than control needs, offers a perspective for a better and deeper understanding of their complexity. This is in line with the general trend in international strategic management research where a combination of theories provides a balanced view of research topics (Bruton *et al.*, 2004).

The need for a multidimensional approach supports the criticisms expressed already by Perrow (1970), concerning the inability of agency theory to fully explain the HQ-S relationship in principal-agent terms. Agency theory does not include the social aspect of the relationship, such as the clan control of Ouchi (1979) or Birkinshaw's (1995) and Harzing's (1999) control

---

[18] Equifinality is the principle that in open systems a given end state can be reached by many potential means. The outcome of equifinal processes cannot be predicted from initial conditions, nor can its specific path of progress. Rather, it depends on the moment-to-moment opportunities available in the immediate environment. Equifinal processes generate emergent structures when living structures are systeming, that is, open to each other's openness'. Source: Croft, 1996.

by socialisation and networks. The social aspect includes vertical as well as lateral integrating mechanisms. This aspect of the relationship, including lateral linkages, creates a basis for the interdependence perspective of Bartlett and Goshal (1987) and O'Donnel (2000). Interdependence is claimed to be important for acquiring and sustaining an international competitive advantage. It has resource and strategy interdependence as modalities.

According to O'Donnel (2000), it may no longer be of primary importance to study and implement the hierarchical headquarters-subsidiary conception, which has been the focus of international strategy research for a long period of time. Her study supports the recent trends in international research of focusing on the role of intra-firm-, inter-unit-relationships that facilitate the implementation of strategy in a global organisation. It also shows the inability of agency theory to accommodate and explain new kinds of peer-relationships, which are not based on the supervisor/subordinate framework. The elements of control aiming at reducing opportunistic behaviour (or better expressed: steering different parts of the organisation) need to be in place so as to avoid chaos and the decline of performance. In this sense agency theory provides a useful departure point for the study of MNE issues (Doz and Prahalad, 1991). But the substitutive choices between monitoring and incentives, for example pay for performance or in monitoring to reduce opportunistic behaviour posited by the agency theory should be abandoned to allow for the addressing of more complex combinations of control types.

Building on the shortcomings of agency theory we proposed complementing it with stewardship theory, especially for including the social aspect of the governance. As Granovetter (1985) stated, all organisation must develop network-kinds of relationships to access resources from, and to provide products or services to actors in their environments. These relationships are difficult to trade or transfer, history-dependent, and time-consuming to nurture (Nahapiet and Ghoshal, 1998). Their development can lower costs and create a sustainable competitive advantage (Powell, 1990; Barney, 1991). Stewardship theory focuses on developing such relationships, without power, and based on the intrinsic motivations of both partners (Davis *et al.*, 1997). In the desired, new kind of interaction mechanisms, intensified communication and personal contacts aim at a faster and extended exchange between the units of a multinational (Martinez and Jarillo, 1991).

The contingency view of the organisation describes the influence of the internal and external contingencies on multinational governance. This approach seems to provide the most complete view of international governance, taking into account internal company strategy and business processes, as well as the influence of national culture and the external business environment. In the next chapter, we will use the general research framework presented in Figure 3.4 to describe the conceptual model for the analysis of HQ-S relationship governance.

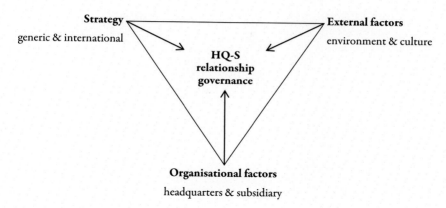

Figure 3.4. General research framework.

Chapter 4. The conceptual model

This chapter presents the operationalisation of the general research framework. Section 4.1 presents the operationalisation of HQ-S governance mechanisms. We discern control and coordination, based on agency and stewardship theory, respectively. Section 4.2 presents the operationalisation of contingency variables in the research model: environment, cultural distance, and strategy and control variables. Section 4.3 presents the development and the theoretical underpinning of proposed relationships between the concepts. Section 4.4 presents the explanation of the relationship of the HQ-S governance mechanisms and performance. Finally, Section 4.5 includes a detailed research model.

4.1 Governance of the HQ-S relationship

As described in Section 3.2 the HQ-S governance mechanisms are developed with four main goals:
1. ensure and control the accomplishment of goals,
2. enable and smooth information flow,
3. align the actions of the individual parts of the MNE,
4. create trust and transparency in the organisation. Based on (Mayntz, 2003).

For the explanation of these goals of the HQ-S governance mechanisms, agency and stewardship theories are used in the present study (see Section 3.2.2 and 3.2.3). In Table 4.1, we classify existing research on organisation control according to agency and stewardship theory. As shown in the first column of Table 4.1, the agency theory based mechanisms rely on formal, bureaucratic, hierarchical and output control and correspond to the first aim of governance. On the managerial level, the goals of the HQ-S governance may be brought under the term of control.

The stewardship theory based mechanisms, as shown in the second column of Table 4.1, include informal, network and empowerment seeking behaviours and correspond to the remaining two goals of governance. In the present study, these mechanisms are called coordination. Below we present the operationalisation of the control and of the coordination concept.

4.1.1 Control

The control in the HQ-S governance model aims at comparing an obtained with a planned output. The principal-HQ has a right to receive information to influence the behaviour of subordinates-subsidiaries. The principal and agent's roles are reflected in mechanistic control. Perrow (1970) and later in Chenhall's (2003) focus on output control and the unbalanced distribution of power between the roles. Galbraith (1976) represented an information

Table 4.1. Overview of agency and stewardship mechanisms.

Authors	Agency mechanisms	Stewardship mechanisms
Lawrence and Lorsch (1967)	Managerial hierarchy, formalisation	Individual/team or departmental integrative devices
Galbraith (1976)	Hierarchy rules and programs, planned targets	Lateral relationship, direct contact, task forces
Ouchi (1979)	Behaviour control, rules and procedures, personal control	Clan control, socialisation, indoctrination
Mintzberg (1983)	Standardisation of output, personal supervision	Mutual adjustment, socialisation, skills standardisation
Child (1984)	Bureaucratic control; formalisation, routine, personal control	Cultural control, socialisation, emphasis on selection, training and development
Bartlett and Goshal (1987)	Centralisation, formal systems and standards	Socialisation, self-development, acculturation
Martinez and Jarillo (1989)	Structural and formal, standardisation, centralisation, output control	Informal and subtle, lateral relations, informal communication, socialisation
Hennart (1999)	Hierarchy, structures, rules and regulations or price through output control	---
Harzing (1999)	Personal centralised control, formal bureaucratic control, output control	Control by socialisation and networks
Chang and Taylor (1999)	Behaviour control, output control	Cultural control
Tosi *et al.* (2003)	Monitoring and reporting, auditing and polices	Empowerment, decision-maker's autonomy, trust
Sundaramurthy and Lewis (2003)	Formal control, monitoring, supervision	Collaboration, empowerment
Covaleski *et al.* (2003)	Efficiency seeking mechanism	Legitimacy seeking mechanisms
Chenhall (2003)	Mechanistic controls, budgets, output control, process controls	Organic controls, broad information exchange, flexible and integrative mechanisms
Gomez and Werner (2004)	Formal control mechanisms, manuals, standards, budgets and schedules	Informal control mechanisms, informal communication, participation in teams

approach to mechanistic control and operationalised it as rules, programmes and procedures, hierarchy and goal setting. In Ouchi's (1979) typology these mechanisms were identified as mechanistic formal bureaucratic rules to control output of work and behaviour. Also Egelhoff (1984) emphasised the measurement of the output and provided operationalisations of control mechanisms for three areas: marketing, manufacturing and finance. Harzing (1999) applied Egelhoff's framework to MNEs, and estimated the subsidiary output of different activities at the headquarters level. This output was measured with the information flow to the HQ in the form of written reports. These control measures have proven their external validity in the above-mentioned studies. Therefore, a similar operationalisation is used in the present study: the frequency of reporting to measure control (see Table 4.2). However, the submission of a report does not mean that its content is analysed, it may only be stored in a central (located at HQ) database. To learn whether the information from the subsidiary's reports is being used or not, we have decided to add a measure of the HQ sensitivity to the information in the submitted reports and by doing so fill in a shortcoming in earlier studies (see second row in Table 4.2). This new item serves as an important indicator as it captures the eagerness in using the information provided to HQ and indirectly measures HQ feedback.

The frequencies of written reports as well as the HQ inquiries on these reports were measured for different activities in a subsidiary, as their frequency may vary according to the strategic function of a certain activity. E.g. HRM (Human Resource Management) might be less frequently reported than financial issues.

The control mechanisms are measured on strategic and operational levels. *Strategic control* is less concerned with the comparison of achieved with planned output but is more related to the capabilities of implementing and adjusting the company's strategy. Thus, it includes the control of long-term strategic objectives as well as the impact of the external environment on, for example, market share change. It provides directions for future actions and anticipates potential developments – it is also referred to as feed-forward control (Preble, 1992). *Operational control* addresses the general question as to whether a subsidiary is operating appropriately. This means that it reports on the operational aspects such as output control and meeting short-term goals by a subsidiary (Merchant and Stede, 2003).

In MNEs the reports and the exchange of information in general may be standardised, meaning that all units (including subsidiaries and HQ) make use of the same policies and operate in a very similar manner throughout the whole MNE network. Standardised procedures and policies may include procedures for hiring new employees or for dealing with reports or communication with customers. Standardisation has traditionally been used to simplify and speed up information flows, but also to increase transparency in a company. Mintzberg (1983), for example, found that larger organisations make more extensive use of standardised policies and procedures. But standardisation becomes inefficient when an organisation is very large and complex. Especially in the international environment, standardisation can make certain units of an MNE inflexible, which in emerging markets can seriously threat the existence of a

Table 4.2. Operationalisation of control.

Control	Author(s)	Item	Scale	Question No.
Strategic control	Egelhoff (1984)	Written reports on: market share development products and process R&D training of personnel	Frequencies from 1-8, scale anchors: 1 = less than once per year, 8 = daily	1c,d,e
Strategic control: HQ sensitivity to information in reports	New item	Inquiries on reports on: sales turnover production volume development of market share training of personnel products and process R&D	7-point Liker scale, scale anchors: 1 = not at all, 7 = always	2a,b,c,d,e
Operational control Output control	Egelhoff (1984)	Written reports on: sales turnover production volume	Frequencies from 1-8, scale anchors: 1 = less than once per year, 8 = daily	1a,b
Standardisation	Hedlund (1984) Harzing (1999)	General use of standardised procedures and policies e.g. concerning hiring new employees or the way the reports are being dealt with	7-point Likert scale, scale anchors: 1 = not standardised at all, 7 = fully standardised	3
Formalisation	Child (1984) Hennart (2001)	The use of formal documents in communication with HQ (including e.g. stamp and signature)	7-point Likert scale, scale anchors: 1 = informal, 7 = formal	4
Expatriate presence	Egelhoff (1984) Harzing (1999)	The nationality of the head of Manufacturing and quality department Marketing department Finance department R&D department	Three groups of nationalities distinguished: Polish Headquarters' country Third country	5

subsidiary, and the MNE as a whole. Standardised documents can be formalised. This means that a document or report is valid or accepted with a name, signature and stamp of the person responsible for a certain task. The formalization aspect of governance has often been included in studies on the management of different parts of an organisation (Child, 1984; Martinez and Jarillo, 1991; Hennart, 2001). Both aspects of standardisation and formalisation are included in the present study (see Table 4.2).

Finally, control involves the expatriate presence. Egelhof, in his several studies on multinational enterprise (Egelhoff, 1984; Gates and Egelhoff, 1986; Egelhoff, 1988; Wolf and Egelhoff, 2002), included the nationality of the CEO and the nationality of the management team as main variables for expatriate control. Harzing (1999) investigated the nationality of the director of a subsidiary as well as the number of expatriates at all levels of a subsidiary. Expatriates play an important role in assuring that the newly set-up subsidiary operates according to the expectations of the headquarters. In a later stage, when the organisational process of founding a subsidiary is accomplished, expatriates may plan an important role in transferring the MNE organisational culture and enhancing MNE-broad learning. The expatriate's presence in the subsidiary during the foundation process has then a clear control function whereas the expatriates presence for a longer period after the foundation process has been completed has a coordinating function. For these two reasons, it is important to include this measure in the study on the international control (Werner, 2002). In the present study we build on the earlier research of Egelhoff (1984) and Harzing (1999) and refer to the control function of an expatriate presence, which is operationalised as the nationality of the CEO and the nationalities of the managers of five different departments (see the last row in Table 4.2). The coordination function of the expatriates is included in mechanisms such as joint task groups and meetings between HQs and across the sub-units of the MNE (see Table 4.3).

4.1.2 Coordination

According to Martinez and Jarillo (1989), pure structural and formal control mechanisms fail to respond to the diverse strategic requirements of global strategy and national responsiveness with increased international competition. As described in Section 3.2.3, for assuring flexibility (also called agility) in international operations, existing control mechanisms (agency-based) are extended with new cross-departmental, informal and subtle coordination mechanisms (stewardship-based). The latter coordination mechanisms in the HQ-S governance focus on establishing concerted actions among different units and the internalisation of norms and beliefs among members of the MNE organisation. In the HQ-S relationship, the mechanisms of mutual adjustment accommodate the complexity of organisation in a dynamic environment. These mechanisms were called organic by Perrow (1970) and Chenhall (2003), and involve low power, coordination by mutual adjustment and high interdependence between work groups. Galbraith (1976) classified these mechanisms as soft control including self-contained task groups and lateral relations. In Ouchi's (1979) typology these mechanisms were subsumed under the informal clan control (recruitment, traditions and ceremonial control).

Table 4.3. Operationalisation of coordination.

Coordination	Author(s)	Item	Scale	Question No.
Stewardship mechanisms				
Personal contacts	Birkinshaw and Morison (1995) Harzing (1999) Bremmers et al. (2003)	Between HQ and S personnel at different functional levels of the subsidiary: CEOs marketing departments R&D manufacturing logistics	Frequencies from 1-8, scale anchors: 1 = less than once per year, 8 = daily	6a,b,c,d,e
Harmonisation of actions	Roth et al. (1991) Luo (2003)	Attuning of: sales turnover production volume development of market share education of personnel product and process R&D	Frequencies from 1-8, scale anchors: 1 = less than once per year, 8 = daily	7a,b,c,d,e
Joint HQ-Sub activities	Martinez and Jarillo (1989) Nobel and Birkinshaw (1998) Harzing (1999)	HQ and S employees' participation in committees or project groups, both temporary and permanent HQ and S employees' business meetings with other subsidiaries	Frequencies from 1-8, scale anchors: 1 = less than once per year, 8 = daily	8 9
HQ-S ICT integration	New item	Based on the speed of the subsidiary-related information availability at HQ, example of stock information	7-point Likert scale, scale anchors: 1 = slowly (e.g. by mail) 7 = at once (e.g. shared database)	10

Coordination activities have a mostly personal character and involve personal contacts, joint actions and the application of liaison devices. For the purpose of this study we combined integration, harmonisation and linking different parts of the organisation in three items: personal communication, joint task groups, training and attuning. The personal contacts contribute to better knowledge transfer and enhance learning. Through personal contacts, employees of HQs and subsidiaries get to know each other and this acquaintance creates a platform for performing a task jointly. Cray (1984) used coordination to describe processes for estimating the intensity of interactions between the headquarters and its subsidiaries in the MNE network. His research did not distinguish between personal (personal contacts) and impersonal (planning) aspects of coordination as he claimed that not the mode but the intensity of coordination is important. Other authors (Birkinshaw and Morrison, 1995; Harzing, 1999) included the 'personal contacts' together with information exchange in 'coordination by socialisation and networks'. In the present research we included the mode and the frequency of personal contacts between the heads of the HQ and subsidiary departments. The measures for coordination are based on the work of Bremmers *et al.* (2003) and are presented in Table 4.3. Linking different parts of an MNE can take place through attuning, i.e. informal usually short ad-hoc e-mail or telephone contact which allows a company to alter and adjust the actions in real-time without retarding it by procedural requirements (Luo, 2003). This flexibility is in turn essential for reacting and anticipating the changes in the environment at low or no additional costs. This was the case in Cray's (1984) study, which measured coordination in nine areas of activities at different operational stages of production and distribution, excluding the strategic areas. The word 'coordination' was purposefully replaced by 'attuning' to underline the harmonisation function of these activities (see Table 4.3). In the present study we also include an indicator for the intensity of joint HQ-subsidiary activities in permanent or temporary task groups and project teams.

Finally, ICT integration is included as a last element in coordination (Table 4.3). The development of information technology has caused the emergence of fast (real-time) communication channels and has enabled almost unlimited interaction between geographically spread units of MNE. The ICT-integration measures how fast information can flow between HQ and subsidiary, varying from very slowly, for example taking a few days, to very fast, for example simultaneous access to the same information by HQ and subsidiary.

Although control and coordination mechanisms are related, we consider control and coordination as separate dimensions. Thus, a company with a weak coordination function does not automatically have a strong control function and vice versa.

4.2 Operationalisation of the contingency concepts

The contingencies which are proposed to have influence over the HQ-S governance mechanisms include the external environment, cultural distance, strategy and performance. External environment is operationalised in three dimensions, each including two variables.

Table 4.4. Operationalisation of contingency factors and performance.

	Authors	Item	Scale	Quest. No.
Environmental uncertainty	Luo and Peng (1999)	Predictability and impact of political changes on business processes	7-point Liker scale, scale anchors: 1 = strongly disagree, 7 = strongly agree	11
		Reliability of governmental organisations – law interpretation		12
Environmental dynamism	Luo and Peng (1999)	Competition intensity		13
		Changes in customer preferences		14
Environmental constraints	Dess and Beard (1984)	In suppliers' network		15
		In availability of resources		16
		In workforce availability		17
Cultural distance	Kogut and Singh (1988)	Distance between HQ and subsidiary in Power Distance and Uncertainty Avoidance	Continuous	X
Generic strategy	Miles and Snow (1978)	Three statements Exploring new areas concerning product, market and operations	7-point scale: 1-2 defenders; 3-5 analysers; 6-7 prospectors	18
International strategy	Bartett and Goshal (1987), Harzing (1999)	Adjustment to local market	7-point Liker scale, scale anchors: 1 = strongly disagree, 7 = strongly agree	19
		Focus on worldwide market		20
		Subsidiary's ideas for international products		21
		Subsidiary developing own export marketing		22
Performance	Choi and Czechowicz (1983) Nohria and Ghoshal (1994) Luo and Peng (1999) Robinson and McDougall (2001)	Subsidiary's perceptions on six dimensions: general satisfaction short-term results performance compared to competitors compared to other subsidiaries in MNE network response to customer requirements long term development	7-point Liker scale, scale anchors: 1 = strongly disagree, 7 = strongly agree	23-28
	Delios and Makino (2003)	Objective measures: market share development, financial indicators on the sector level	% in own product division database	29

Including multiple (three) dimensions in the analysis of external environment allows for a deep analysis of the environment, as described in Section 3.4.2. The first dimension, *the environmental uncertainty,* refers to the transition economy and was earlier used by Luo and Peng (1999) to evaluate the influence of regulatory stakeholders. For this concept, the present study includes two items: the predictability of law change and the reliability of governmental organisations. The second dimension, *environmental dynamism,* measures the predictability and variability of the environment and allows for estimating the intensity of competitiveness and the variability of customer tastes (expectations). Similar to the environmental uncertainty, the measure of Luo and Peng (1999) is also used here by including two questions concerning the intensity of competition and the predictability of customer tastes. Finally, a third item, *environmental constraints,* is an adjusted and a reverse-scaled measure of munificence used earlier by Dess and Beard (1984) and Castrogiovanni (1991). In the present study the environmental constraints measure the difficulties in acquiring resources from the market in general, the scarcity of workforce and the difficulties in assuring cooperation with a supplier's network in particular. As previous research suggested that the subjective measures of the environment such as management perceptions are more relevant than archival measures of the environment (Miller and Friesen, 1983; Boyd *et al.,* 1993), we use the CEOs' perceptions for the evaluation of environment.

Cultural distance

Two of Hofstede's five cultural dimensions are particularly relevant for the HQ-S relationship governance (see Section 3.3.2). Therefore, for measuring cultural distance we adjust the formula of Kogut and Singh (1988) by reducing the number of dimensions to two: power distance and uncertainty avoidance.

$$CD = \sum_{i = 1 \text{ to } 2} [(D_S - D_{HQ}) / \sigma_i] \text{ where}$$

D_S represents the subsidiary's country value on cultural distance,
D_{HQ} represents the headquarters' country value on Hofstede's dimension
σ_i is the standard deviation of the scores on the cultural dimension of countries participating in the present study

Table 4.5 presents the cultural distance estimation based on the data from Hofstede's research published in 2001.

Table 4.5. Calculation of cultural distance for the countries included in the sample.

HQ country	Hofstede's scores[1]		Distance[2] to Poland divided by s.d.		SUM of PD & UA distances
	PD[3]	UA[3]	PD	UA	
Denmark	18	23	2.89	3.33	6.22
Sweden	31	29	2.14	3.05	5.19
Austria	11	70	3.30	1.09	4.39
Norway	31	50	2.14	2.05	4.19
USA	40	46	1.62	2.24	3.86
Australia	36	51	1.85	2.00	3.85
Finland	33	59	2.02	1.62	3.64
Netherlands	38	53	1.74	1.90	3.64
Swiss & Lichtenstein	34	58	1.97	1.67	3.63
Germany	35	65	1.91	1.33	3.24
Italy	50	75	1.04	0.86	1.90
Czech Republic	57	74	0.64	0.90	1.54
France	68	86	0.00	0.33	0.33
Belgium	65	94	0.17	0.05	0.22
Poland	68	93			
Standard deviation (s.d.)	17.29	21.02			

[1] Hofstede's scores have continuous scales, usually from 0 to 100.
[2] Distance is quoted in absolute values.
[3] PD = power distance, UA = uncertainty avoidance.

Generic strategy

For a generic strategy of a subsidiary, an adjusted measure from Shortell and Zajac (1990) is used based on the respondents' opinion – so called self-typing. The measure consists of the evaluation of innovation orientation of the subsidiary in three areas concerning product, market and operations. Similarly to Shortell and Zajac (1990) we use a 7-point Likert scale for this evaluation but we changed the scale's anchors from '1' and '7' to a value of '3' for both anchors and a '0' as a neutral value (see Table 4.3). This was done in order to avoid a perception scale bias and also to emphasise the neutral character of the middle values to the respondents (Buchko, 1994).

International strategy

Measuring international strategy has a relatively short history in management literature. Most research uses measures based on the work of Bartlett and Goshal (1987). This work was later updated and validated by a number of researchers such as Zou and Cavusgil (2002), Gomez and Werner (2004) and Yeniyurt *et al.* (2005). Global strategy measures have been used for longer and more often in the literature (Kogut, 1984; Doz and Prahalad, 1991; Kobrin, 1991; Roth and Morrison, 1992) but they often use different contexts and a higher abstract level. For example, Roth *et al.* (1991) measured the global subsidiary mandate with a 4-item statement, and then used the summed score for classifying the subsidiary as having a global mandate. A global subsidiary with a mandate resembles subsidiaries in the transnational network as developed by Bartlett and Goshal (1987). 'The mandate' gives the subsidiary an important (influencing) function in the MNE's network. Harzing (2000b) applied a modified extended measure and investigated the validity of Bartlett and Goshal's (1987) three-strategies typology: multidomestic, global and transnational. Harzing (2000b) confronted the respondents with four statements: the first concerned achieving economies of scale, the second focused on global competition, the third focused on local competition and the last one included local differentiation. Multidomestic subsidiaries combined strong local competition with national responsiveness. Global subsidiaries showed exactly the opposite picture, focusing on global competition and achieving economies of scale. The third group, transnational subsidiaries attempted to combine national responsiveness with economies of scale. These subsidiaries competed mostly on global markets but also showed a strong focus on domestic market competition. In the present study, we combine the measures of Roth *et al.* (1991) and Harzing (2000b). The expected scores for the three strategies are presented in Table 4.6.

Table 4.6. Operationalisation of international strategy concept.

		Expected score for		
Variable	**Q No.**	**Global strategy**	**Multidomestic strategy**	**Transnational strategy**
Focus on local market	19	Low	High	High
Focus on worldwide market	20	High	Low	High
Subsidiary's ideas for international products	21	Low	Low	High
Subsidiary's control over export	22	Medium	Low	High

Performance

In the contemporary management research, performance is one of the most difficult concepts to measure due to the problems in acquiring data. Companies easily claim confidentiality on any information concerning their performance. In the present study, performance is measured at the subsidiary level. This measurement level helps us to isolate the specific effect of parent strategies (for example, global vs. multidomestic) on the HQ-S governance mechanisms (Luo, 2003). Although, traditional accounting measures for performance have been widely applied to evaluate the performance of business units and subsidiaries, non-financial measures receive better recognition in evaluating the long-term development of an MNE. Watty and Terzioglu (1999) found support for the increasing importance of non-financial measures such as customer satisfaction, productivity and service quality assurance, which determine the competitiveness of a business and its ability to sustain profitability in the future. Non-financial measures may compensate some of the shortcomings of the traditional measures of performance such as: the scope of accounting manipulation, and the short-term oriented, myopic, evaluation of a company's performance (Merchant and Stede, 2003). Moreover, accounting measures record mostly the history of a firm, while non-financial indicators may predict the potential growth of a company. Monitoring a firm's strategy requires measures that can also capture its potential for performance improvement in the future (Chakravarthy, 1986). For example, to capture the innovativeness and growth potential of organisations, a multidimensional approach to performance evaluation is suggested, e.g. Kaplan and Norton's (1996) Balanced Scorecard. The drawback of performance evaluation frameworks is that it is hard to make comparisons between companies due to a large amount of qualitative data[19] (Epstein and Manzoni, 2002) and the validity of these instruments have still to be tested. Changler and Hanks (1993) showed advantages of combining subjective (non-financial) with objective (financial) performance measures: such as a company's position compared to its competitors and profitability indicators. Subjective (non-financial) performance measures are particularly useful in studying emerging businesses, moreover they correlate with the objective measures with a high degree of reliability (Dess and RobinsonJr, 1984; Gonzalez-Benito and Gonzalez-Benito, 2005). Such measures were successfully applied by Luo and Peng (1999), who measured performance using management perceptions on four factors concerning the competitive position of a company and the managers' satisfaction about the company's operations. In the present study we measure performance on the various perspectives of the Balanced Scorecard. These perspectives are adjusted to the special character of the HQ-S relationship governance, as we focus on the effect of the managerial influence of the HQ on the subsidiary. The survey character of the study which implies a quite abstract measurement level (as opposed to a case study), has a proven high validity (Venkatraman and Ramanujam, 1987). We combined a number of measures (Choi and Czechowicz, 1983; Nohria and Ghoshal, 1994; Birkinshaw and Morrison, 1995; Luo and Peng, 1999; Robinson and McDougall, 2001; Delios and Makino, 2003) and built a multi-item measure of operational and strategic

---

[19] For discussion on the applicability of different measures see Epstein and Manzoni, 2002.

performance. In the questionnaire we focused on the subjective measures of the performance based on the perceived satisfaction of the subsidiary's CEO on six dimensions: general, short-term, market, network, customer and learning (see Table 4.4). Financial indicators on the industry level were acquired from the secondary data sources such as the Central Statistical Office (GUS).

4.2.1 The operationalisation of control variables

Table 4.7 presents the overview of control variables. In the present study, the *size* was measured by the number of employees in full-time equivalents (fte) in the headquarters and subsidiary. In the analysis, the natural logarithm of the number of employees was used. In the earlier study of Egelhoff (1984), the nominal number of employees was used. Later studies, however, used the natural logarithm of the number of employees for measuring the size (Roth and Morrison, 1992; Harzing, 1999). As to Miller and Droge (1986) this logarithmic scale normalises the variable, which might otherwise be skewed.[20]

Relationship duration with the headquarters is in some studies equal to the subsidiary age, e.g. Egelhof (1984) and Chang *et al.* (1999). The relationship duration and the subsidiary age have the same length when we talk about the Greenfield investment (see Section 2.1.1). Then a foreign company (MNE) establishes and builds a new company from scratch, which implies that the investment moment and the foundation date are the same. In the case of an investment in an existing subsidiary, the investment date constitutes the beginning of the relationship but the foundation of a subsidiary had taken place much earlier. Harzing (1999) used a two-item measure including the foundation year of a subsidiary and the date of acquiring the majority of capital by the headquarters, but did not register when the entity actually became a subsidiary of this headquarters. For measuring the relationship duration in the present study, we include

Table 4.7. Operationalisation of control variables.

Item	Scale	Q No.
Headquarters and subsidiary size	Number of employees in FTE – full time equivalents	34,35
Relationship duration	2004 minus the investment date	32, 33
International sale	% export of production	37
HQ capital share in subsidiary	%	31

---

[20] Skewness (this term was first used by Pearson, 1895) measures the deviation of the distribution from symmetry. If the skewness is clearly different from 0, then that distribution is asymmetrical, while normal distributions are perfectly symmetrical. Source: http://www.statsoft.com/.

two variables: the investment date and the foundation year of a subsidiary. The duration of the HQ-S relationship is then calculated by the negative of the year in which the largest capital stake was acquired and the year of data collection.

Subsidiary's international sales are measured by asking the respondents to state the percentage of the subsidiary's sales in the international and domestic market. The answers had to total 100%. Moreover, we included an item on the intra-company sales by asking how much of the production is sold directly to the market, and how much to the headquarters – identifying a subsidiary dependence of the headquarters in the international market. Similar measure was used by Kobrin (1991), who applied intra-firm international sales to measure the transnationality of a subsidiary.

Headquarters' capital share is measured by the percentage of foreign HQ capital in the subsidiary. Other studies, e.g. Chang and Taylor (1999), measured the concentration or dispersion of the capital among different shareholders by the proportion of stock held by each MNE owner on five levels: single owner, 50-100% majority owner, 20-50% minority owner, <20% executing a small influence (because of more than 10% share) and the last group with multiple owners. As we learned from secondary data sources, the situation in this study is different, and in each case one dominant foreign investor is present, therefore a continuous scale from 0 to 100% of foreign capital share is used.

4.3 Propositions for the contingency model

As described in Chapter 3, HQ-S governance mechanisms are a function of a number of factors such as the business environment, the culture, and the MNE's strategy and size. In this section the influence of these contingencies will be discussed.

4.3.1 Environment

Looking at the influence of the external environment from the contingency theory point of view, a company will try to predict as well as possible, and build in flexibility to hedge against the uncertainties of the environment and their operations. Porter (1985) showed the impact of the institutional environment on a subsidiary's responsiveness, thus the ability to adjust products and operations to the needs of a local market. A number of studies have explored the influence of institutional instability on the level of integration of foreign operations into the structures of headquarters. It has been shown that the higher the uncertainty about the institutional environment the more integrated foreign operations are and the stronger the supervision of headquarters is (Anderson and Gatignon, 1986; Henisz, 2000). Besides the institutional dimension, environmental forces affect the firm's ability to secure necessary resources, which in turn influence organisational performance (Pfeffer and Salancik, 1978). Luo and Peng (1999) showed that the environmental factors such as hostility, dynamism, and complexity moderate the relationship between the experience and performance of a multinational enterprise. Given that the institutional, economic, and socio-cultural environments in transition economies are dramatically different from those in developed economies (Peng and Heath, 1996), we can expect that these environmental factors will serve as mediator or moderator variables in the governance model of a HQ-S relationship. A moderator variable influences the strength of the relationship, and a mediator variable explains the relationship between the two variables (Baron and Kenny, 1986).

As presented in Chapter 2, similar to other former planned economies, the Polish economy used to be ruled by power relations and bureaucratic control (Peng and Heath, 1996). Such a transition, from a planned to a market economy, is characterised by a weak regulatory regime, poorly protected property rights and relatively strong political interference in the economy (Slangen, 2000). During the transition period the state gradually relinquishes its influence, and the need for a well-developed institutional framework becomes important. The development of an institutional framework and the creation of solid property rights protection usually take a longer time-span and are characterised by strong dynamics. In organisation theory, dynamism increases the task uncertainty which results in the need for more information to achieve a certain level of performance (Galbraith, 1976). In this period, the uncertainty and the risk of opportunistic behaviour are high. Therefore, headquarters will try to decrease the uncertainty and potential risks by adjusting the HQ-S governance. For example, Haley (2000) proposed implementing a special auditing procedure (so called CETA – the Cross-Environmental Technology Audit) for assuring the protection of property rights in new FDI ventures. From the subsidiary perspective, it will appreciate headquarters' legal assistance and advice. A subsidiary may also benefit from the MNE's network of international contacts and knowledge of developed institutional structures. As Luo and Peng (1999) posited, in highly uncertain environments, the support of HQ and other subsidiaries is a valuable resource. The influence of the internal network of an MNE may be strong enough to withstand the pressures of the external environment. In doing so, HQs influence the subsidiaries' institutional environment by lobbying for more favourable decisions, and thus make the sub-environment of the subsidiary less uncertain (Peng and Heath, 1996). Extended networking with other companies and creating (e.g. personal) linkages with the HQ can provide useful feedback and exchange of knowledge and through this help to cope with an uncertain environment (Lyles et al., 2004). Luo and Peng (1999) found that in dynamic environments, a company's international experience positively contributes to its performance. But what if HQ does not have much previous internationalisation experience, especially in the case of the post-communist economies, which have just recently been opened to foreign investors? Then, it needs to exercise additional efforts so as to collect as much information as possible in order to build on knowledge and expertise in managing their new subsidiaries and their business environments. The HQ-S governance mechanisms may aim at supporting an intensive information exchange and promote subsidiary's initiatives. These mechanisms are related to the last two aims of governance (as mentioned in 3.1.1): information exchange and aligning actions.

Environmental constraints are the scarcity of critical resources required by one or more firms within a business environment (Castrogiovanni, 1991). The opposite situation, the environmental munificence (Starbuck, 1976) or Aldrich's (1979) environmental capacity, are said to be able to support the sustained growth of a company. By sourcing from a rich environment, companies can build in flexibility to survive periods of relative scarcity or provide means for sustaining coalition and conflict resolution (Dess and Beard, 1984). Firms operating in highly munificent environments have maximal strategic options, minimal competitive pressures and relative harmony among their organisational constituencies (Sutcliffe, 1994; Goll and Rasheed, 1997). On the contrary, environmental constraints may have a negative effect on the current condition of a company, and also endanger company growth in the future. In such an environment, focusing on strengthening the agency relationship would have no effect and might even work in an adversarial way, as it does not unveil new resource opportunities. In the presence of environmental constraints, interaction with headquarters can contribute to solving shortage problems and HQ may support the subsidiary in searching and acquiring new resources. But before such support takes place, the mechanisms should enable information flows and help recognise and estimate the needs. The coordination mechanism in the HQ-S governance may fulfil this task. This positive effect holds possibly only for a limited period; long-term scarcity in the external environment deters performance and has negative consequences for the whole MNE.

Therefore, we can put forward one general hypothesis for the influence of the external environment which is a result of operating in the turbulent transition environments:

Proposition 1

In turbulent environments, HQ-S governance mechanisms that primarily rely on coordination (in terms of attunement and personal contacts) will be positively associated with performance.

4.3.2 Culture

Governance mechanisms become more complex when organisations cross national borders and set up their subsidiaries in culturally distant countries (e.g. a Dutch company with a subsidiary in Poland). The HQ-S governance mechanisms carry cultural values that are developed in a particular socio-economic and historical setting (Hofstede, 1980). At the same time, Hofstede (2001) stresses the importance of the selective adoption of different governance mechanisms. For example, stronger uncertainty avoidance supports a need for more detailed planning and short-term feedback. A large power distance requires personal control rather than impersonal control systems, as the behavioural obedience is person/principal – not rules – related. Sometimes there is no formal planning at all, political thinking (instead of strategic) is supported and bilateral trust in the relationship between headquarters and subsidiary is missing (Paik and Sohn, 2004). The differences in power distance seem to be more manageable than differences in uncertainty avoidance (Zaheer and Mosakowski, 1997; Chen, 2006). Local managers can adopt more authoritative management practices when the subsidiary is established in a country with a larger power distance than the headquarters, regardless of the participative attitude of their international chiefs. In general, the HQ's ability to manage culturally-distant subsidiaries depends not only on the distance between the cultures but also on the awareness and the knowledge of the foreign culture (in this case – the subsidiary's culture). For example, in the case of HQ managers working as expatriates at the subsidiaries' locations, the knowledge of the subsidiary culture has a significant positive relationship to performance (Burton *et al.*, 2000). The differences between HQ's country and a subsidiary's country in power distance and uncertainty avoidance may have an effect on the HQ-S relationship governance. The focus on control in HQ-S governance can create transparency and culturally compromised instruments for data exchange and for building relationships to reduce uncertainty (related to the liability of foreignness as in Govindarajan and Gupta, 1985), and also provide information for creating knowledge and learning about the two cultures. Therefore, we can formulate the following proposition:

Proposition 2

In case of a large cultural distance, the HQ-S governance mechanisms that primarily rely on control (operational and strategic) will be positively associated with performance.

4.3.3 Generic strategy

The three strategies: prospector, analyser, defender presented in Section 3.3.3, are pursued depending on the extent to which a company is willing and able to explore new markets, develop new products and take the new opportunities in the market. Burton *et al.* (2000) showed that being extremely innovative and pursuing a prospector strategy cannot take place under highly formalised, strictly regulated governance structures. In this case new ideas, if ever allowed to emerge, will be rejected as they display much higher risk with uncertain returns. For this reason innovative-prospector (see Table 3.3) subsidiaries will require a large amount of freedom from their HQs to foster the creation of new initiatives. This is supported by the studies of Govindarajan and Gupta (1985) and Bruggeman and Stede (1993) which demonstrated that innovative companies (with a differentiation strategy according to Porter's (1985) classification) are less intensively controlled financially and may undergo numerous budget revisions, showing flexibility in their financial decision-making. However, Porter's definition, discussion, and examples are deliberately devoid of environmental characteristics, while the Miles and Snow typology, which is used in the present study, lends itself better to evaluating environmental variables (Segev, 1989). Porter assumes that the generic strategy types hold no matter what kind of environment a company operates in, while Miles and Snow's strategies accommodate the differences in the external environment.

In line with the criticism of the agency theory presented in Section 3.2.2, HQ-S governance relying on an agency relationship may have a counter-motivating effect or even become adversarial, as it would exhibit the classical 'headquarters hierarchy syndrome', which indicates a clear superior-subordinate relationship (Bartlett and Ghoshal, 1998). In such a relationship, subsidiaries are only implementers of headquarters' decisions and are strictly controlled for their outputs. There is hardly any space or resources for exploring new initiatives. Bearing in mind the above consideration, we can expect that the prospector strategy will be better served by an informal, horizontal relationship thus stewardship mechanisms, with the HQ contribution as an experienced idea-developer, not as a strict-controller. The study on knowledge-intensive firms performed by Ditillo (2004) suggests that, in a strong-knowledge complexity, as may be the case for companies pursuing a prospector strategy, the governance mechanisms include informal communication, joint action, output exchange and development of shared values/ beliefs. Also for companies which combine their competitive strategy with socially responsible operations as described in the corporate responsibility framework by Porter and Kramer (2006), these mechanisms may contribute to effective strategy implementation. Thus, in line with the contingency theorists such as Govindarajan and Gupta (1985) and Burton *et al.* (2000) we can expect:

Proposition 3

For subsidiaries pursuing a prospector strategy, the HQ-S governance mechanisms that primarily rely on coordination (in terms of attunement and personal contacts) will be associated with better performance.

4.3.4 International strategy

Section 3.3.4 presented three strategies for competing in the international environment: global, multidomestic and transnational. Each strategy denotes different strategic subsidiary roles (Cantwell and Mudambi, 2005) with each requiring specific governance mechanisms as a result of different HQ-S relationship contexts (Kogut, 1984). The evolutionary view of the MNE notices shifts in the international strategies, for example from global to transnational. These strategy shifts require adjustments in the governance mechanisms (Bartlett and Goshal, 1987). The roles of MNE subsidiaries shift along with the changes in the international strategy, for example from competence-exploitive to competence-creative subsidiaries (Bartlett and Ghoshal, 1998). Globalization, in combination with advances in information technology and the Internet are driving multinational companies towards the integration of business processes across countries (Martinez and Jarillo, 1989). Perhaps for the first time in history, the strategies of MNEs have to achieve worldwide coordination and efficiency while optimizing local responsiveness and organisational learning (Martinez and Jarillo, 1991). This strategy combining global efficiencies with local responsiveness is served by a network structure of MNE in which subsidiaries play a strategic role and actively contribute to the overall strategy of a multinational. The evolution and shifts in strategy cannot be performed without consecutive changes in governance. As Prahalad (1976) claimed in his early work, the two strategic options, global and multidomestic, are subject to internal pressures, such as demands for managerial diversity and managerial interdependence.

The primary motivations driving the globalization of the firm are the comparative and competitive advantages that are gained by the integration of various value-added activities performed throughout the organisation (Calori *et al.*, 2000). Multinational enterprises pursuing a global strategy strive for global efficiency as they treat national markets as one global village with worldwide consumer demand (Roth *et al.*, 1991). Under the pressure of globalization forces, the mechanisms for centralizing the decision-making authority and the integration of activities across national boundaries are essential (Kim *et al.*, 2005). In these companies, many activities such as strategic and operational decision-making are centralized at HQ or are headquarters-based. HQ management treats foreign operations as 'delivery pipelines' to a unified global market. The HQ-S governance shows a strong dependence of the subsidiary on the HQ with tight central control of decisions, resources, and information (see scheme in Figure 4.1). This is a result of greater needs for sharing global economies of scale and optimizing factor costs across countries. Global companies like Nike and Mars tightly control the outputs of their international activities (Luo and Zhao, 2004).

The aim of governance under a global strategy is to enable resource sharing and ensure the required output. These aims can be reached by strengthening the agency mechanisms in the HQ-S governance. Therefore:

Proposition 4

For subsidiaries pursuing a global strategy, the HQ-S governance mechanisms that primarily rely on control (operational and strategic) will be associated with better performance.

Although extant research is mainly concerned with the structural and formal mechanisms of governance (Roth *et al.*, 1991), recent studies emphasize the importance of informal inter-

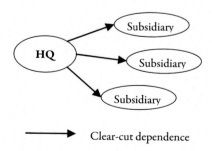

Figure 4.1. HQ-S relationships in global strategy.

functional relationships. These play a special role for MNEs with a transnational strategy, in which a coordinated set of actions is pursued worldwide and controlled by the HQ and key subsidiaries (Kim *et al.*, 2005). In this role, the focus of the governance is not on agency mechanisms, but on activities building transparency, shared identity and values. These mechanisms include: lateral relations, informal communication and the organisational culture (Birkinshaw and Morrison, 1995). In the MNE network, a subsidiary enjoys a world mandate (a concept introduced by Birkinshaw and Morrison, 1995) and actively contributes to strategy development and is interdependent on different units of the MNE (see Figure 4.2). HQ-S governance mechanisms focus on stewardship mechanisms (as opposed to control agency) demonstrate an alternative way for re-alignment of the interests of MNE actors, and shorten the cycle for reinvestment of capital into productivity and growth. These mechanisms facilitate information sharing, learning and innovation that ultimately bring comparative advantage[21] to the MNE (Todeva, 2005). Especially in the era of rapid information technology development allowing for interconnectedness (i.e. linking geographically-dispersed parts of the organisation via intranets, extranets, etc.) best practice repositories and lead centres of excellence enhance a company's performance (Yeniyurt *et al.*, 2005).

For the transnational strategy, a cross-border form of governance is suggested that combines elements of global and local strategy; e.g., Nestle implying that a combination of tight and loose coordination would be characteristic for that type of strategy (Calori *et al.*, 2000).

Proposition 4a

For subsidiaries pursuing a transnational strategy, the HQ-S governance mechanisms that primarily rely on coordination (in terms of attunement and personal contacts) will be associated with better performance.

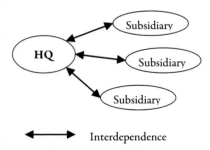

Figure 4.2. HQ-S relationships in transnational strategy.

---

[21] In economics, the theory of comparative advantage (sometimes known as 'Ricardo's Law') explains why it can be beneficial for two parties (countries, regions, individuals and so on) to trade, even though one of them may be able to produce every item more cheaply than the other. What matters is not the absolute cost of production, but rather the ratio between how easily the two countries can produce different goods.

4.4 Concluding remarks

In the elaborated propositions on the influence of the external business environment, cultural distance, generic and international strategy on the HQ-S governance mechanisms, we propose that accounting for these influences will be associated with better performance. Figure 4.3 presents the model for the proposed relationships. Creating a balance between external and internal factors and the HQ-S governance mechanisms may enhance an MNE's performance. These relationships are viewed in terms of a contingency fit. The MNEs that manage to create the fit between their internal and/or external factors show better performance than companies with mis-fit(s) (Burton *et al.,* 2000). This fit is also related to the diverse objectives of the MNEs' expansion into international markets (Geringer, 1989). For example, in industrialised countries these goals are learning, knowledge acquisition and the strengthening of corporate image, while in developing countries natural resources and raw materials acquisition are often mentioned (Luo, 2003). Evaluation and feedback provided on meeting these goals constitutes an important part of the fit evaluation. MNEs that manage to achieve and sustain fit will outperform their competitors. In that sense, fit is a dynamic concept and single (one-time) fit estimations must be interpreted with caution.

The challenge of the present study is to develop a model based on the strategic intentions of the organisation simultaneously accounting for the influence of the environmental factors, the associations between the established coordination-control mode and performance.

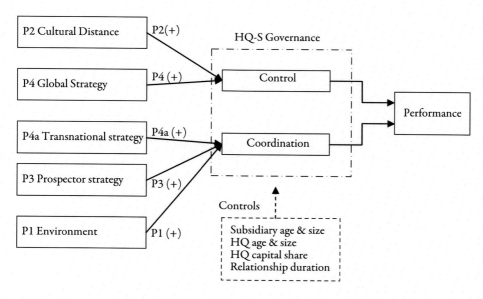

Figure 4.3. Detailed research model for the HQ-S relationship governance.

Chapter 5. Research design

'Statistics is a tool to make order out of the apparent chaos of our environment'

(Child, 1970)

This chapter describes the methodology applied for collecting and analysing the data and is organised as follows. Section 5.1 presents the survey and Section 5.2 the in-depth interview methodology. The survey study methodology describes the issues concerning the level of data collection, the choice for the respondents, survey population and sample and finally the design and pre-test of the questionnaire. As the in-depth interviews are performed after the survey and a similar methodology is applied, only the changes in the in-depth interview methodology as compared to the survey study are discussed in Section 5.2. The remaining part of the present chapter, Section 5.3, presents the methods of data analysis, dealing with missing data in the study, the validity and reliability of the concepts, the classification techniques and the modelling approach.

A research strategy provides the overall direction of the research, including the process by which the research is conducted. It is common practice in management to rely on empirical data when testing propositions and developing conclusions (Romeneyi *et al.*, 1998). This includes being aware of the ontological assumptions that each different research methodology shares (Morgan, 1980). To get a better understanding of the governance issues, we decided to complement the survey research with several in-depth interviews. Combining survey and in-depth interviews is a widely accepted method in management and business research. Romeneyi *et al.* (1998) point out that due to the complexity and dynamic character of business and management problems nowadays, questionnaires alone are increasingly regarded as inadequate in providing the type of evidence needed in management studies.

The choice of a particular strategy is determined by four key factors (see Figure 5.1): research question, time-range of the study, skills of the researcher and costs. The research question or a problem is probably the most important choice and it also determines the other choices.

Figure 5.1. Factors affecting research strategy. Source: Romeneyi et al. (1998: 45).

5.1 Survey research of Polish subsidiaries

Survey research design is a quantitative empirical strategy for gathering data. A survey is defined as the collection of a large quantity of data, usually numeric, or evidence that will be converted to numbers, usually by means of a questionnaire (Romeneyi *et al.,* 1998). This provides a broad overview of the research issue and allows for generalisability of the results (Verschuren and Doorewaard, 1999). Furthermore, survey research has the advantage of representing a relatively time-efficient data collection process. In survey research, the selection of the study sample is a critical decision for the generalisability of the results (Myers, 2000). In international management, the issues around the response rate and generalisability of the results evoke much discussion. In the present study we applied a cross-sectional survey design, which means that the data were gathered at one time and from one population.

In the view of the objective of our study, we expect subsidiary managers to have a good knowledge of the operations of the subsidiary and its daily management. And assuming strategic issues are efficiently communicated throughout the MNE, subsidiary managers will be able to provide information on strategy issues as well. Therefore, we decided to choose the subsidiary level for data collection. For completeness of the view, the mail survey in Poland was supplemented with a number of in-depth interviews at headquarters level.

Having chosen the level of data collection, in the next step we identified potential respondents. We decided to choose one key informant in the person of the managing director (CEO) of the subsidiary. We are aware of the fact that having more respondents, for example the HR manager or financial manager might be more suitable for gathering information on the subsidiary. But it would be difficult to realise because of the additional time and costs involved and the risk of incomplete questionnaires. We assume that the managing director is the best person, aware of both operational as well as strategic issues, and has the most complete information on the relationship with its headquarters.

5.1.1 Survey population and sample

Research into the governance of the HQ-S relationship with a subsidiary based in Poland forms a challenging task. We encountered serious difficulties in finding a suitable sample for our research as the FDI flows are registered only at macro levels by national banks. Moreover, during several interviews with managers from MNEs in Poland, we learned that they are not willing to share any information with researchers and external parties in general. They make an exception for large consultancy offices providing them with company information in return for consultancy services. Unfortunately, these data are unavailable for university research. As a consequence, Polish universities seldom perform empirical research on the micro level and focus on macro-level research, relying on secondary data sources. Not only are MNEs a recent phenomenon there, but the research techniques and traditions also emerged together with the inflow of foreign capital, which means they have a very short history. In the search for a solution to these problems and in view of constrained resources such as time and costs (see Figure 5.1), we contacted the Centre for Economic Information (CEI) and asked for support in the research. CEI is a research division of the Ministry of Labour and Social Affairs in Poland, a centre which takes care of collecting economic and financial data on companies seated in Poland. They had access to a database of companies and agreed to cooperate with our university. The CEI database relies on the evidence from statistical office registration (REGON) which contains 200,000 companies and is updated every three months. Companies are categorised according to Polish EKD[22] classification which conforms to the NACE- Classification of Economic Activities in the European Community. From this database we selected manufacturing subsidiaries based on the criterion of the presence of a significant share of foreign capital (more than 10%) and a size larger than 10 employees.

5.1.2 Questionnaire design and pre-test

The design of the questionnaire is probably the most important stage of the research process. The quality of the instrument has an enormous impact on the quality of the analysis and later on the quality of the conclusions (Romeneyi *et al.,* 1998). With desk research and an extended literature review, we identified a number of concepts relevant to the general framework of the study. In the next step, these concepts and preliminary designs were discussed with four company professionals (CEOs of MNEs). The primary questionnaire was then used in a pilot study on 24 Dutch subsidiaries in Poland in 2002.[23] Comments from respondents, as well as the experiences during this data collection were taken into account in the design of the final questionnaire. In a next step, an adjusted questionnaire was discussed within the Wageningen Business Administration department, with three experts on strategic and financial management, as well as a methodology specialist. To avoid semiotic bias and minimise the influence of the researcher, after designing and translating the questionnaire in Polish, the questionnaire was retranslated into English by an independent translator. The cover page of the questionnaire included a statement on confidentiality of the data and anonymity of the respondents, as well as the institutions engaged in the project and the name and contact data of the researcher. On the last page of the questionnaire, a space was available for comments from the respondents and a box for filling in their e-mail address, in case they were interested in receiving the results of the study. To each questionnaire we added a cover letter explaining the purpose of the study and mentioning potential benefits for the subsidiary management.

5.1.3 Data collection process

The questionnaire together with the covering letter signed by the head of the Business Administration Department, other senior lecturers and the researcher were sent from The Netherlands to the respondents in Poland. The package also included a return-envelope with

---

[22] Europejska Klasyfikacja Działalności.

[23] The results of this study are published in Gusc *et al.* (2003)·

the return address of the Agricultural University in Warsaw, Poland, as we believed it would increase the return rate.

In May 2004 we sent 3,126 surveys to manufacturing subsidiaries in Poland. We decided to send the questionnaire just after Poland had entered the European Union in May 2004, as it was a very good zero-moment for the measurement of the effects of EU entrance. We followed Armstrong and Overton's (1977) widely adopted method of checking non-response bias such as early and late respondents group comparison. The non-response and eventual bias are described in the results in Chapter 6.

5.2 In-depth interviews with Dutch and French headquarters

Contrary to survey design, in-depth interviews form a qualitative research strategy and are similar to case studies, which allow for in-depth detailed analysis of the researched objects (Yin, 1984). In our research, in-depth interviews were conducted after the survey and at a different level, namely at the headquarters. In this way, additional information allowed for an exploration of the perceptions of governance from the headquarters' perspective. Furthermore, it was expected to provide explanatory notes to illuminate the survey findings. To provide for a valid comparison of the views of the subsidiary and headquarter managers, an identical theoretical framework to that in the survey research was applied.

As the in-depth interviews were planned after the survey, we were able use the data from the survey to identify suitable candidates for the in-depth interviews research. For between-countries comparison, we selected headquarters from the Netherlands and France. In both countries we performed several structured interviews, by telephone or by person. For performing interviews, researchers used translated versions of the questionnaire (in Dutch and in French). The data collection in France took place from October to November 2004 and in the Netherlands in December 2005. In contrast to the survey study, here the key informant was the manager responsible for the management of the MNE's foreign operations.

Based on the information we received from the subsidiaries, we were unfortunately not able to trace all the headquarters of the subsidiaries that participated in the quantitative study. In a few cases, headquarters refused to contribute to the research although we had a response from the subsidiary and explained to the headquarters the importance and contribution of this double perception check, for the management of company as well. Finally, we included Dutch and French headquarters which were not the headquarters of the subsidiaries included in the quantitative part of the study. This is important to bear in mind when interpreting the further described comparisons.

5.2.1 Topic list for the in-depth interviews

There was another advantage to performing in-depth interviews after the survey. The survey provided us with a set of operationalised and validated variables. The topic list included the following items:

1. General information on the headquarters.
2. Number and locations of foreign subsidiaries.
3. Date and mode of investment.
4. Headquarters' control configuration and intensity over Polish subsidiary.
5. Headquarters' coordination with Polish subsidiaries.
6. Performance results.

In addition to the above-presented elements, the nationality of the manager directly responsible for the management and performance of a foreign subsidiary was included in the analysis.

In the next section we provide a short description of the methods of analysis applied in the study.

5.3 Methods of data analysis

The data collected by means of questionnaire described in Section 5.2. is used for testing the relationships between several concepts such as strategy, environment, governance and performance in the research model described in Chapter 4. The methods for analysing the relationships and grouping variables in the present study include: descriptive statistics, correlation analysis, cluster analysis and finally a multivariate test of the proposed relationships using partial least squares method (PLS). However, before describing these methods, a problem of dealing with missing data in survey research will be briefly presented.

5.3.1 Dealing with missing data

Despite the careful design and the pre-test of the questionnaire, some of the returned questionnaires showed missing values. Generally, all survey research in the international business environment suffers from missing data in the returned questionnaires (Leung *et al.,* 2003). Instead of commonly applied deleting cases with missing data or replacing missing values with a mean, we decided to use the Expectation-Maximization (EM) estimation technique for replacing the missing values, which allows for avoiding pitfalls of other methods such is their influence on the data distribution and by this increases the reliability of multivariate analysis based on these data. The Expectation-Maximization (EM) approach belongs to the model-based missing data analysis techniques, where the missing data are replaced whether through a specifically designed procedure or as an integral portion of multivariate analysis (Hair *et al.,* 1998). The EM method is an iterative two-stage method (the E and M stages) in which the E-stage makes the best possible estimates of the missing data, and the M-stage then makes estimates of the parameters (means, standard deviations, or correlations) assuming the missing data were replaced.

The E-step finds the conditional expectation of the 'missing data' given the observed data and current estimated parameters, and then substitutes these expectations for the 'missing data'. The EM process has an iterative character and continues re-estimating parameters until a convergence is reached (Little and Rubin, 1987).

5.3.2 Construct validity and reliability

The validity of a construct is the extent to which the answer to a question is a true measure and a true reflection of the operational definition, whereas the reliability refers to the extent to which respondents in comparable situations will answer the questions in similar ways (Carmines and Zeller, 1979; Churchill, 1979; Fowler, 2002: p. 88-89). Construct validity refers to establishing correct operational measures for the concepts, ideas and relationships being studied. It is also called a scale valuation criterion and it relates to the two steps:
a. carefully identifying ideas, concepts and relationships and issues to be studied;
b. demonstrating that the selected measures actually address the ideas, concepts, relationships and issues being studied.

Some of the concepts used in the present study were drawn from the literature (see Sections 4.1 and 4.2) and their validity was analysed in earlier studies, e.g. the concept of international strategy in the study of Harzing (1999).

Face validity, also known as content validity, excludes the possibility of a construct being valid as a result of a superficial enquiry or inspection. It assesses the correspondence of the variables to be included in a summated scale and its conceptual definition (Hair *et al.*, 1998). Internal validity is of concern in all causal and explanatory studies. It is the degree of validity of statements made about whether X causes Y (Rosenthal and Rosnow, 1991).

Reliability is a measure of consistency between multiple measurements of a variable. Nunnally (1978: 206) defined reliability as '*the extent to which measurements are repeatable and that any random influence which tends to make measurements different from occasion to occasion is a source of measurement error.*' There are number of possible tests for internal validity e.g. test-retest, item to total correlations or internal consistency tests. We will describe one of the internal consistency tests; namely the Cronbach's alpha, which is based on inter-item correlation and allows for measuring reliability of the entire scale (Nunnally, 1978). The Alpha gives us information about the extent to which each item in a set of items correlates with at least one other item in the set (i.e. the communalities of the items). Generally the agreed minimum level for Cronbach's Alpha is .70, however it may decrease to .60 in exploratory research (Hair *et al.*, 1998). Although alpha is sometimes referred to as 'the estimate of reliability', researchers must be cautious in its application for its positive relation to the number of items, the more items that are in the scale, the higher the reliability value is, even with the same degree of inter-correlation (Hair *et al.,* 1998). For example, if a scale has many items (i.e. more than 20), then it may show the alpha greater than .70 even when the correlation among individual items is very small (Cortina, 1993). Cronbach's alpha is used for measuring reliability inside one factor. In a uni-dimensional scale (such as applied in the present study) an average item inter-correlation of .50 yields alphas that are acceptable by convention (i.e. greater than .75) regardless of the number of items. Cortina (1993) suggested applying different lower levels for the alpha coefficient depending on the number of items and the level of inter-item-correlation (see Table 5.1).

In the present study the construct validity and reliability analysis are integrated in the PLS model estimation.

5.3.3 Cluster Analysis

Cluster Analysis (CA) is used in the present study to create strategy groups and thereby get better insights into differences between these groups. CA is a restrictive method for dividing a group of objects into subgroups called clusters in such a way that objects in the subgroup are more similar than objects in different subgroups. CA in the present study allowed for classifying three international strategy groups of objects: multidomestic, global and transnational. This grouping method has similarities with factor analysis, except that there the variables are grouped and not the objects. The results of cluster analysis contribute directly to the development of classification schemes (Anderberg, 1973). Central questions that we ask before performing CA are:

> *How to measure the similarity?*
> *Which variables should be used?*
> *For which objects or subgroups should clusters be created?*

Table 5.1. Alphas and precision estimates. Source: Cortina (1993).

No. of items	Average item inter-correlation in one dimension		
	r = .30	r = .50	r = .70
	α	α	α
6	.72	.86	.93
12	.84	.92	.96
18	.88	.95	.98

There are two methods for creating clusters: hierarchical (agglomerative) and non-hierarchical. In hierarchical cluster analysis each object starts as a cluster and in successive steps these single clusters are merged based on the highest possible similarity, e.g. score on a certain question. On the contrary, in the non-hierarchical method a number of clusters including cluster centres are specified beforehand. Non-hierarchical methods are very sensitive to the choice of the seed points – cluster centres. This sensitivity can result in instability (inreplicability) of a cluster solution (Lorr, 1983). The most stable clusters are those based on the so-called 'natural' grouping which emerges from the measure and the method used. But if the natural grouping is known why perform cluster analysis? This question is known as 'cluster analysis paradox' (Everitt, 1993). To avoid this cluster analysis paradox as well as to acquire stable cluster solution, the combination of hierarchical and non-hierarchical methods is used in the present study. That means that we first subject the data to the hierarchical method and search for natural groups and so identify the cluster centres. In the hierarchical method, the similarity calculated as the sum of squares between two clusters is summed over all variables to create clusters (in SPSS it is Ward's method). This method minimizes the within-group variation and creates clusters of approximately similar sizes. The cluster centres (here the value on the strategy question) evolved from the hierarchical method are then compared to the cluster centres as suggested by earlier research on the international strategy (see (Roth *et al.,* 1991; Harzing, 2002; Wolf and Egelhoff, 2002). In the next step we use those cluster centres (centroids) as pre-specified seeds for the non-hierarchical method (K-means cluster) and build clusters around these centres. Finally, we place the results of both hierarchical and non-hierarchical clusters in a cross table; when they converge the final cluster solution is stable and valid (Everitt, 1993; Hair *et al.,* 1998). Between-clusters comparisons are performed applying Kruskal-Wallis (1952) tests for non-parametric data.

5.3.4 Partial Least Squares (PLS)

For exploring the paths between constructs in the research model (see Figure 4.5), a partial least squares method was applied. PLS is a second generation multivariate technique developed by Wold (1975, 1985). It estimates path models involving latent constructs indirectly measured by multiple indicators. PLS is an iterative technique which encompasses the following statistical methods:
- canonical correlations;
- redundancy analysis;
- multiple regression;
- multivariate analysis of variance;
- principal components.

It is particularly suitable for larger model estimations, when the importance shifts from individual variables and parameters to packages of variables and aggregate constructs (Wold, 1985). As compared to the better known factor based-covariance fitting approaches (i.e. LISREL), the component-based PLS avoids two serious drawbacks: inadmissible solutions (such as negative variances) and factor indeterminacy (Fornell and Bookstein, 1982). Instead, it estimates latent variables (LV) as exact linear combinations of the observed measures (manifest variables) and provides exact definitions of component scores. Unlike structural equation modelling or general least squares methods, PLS does not require a strong prior theory of existence and full-information estimation, which makes it suitable for early stage research models with emphasis on theory exploration and prediction (Hulland, 1999). In PLS, it is assumed that all measured variance can be explained (Marcoulides, 1998; Chin and Newsted, 1999).

The PLS method developed by Wold (1980, 1982) has several considerations:
- allows working with small sample size and therefore the researcher does not have to bother about assumptions of maximum-likelihood estimation (MLE);
- only the basic assumptions of least-squares estimation must be satisfied;
- the estimation is distribution-free;
- does not pose identification problems;
- can be used with small samples; and
- has the same freedom with measurement scales as ordinary regression.

The path coefficients in PLS are standardised regression coefficients and the loadings of items on the constructs are the same as factor loadings. In PLS, the analyst specifies the residual variances to be minimized and the estimation is accomplished via an iterative procedure in which each step involves minimization of residual variance with respect to a subset of the parameters, given a fixed-point constraint on the other parameters.

The application of PLS has a relatively short tradition in management literature and as a second generation multivariate technique is slowly increasing in popularity among social science researchers. Table 5.2 presents an overview of PLS application in management studies.

Table 5.2. Application of PLS in management literature.

Authors	Sample
Cool *et al.* (1989)	21 commercial banks
Fornell *et al.* (1990)	67 Swedish and Norwegian industrial firms
Johansson and Yip (1994)	20 American and 20 Japanese companies
Birkinshaw *et al.* (1995)	124 businesses from 10 industries
Steenkamp and Trijp (1996)	192 meat-purchasers for the household
Howell *et al.* (2005)	101 senior managers

A PLS Path model is described by (1) a measurement (outer) model relating the manifest variables to their latent variable, and (2) structural (inner) model relating some endogenous latent variables to other latent variables.

In the **measurement model**, two ways exist to relate manifest variables to their latent variables: reflective and formative. In the reflective way each latent variable ξ is indirectly observable by a set of manifest variables x_{jh} (h-$_{th}$ manifest variables related to the j-$_{th}$ latent variables). Each manifest variable is related to its latent variables by simple regression:

$$x_{jh} = \pi_{jh0} + \pi_{jh}\,\xi_j + \varepsilon_{jh}$$

where ξ_j has mean m_j and standard deviation 1. It is a reflective scheme: each manifest variable x_{jh} reflects its latent variable ξ_j. The usual hypotheses on the residuals are made (Chatelin *et al.,* 2002). Reflective indicators (measures) reflect an unobserved, underlying construct giving rise to (or 'causing') the observed measures (Diamantopoulos and Winklhofer, 2001). Reflective constructs have arrows directed towards the indicators, and each indicator in each block would be individually regressed on its respective latent variables (i.e. inside approximation score). If the constructs are unobservable they must be inferred from measured variables. In this case each construct called a 'latent variable' is explained by a number of indicators (combination of variables) that can be empirically measured. This design enables us to evaluate the incidence of construct measurement error (convergent and discriminant validity) in addition to error in the structural equations among constructs.

In the formative way, the latent variable ξ_j is generated by its own manifest variables. The latent variable ξ_j is a linear function of its manifest variables:

$$\xi_j = \Sigma_h\,\varpi_{jh}\,x_{jh} + \delta_j$$

The formative construct has the arrows directed towards itself and multiple regression on the indicators is performed (Chin and Newsted, 1999). The manifest variable x_{jh} is an observed variable describing an underlying concept measured by a latent variable ξ_j. They are usually built in such a way that each manifest variable x_{jh} is positively correlated to its latent variable ξ_j. This implies that expected signs of the loadings π_{jh} and the weights ϖ_{jh} are positive. There are no signs constraints on loadings and weights in the PLS algorithm, but unexpected signs of the loadings and/or weights show problems in the data and some action must be taken. For example, manifest variables related to estimated parameters with wrong signs can be removed from the data (Chatelin *et al.,* 2002). Formative indicators define or (cause) the construct. Cause measures, first introduced by Blalock (1964), are measures that form or cause the creation or change in the LV (i.e. formative relationship). An example is social economic status (SES), where indicators such as education, income and occupational prestige are the items that cause or form the LV social economic status. If an individual loses her job, the SES will be negatively affected. But to say a negative change has occurred in an individual's SES does not imply that there was a job loss. Furthermore, the change in an indicator (say income) does not necessarily imply a similar directional change for the other indicators (say education or occupational prestige). As explained by Chin (1998), formative indicators need not be correlated nor have high internal consistency such as a high Cronbach's alpha. A researcher must think and make a choice beforehand as to whether the underlying construct causes the observed measures (i.e. reflective relationships) or the manifest variables cause (or define) the construct (i.e. formative relationship).

The measurement model enables us to evaluate whether the constructs are measured with the satisfactory accuracy: convergent and discriminant validity. Convergent validity of a construct is measured by the ratio of the amount of variance of its indicators captured by the construct (factor loading), relative to the total amount of variance, including the variance due to the measurement error ('average variance extracted' AVE). As a general rule, a ratio of less than 0.50 is judged inappropriate as more variance is due to error (Calantone *et al.*; Bagozzi *et al.*, 1991). Constructs are considered to have adequate discriminant validity, if the square root of the AVE (average variance extracted) for each construct is larger than the correlation between the construct and any other construct in the model (Chin, 1998). This implies that the variance shared between any two constructs is less than the variance shared between a construct and its indicators (Bagozzi *et al.*, 1991).

The **structural (inner) model** specifies the relations among the constructs (or latent variables):

$$\xi_j = \beta_{j0} + \Sigma_i \, \beta_{ji} \, \xi_i + v_j$$

A latent variable which never appears as a dependent variable is called an exogenous variable; otherwise it is called an endogenous variable. The causal model must be a causal chain, which means that there is no loop, or in other words the model is recursive. The path coefficients in a PLS model are standardized regression coefficients, and the loadings of items on the constructs are the same as factor loadings (Birkinshaw *et al.*, 1995).

PLS estimation proceeds in two stages. First, the latent variables are estimated in an iterative manner by finding successive approximations. The algorithm involves alternations between the measurement and the structural model where parameters estimated in either part of the model are treated as fixed just as the parameters in the other part are estimated. Second, upon a convergence, the measurement and structural relations are estimated by OLS regression using the latent variables estimated in the first stage (Chatelin *et al.*, 2002). This method has an important advantage compared to regression analysis for two reasons: first, it considers all path coefficients simultaneously, including direct, indirect and also false relationships, second it estimates the factor weights in the context of the theoretical model rather than in isolation.

As PLS does not require multivariate normality for estimating parameters it is suitable for use with **smaller samples** and is less affected by changes in the distributional properties of the sample (see Wilcox, 1998 for a discussion on the normality assumptions). In the model specification and in the estimation process, the PLS requirements for sample size become reasonably clear for all stages of the estimation process. This has to do with the fact that either simple (reflective indicators) or multiple regressions (formative indicators) are performed depending on the mode for each block of indicators and the inner weighting scheme. Due to the partial nature of the estimation procedure where only a portion of the model is involved at any one time, only the part that requires the largest multiple regression becomes important (Jöreskog and Wold, 1982).

In PLS, **the model fit** is evaluated based on the strength of the structural paths and the loadings in the measurement model. The loadings should be at least 0.60 (and better at 0.70) or higher, indicating that each measure accounts for 50 percent or more of the variance of the underlying LV (Latent variable). Meaningful standardized paths in the structural model are those of at least 0.20 and ideally above 0.30, anything lower is due to the 'crude factor' when everything correlates with something to some extent 'because of some unknown complex environmental factors' (Meehl, 1990: 209). Furthermore, paths of .10, for example, represent at best a 1 percent explanation of variance. Thus, even if they are 'real', constructs with such paths are theoretically not interesting (Chin, 1998). In the present study Partial Least Square analysis was performed with software PLS Graph 3.0 under the license from W. Chin.

5.4 Concluding remarks

This chapter described the methods and procedures for data collection for both the quantitative survey and the qualitative in-depth interviews in our research. We described the population of our study and measurement levels. We briefly described data analysis methods applied in the present study and described some of the advantages and disadvantages of the particular research method asserting mentioning its utilisation for the present research. In the present study, we use the following software packages for the data analysis: SPSS 12.00, PLS graph 3.1 and Microsoft Excel.

Chapter 6. Survey results

This chapter presents the results of the analysis of the survey research. Section 6.1 describes the response and the non-response in the present study. Next, a baseline description of the subsidiaries is presented in Section 6.2. This section includes the characterization of subsidiaries' markets, strategy and autonomy in decision making. Section 6.3 describes the characteristics of the participating MNEs. In Section 6.4 the different HQ-S governance mechanisms are addressed. Sections 6.5 and 6.6 present the respondents' perception of the external environment and the calculation of cultural distance between MNE's and subsidiary's countries based on the scores of Hofstede's (2001) dimensions. We close the baseline description of the study sample with an estimation of the performance of the subsidiaries (Section 6.7). Section 6.8 presents the PLS model in which the results of a simultaneous evaluation of the proposed relationships are described. The last Section 6.9 presents the results of the international strategy clusters and reveals several interesting differences between the clusters.

6.1 Response rate and analysis of non-response

The research population included 2,872 manufacturing companies with foreign capital participation registered in the database at the Centre for Economic Information (CEI) in Warsaw, Poland. We were informed that the database would probably not be entirely up-to-date. For that reason we decided to include the whole population in the mailing. Indeed, after the first mailing in May 2004, we received 541 survey questionnaires back which were non-eligible. These 541 companies were terminated or moved to other addresses without having left their new address for new mail to be forwarded. At that moment we learned that the database-update performed by the Centre for Economic Information (CEI) included the input of new companies, but terminated companies had not been removed. In consequence, it contained many more companies than in fact were operating. After the first mailing we received 61 surveys. Out of these 61 companies, 7 companies had to be excluded as there was no foreign capital present, or the capital was brought in by a Polish private individual with a foreign nationality. These companies returned empty questionnaire forms, so no additional information was available. Another 6 companies returned the questionnaire and declined participation in the research. We were therefore forced to adjust the research strategy to increase the response rate.

To support the data collection process and reveal the reasons for non-response, the researcher stayed for a couple of weeks at the Agricultural University of Warsaw, in Poland. During the stay, 151 selected companies were contacted by telephone to remind them about the survey. When selecting companies for the telephone calls, the focus was on the food sector as one of the purposes of the study was exploring differences between food and non-food companies. For approaching non-food companies, a network of personal contacts in Poland appeared to be the most effective way of reaching the appropriate person for answering the questionnaire. The first important finding from these telephone calls shows that despite the fact that the survey was addressed to the General Director (CEO), it did not always reach the right person. Each time we learned about this problem, we sent the survey questionnaire again addressing it directly to the right person. The second finding is that the questionnaire was well-understood and the researcher's assistance in filling it out was seldom required. Interestingly, some of the CEOs were not authorised to quote any information externally about the company. They needed permission from the headquarters to fill out the questionnaire. In some cases we received mailings with multiple authorisation signatures or sent from the headquarters' offices. Finally, the telephone conversations revealed additional information about the organisational structure of the companies in Poland. For example, Danone has a number of production plants spread all over Poland, which all were included in the database as separate companies with foreign capital share. In fact these production plants were subsidiaries of the Polish headquarters seated in Warsaw, which in turn were subsidiaries of the French headquarters. As the subject of the study was the analysis of the cross border HQ-S relationship governance, Polish subsidiaries of headquarters seated in Poland were excluded from the research.

Finally, the response after the telephone calls resulted in another 28 completed questionnaires. Moreover, it revealed the reasons for non-response of 123 other respondents (see Table 6.1). The non-eligible respondents were removed from the population and this resulted in a response rate of 34%.

The response from the telephone-contact procedure together with the response from the first mailing provided 89 questionnaires, 76 of which were useable for the analysis. The comparison of early and late respondents did not show any significant differences. The industry distribution of the subsidiaries and the industry distribution in the population are shown in Table 6.2.

Comparing the results from the telephone calls with the original composition of the CEI database, we can classify as much as 44% of the companies as non-eligible. This decreases the

Table 6.1. Non-response during the telephone calls.

Non-response	Count	Percent
Refused to fill out	22	18%
Agreed to respond, but did not send the questionnaire back	35	28%
Non-eligible subsidiaries*	66	54%
	123	100%

The main causes were wrong address, telephone number could not be traced, company did not exist at all or was under liquidation, it was a sub-subsidiary or did not have a production function.

Table 6.2. Industry distribution according to NACE¹/EKD code N=76.

Description of manufacturing sector	Sample		Population	
	Count	Percent	Count	Percent
Food and beverages	24	32%	369	13%
Textiles	6	8%	363	13%
Paper and paper products and printing	5	6%	219	7%
Chemicals and chemical products	4	5%	130	5%
Rubber, plastic, and non-metal products	12	16%	519	18%
Fabricated metal, machinery and equipment	9	12%	623	22%
Electric, audio, medical equipment	6	8%	237	8%
Transport equipment	7	9%	184	6%
Furniture	3	4%	228	8%
Total	76	100%	2,872	100%

¹ The EC statistical office (Eurostat) classification scheme of economic activities. ('Nomenclature générale des activités économiques dans les communautés européennes' [General Industrial Classification of Economic Activities within the European Communities. EKD is Polish equivalent of NACE.

population to 1608 companies. With a population of 1608 companies and 89 questionnaires returned the response rate accounted for about 6%, which is within the range generally found in international management studies (Harzing, 1997; Harzing, 2000a).

We can speculate on the reasons for the relatively low response rate. First, the questionnaire was sent at the moment that Poland entered the EU. Although, important as a zero-measurement moment, it definitely lowered the response rate. During the telephone conversations with the directors and managers, we noticed a high degree of uncertainty about the future developments of their companies with the new EU legislation and requirements. Secondly, while we anticipated that performing this research from an EU-country university would work in favour of the response, in 2004, it definitely engendered even more anxiety. For this reason our response placed itself at the lower boundary of the response range in international management studies.

In the telephone enquiries, lack of interest because of questionnaire weariness and time consumption were the most often mentioned other reasons for non-response. About one third of the CEOs in the non-response group indicated that they would participate at another time or stated that their companies were successful and did not need to compare their governance mechanisms, which we proposed in the cover letter, as appreciation for their participation in the survey.

6.2 Profile of the subsidiaries

The majority of foreign subsidiaries was characterized by homogeneous private ownership. Most of the subsidiaries with mixed ownership (private/state) were (partially) privatized state-owned companies (described in Section 2.4.1), in which the State Treasury held a minor capital stake and employees together with foreign shareholder(s) had a majority share (see Table 6.3).

The effect of the introduction of the economic transformations was clearly noticeable from the date the subsidiaries were established. Most of them were established after the market liberalisation process had started in 1990, and only a few companies (15%) had a longer tradition. Two companies had a more than a 100-year tradition and dated from the 19th century. The largest group of subsidiaries (47%), represented those founded in the early transformation period 1990-94 (see Figure 6.1).

Table 6.3. Ownership distribution in the sample (N=76).

CEI Code	Ownership type	Percent
216	Private with foreign capital share	70%
226/236	State or mixed state/private with foreign capital share	30%

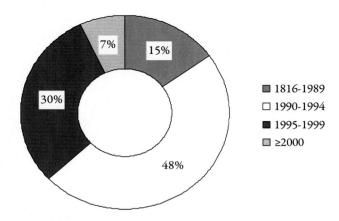

Figure 6.1. Establishment year of the companies [N=76].

When we compared the subsidiaries founded before and after the transformation began in year 1989, we noticed that in the groups of subsidiaries founded in the early transformation process, the acquisition of capital by a foreign shareholder took place gradually and foreign capital share was significantly lower than in the rest of the subsidiaries.

If we look at the entry foundation mode, we see that Greenfield investments clearly prevailed (52% of cases). These wholly-owned subsidiaries were established from scratch by the headquarters (see Figure 6.2). Next to acquisitions (15% of cases), a special kind of acquisitions – 'Brownfield' – investments were identified in 11% of the cases. This particular entry mode, characteristic for a transition economy (see in more detail: Meyer and Estrin 1998), implies a huge resource transfer from the investment company to the acquired company. This situation takes place particularly if the privatisation process is started with the aim of restructuring a subsidiary or if a subsidiary owns or controls special kind of resources which cannot be purchased in the market (e.g. licences to produce).

Although subsidiaries had a relatively large mean size (223 employees), the majority was small; 76% employed less than 250 workers (see also the positively skewed distribution in Table 6.4). The skewness shows a lower value for the year 2004 and 2006, indicating a more equally spread distribution of subsidiaries' sizes.

A deeper investigation of the employment change from 2002 through 2006 showed that the average subsidiary became smaller (see mean value in Table 6.4), although the median size increased. This higher median size means that the number of large subsidiaries in the period 2004-06 increased. At the same time the maximum size of subsidiaries decreased. This decrease may be the result of reorganisation processes or expiration of initial contractual commitments

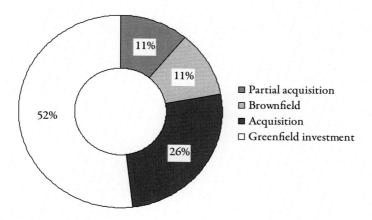

Figure 6.2. FDI entry mode in Poland [N=76].

Table 6.4. Employment in subsidiaries (N = 76 for 2002 and 2004; N = 59 for 2006).

Statistics	Employees		
	2002	**2004**	**2006 (projected)**
Median	85	91	110
Mean (SD)	255 (526)	223 (356)	237(326)
Min/Max	10/3900	10/2400	8/1600
Skewness	5.19	3.84	2.72

obligating headquarters to sustain employment for a certain period of time[24] in the privatised companies. As shown in Table 6.5, employment increased in 56% and decreased in 34% of the subsidiaries during the period 2002-2004. Interestingly, the respondents had a positive opinion of the future, as 71% of the companies expected growth in 2006.

We found two especially interesting subsidiaries: one operating in the manufacture of wearing apparel, dressing and dyeing of fur and the other in the food industry. The manufacturer of wearing apparel more than doubled its size in the period 2002-2004 (increase in employment by 220%), and planned a more moderate increase of 18% for the period 2004-2006. The second subsidiary, operating in the food industry, showed the opposite picture and had a moderate 15% expansion in the period 2002-2004 and expected to grow by 200% in the period 2004-2006. Such a large change in employment is usually a result of an important strategic decision or event that has a strong impact on current subsidiary operations.

Table 6.5. Employment in subsidiaries 2002-2004 (N=76); 2004-2006 (N=59).

Subsidiaries	Change 2002 through 2004	Change 2004 through 2006
Expand	56%	71%
No change	10%	15%
Decrease	34%	14%
	100%	100%

---

[24] This was usually the consequence of privatisation or special economic zones regulations (see Section 2.4.1).

6.2.1 Subsidiaries' markets served

Most subsidiaries concentrated on B2B (business-to-business) markets, 48% sold their entire production and another 18% the majority of their production to business customers. Only 16% of subsidiaries directed their sales purely at private consumers (see Figure 6.3).

In line with the general idea that companies with foreign capital share show strong international activity as they profit from faster and easier access to international markets (Durka *et al.*, 2003), the subsidiaries in the sample also showed strong international activity. Figure 6.4 shows that a large group of companies (64%) exported a major part of their production and 11% sold exclusively to the international market. Only 6% of the subsidiaries focused entirely on the domestic market.

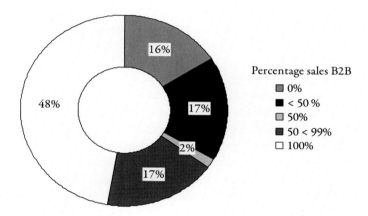

Figure 6.3. Sales to B2B customers by Polish subsidiaries [N=63].

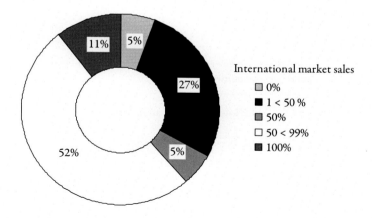

Figure 6.4. Subsidiaries sales in the international market [N=73].

International sales of the Polish subsidiaries were mostly organised through headquarters, which is shown by the strong positive correlation between international sales and sales to the headquarters ($r = 0.8$, $p < 0.01$). Polish subsidiaries selling more than 67% of their products internationally enjoyed little autonomy from their headquarters in strategic planning and in setting performance standards. Also the marketing decisions took place at the headquarters and were then imposed on subsidiaries. The more interesting differences between groups of subsidiaries are presented in Section 6.9.

6.2.2 Generic strategy – innovativeness

Generally, subsidiaries showed rather low scores on innovation in three areas: products, operations and markets (see mean values in the bottom row in Table 6.6). Most of the subsidiaries (53%) pursued a defender strategy, concentrating on the current areas of operations and on current markets. Only one area of operations shows a slightly higher mean value for innovations. This may be interpreted as subsidiaries implementing improvements or new solutions once these had been successfully applied in HQs first, which indicates knowledge-sharing in the MNE network.

The most innovative prospector companies formed the smallest group of subsidiaries (11%), but at the same time were on average the most successful. In this group 80% of the subsidiaries showed above-average performance. A group of 28 subsidiaries pursued an analyser strategy. These subsidiaries postponed the implementation of an innovative solution till it had proven its quality elsewhere, or they focused on innovation in one area at a time, either on a new product, or on improving operations, or on entering new markets. A possible explanation for these results is that by selectively choosing their innovation areas these subsidiaries were better able to cope with uncertainties and seize the opportunities in the transforming market. Defenders, only exploiting the existing market and bringing hardly any changes to their operations and product portfolio, formed the largest group with 40 subsidiaries.

Table 6.6. Generic strategies of subsidiaries.

Strategy	Innovative orientation*			N	Indicated above average performance
	Products	Markets	Operations		
Prospectors	6.50 (0.53)	6.38 (0.52)	6.38 (0.74)	8	80%
Analysers	2.54 (1.73)	3.64 (2.31)	4.21 (1.85)	28	70%
Defenders	1.55 (0.78)	1.50 (0.78)	1.50 (0.64)	40	65%
Whole sample	2.43 (1.90)	2.80 (2.08)	3.01 (2.11)	76	69%

Scale: $x \le 2$ defenders; $2 < x \le 5$ analysers; $5 < x \le 7$ prospectors

*question no 18 in the questionnaire see Appendix 1

Interestingly, the innovations in the operations were positively associated with international strategy variables. Subsidiaries showing high scores for operations innovativeness controlled the marketing of their export products (r = 0.3, p < 0.01, N=76) and more often developed ideas for international products (r = 0.2, p < 0.10, N=76).

Prospector subsidiaries were particularly interesting as they showed much higher autonomy in decision making than the other subsidiaries. Decisions concerning strategy, setting performance standards and manufacturing and control quality took place locally at the subsidiary level (see Table 6.7). These subsidiaries sold independently of the HQs a much higher percentage of their products in the international markets; 26% compared to the 14% for analysers and defender firms. Interestingly, the directors of these subsidiaries perceived higher dynamism of the environment in the customer dimension. In view of the observation that prospectors showed better performance, we may think that this group put more effort into tracing changes in customer needs and tastes, and therefore was better informed about market developments. Finally, prospectors had headquarters from more culturally distant countries. This is in line with the comments of the subsidiary directors about the quality of the cooperation (see Section 6.5.). The directors of subsidiaries with more culturally distant headquarters' countries showed greater satisfaction with the relationship with headquarters than culturally close headquarters.

Table 6.7. Prospector subsidiaries.

	Others (N = 68)	**Prospectors (N = 8)**
Autonomy in strategic decision-making [39a]	3.18 (1.73)	4.63 (2.00)
Autonomy in setting performance standards [39b]	3.67 (1.77)	4.88 (2.03)
Autonomy in manufacturing and quality decisions [39d]	5.50 (1.40)	6.50 (1.07)
Independent of the HQ international sales [37a]	14% (24.77)	26% (23.71)
Market dynamism: customers' needs change [14]	4.12 (1.83)	5.92 (1.05)
Cultural distance between HQ and subsidiary	3.30 (1.12)	4.07 (1.91)

Kruskal-Wallis tests significant at p < .05, *p* < .10

6.3 Baseline description of headquarters

Headquarters had a relatively short experience of operating in Poland; only four HQs entered Poland before the beginning of the transformation process, so before 1989. Most of the HQs (67%) started their operations in Poland after 1995 and quite a few (24%) invested after 2000 (see Table 6.8).

Table 6.9 presents the country of origin of the headquarters as well as the distribution of the investor capital in the total study population. Germany, the neighbouring country of Poland seated the most headquarters. The second and third largest group originated from the Netherlands and the US. French headquarters were clearly under-represented in our sample with 3% as compared to 11% in the population of foreign investors in Poland (see Table 6.9).

Concerning the area of activity, it should be mentioned that many of our respondents (subsidiaries' representatives) found it difficult to classify their HQs activities even though we left an open space for a description instead of using a four-digit NACE[25] code. Eventually we collected the activities of 55 HQs (see Table 1 in Appendix 4). Most of the HQs invested in a subsidiary in the same branch, but also a few so-called supply chain investments were found, such as a retailer in 6 HQs investing in manufacturing facilities in Poland which operated as an intermediary or a wholesale trader, not as a manufacturing company.

We found mainly large HQs investing in Poland. Nearly 45% employed more than 250 employees, while the largest headquarters had more than sixty thousand employees. The group of small investors, with less than 50 employees in the headquarters, counted for 30% of the sample. Large headquarters had usually larger subsidiaries (r = 0.56, p < 0.00, N =

Table 6.8. Year of capital acquirement in a subsidiary (N=67).

Capital acquired	Percent
before 1991	7%
1991-1995	25%
1996-1999	43%
after 2000	24%
	100%

---

[25] The EC statistical office (Eurostat) classification scheme of economic activities. ('Nomenclature générale des activités économiques dans les communautés européennes' [General Industrial Classification of Economic Activities within the European Communities.

Table 6.9. Headquarters origin (N=74).

Countries	Headquarters in the sample	Percent	Total investors in Poland	Percent of investors
EU members				
Germany	27	36%	258	28%
Netherlands	8	11%	126	14%
Italy	5	7%	27	3%
Denmark	4	5%	50	5%
Finland	3	4%	20	2%
Belgium	3	4%	67	7%
Austria	2	3%	40	4%
Sweden	2	3%	60	7%
France	2	3%	101	11%
Czech Republic	1	1%	5	1%
Non EU members				
Norway	5	7%	14	2%
Switzerland	4	5%	28	3%
USA	7	10%	118	13%
Australia	1	1%	3	0%
Total	74	100%	917	100%

65). HQs held mostly 100% ownership of their subsidiaries (76%), or majority ownership (21%). In only two cases (3%), headquarters had less than 50% capital share. The results of the comparison of the wholly-owned (100% capital share) and the partially-owned subsidiaries show that governance mechanisms in the wholly-owned subsidiaries were more standardised, and often imposed by the headquarters (see Table 6.10). The marketing departments of the wholly-owned subsidiaries contacted their headquarters more frequently than departments in partially-owned subsidiaries. Interestingly, their CEOs had different perceptions of the external environment depending on whether their subsidiary was wholly or partially-owned. In the wholly-owned subsidiaries, subsidiaries' CEOs perceived more constraints upon access to resources in general, and stronger dynamics of the environment. A probable explanation for these differences in perceptions may be that without Polish capital more uncertainties around the resource supply may arise as the participation of Polish capital contributed to securing the procurement of resources. Another explanation may be that wholly-owned investment bears higher risks as a result of higher investment and therefore the perception of the uncertainties in the environments is higher.

Despite the fact, that the wholly-owned subsidiaries perceived the business environment as more competitive they showed greater satisfaction in their customer relations (question 27

Table 6.10. Significant differences between wholly- and partially-owned subsidiaries.

	Foreign capital share	
	< 100% (N = 17)	= 100% (N = 57)
Personal contacts between marketing dept. [6b]*	3.89 (1.44)	4.33 (1.48)
Standardisation imposed by the HQ [3]**	2.93 (1.46)	3.76 (1.22)
Availability of qualified workforce [17]	5.00 (1.84)	4.34 (1.93)
Availability of other resources [16]	5.88 (1.22)	4.95 (1.73)
Subsidiary performance as compared to other subsidiaries [20]	4.45 (1.21)	5.31 (1.19)
Success in response to customer requirements [27]	5.00 (1.27)	5.65 (1.29)

Kruskal-Wallis tests significant at p < .05, p < .10.
* scale 1-8; 1 less than once a year, 2 yearly, 3 semi-annually, 4 quarterly, 5 monthly, 6 semi-weekly, 7 weekly, 8 daily.
** [...] question number in Appendix 1.
All questions 7-point Likert scale; 1 strongly disagree to 7 strongly agree.

in Table 6.10). There are growth opportunities in dynamic environments but the dynamism certainly causes difficulties in catching up with the customer. It may be concluded from our results that HQs may play an important role in dealing with customers, because they can collect information about the customers from multiple international markets and may also have more experience in dealing with customers. However, this relationship should be investigated in-depth to validate this conclusion.

6.4 Baseline description of governance mechanisms

As explained in Section 4.1, governance mechanisms deal with the processes and systems which guide and supervise organisational operations and as a result lead to desired organisational outcomes. The mechanisms included in the present study are expatriate presence, written reports, attunement, personal contacts, but also ICT integration, as well as formalisation and standardisation (see the operationalisation in Table 4.2).

6.4.1 Expatriate presence

Expatriates are headquarters' employees detached for a certain (usually short) period of time to work at a subsidiary location. Expatriates are usually appointed in the founding phase of a subsidiary with the task of organising it according to the strategic intent of the headquarters.

They are often involved in educating and training employees of subsidiaries and perform personal control of the subsidiary's activities.

In the investigated sample, the expatriate presence was low. In the majority of subsidiaries local (Polish) managers held management and director positions. There were more expatriates among CEOs (27%) than in operational management positions (7%). A small group of CEOs – 5% – had a third-country nationality. From the interviews with managers we learned that some companies regularly transferred managers from one subsidiary to another. These transfers probably explain the 5%-presence of third-country nationalities among subsidiary managers.

Many subsidiaries, especially the smaller ones, did not discern separate departments, for example only 53% of the subsidiaries appointed own R&D managers. Management functions were consolidated and held jointly by one person, e.g. both financial and general management was performed by the CEO. Alternatively, these functions were centralized at headquarters. The nationality of the CEO varied according to the size of the subsidiary, as shown in Figure 6.5. In subsidiaries – up to 100 employees, most of the CEOs were Polish (79%), whereas in the medium-size subsidiaries a relatively large group of managers came from third countries (12%). Furthermore, medium-size companies had Polish CEOs in 47% of cases, which represented the smallest share of Polish managers among the three size-groups.

The advantages of sending expatriates to newly acquired or established subsidiaries are being questioned nowadays, especially as a result of acculturation and expatriate family problems (Werner, 2002; Paik and Sohn, 2004). This decreasing trend of expatriate presence was also visible in our sample. In the recently founded subsidiaries (in 2000 or later 7% of the sample see Figure 6.1), hardly any expatriates were present. At the top of marketing, manufacturing and financial departments there were no expatriates at all. Furthermore, there were no

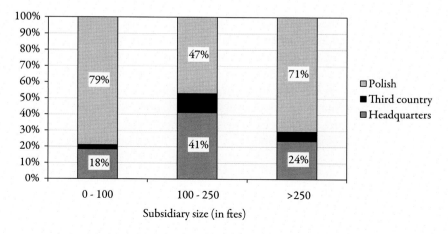

Figure 6.5. Nationality of the CEO and size in 2002 (N=72).

headquarters' representatives in the CEO positions. A few foreign CEOs originated from a third country. The only headquarters' expatriate in subsidiaries founded after 2000 was the head of the R&D department.

When exploring the expatriate presence from the perspective of the duration of the foreign capital presence, the results show that in the subsidiaries with the longest relationship with their HQs all management positions were filled by Polish managers. We observed the largest participation of foreign managers in the group of companies in which investments took place between 1995 and 1999: 35% of the CEOs, 13% manufacturing and 14% financial.

In conclusion, the results show a low presence of expatriates in Polish subsidiaries. At each functional level Polish managers prevailed; only in the director's position was a larger share of foreign nationalities present. In total, only 13% of all positions including the CEO and the heads of four departments manufacturing, marketing, finance and R&D, were staffed with headquarters' expatriates, and 3% with third-country representatives; the remaining 84% was Polish.

6.4.2 Control

The results show a higher frequency of operational compared with strategic control. Production volume and sales turnover were reported monthly in the majority of cases (respectively 52% and 65%). The frequency of reporting on strategic aspects was significantly lower. Reports on market share development were submitted on a quarterly basis, and the reports concerning training of the personnel and R&D activities even more rarely with a semi-annually or yearly frequency (see Table 6.11).

The HQ reactions and questions in these reports showed a similar pattern. HQ inquired about the operational issues such as sales turnover and production volume more often than about for instance R&D and the training of the personnel. This question captured what actually happened with the information. There is a chance that written reports submitted to headquarters end up unread in the archive and in those cases they fail to perform their control task. The reports on sales turnover and production volume received most attention from headquarters, with 17% of subsidiaries always receiving inquiries on submitted reports and 70% being interviewed at least about every second report. Reports on training of the personnel received hardly any attention from headquarters, 50% of the subsidiaries' managers seldom received inquiries about these reports, of which 25% had never been asked to provide any additional information.

MNEs often apply standardised procedures across the entire organisation, including all subsidiaries. Such standardised procedures may concern hiring employees, reward systems, communication with suppliers or negotiating contracts. In our sample, 67% of the subsidiaries confirmed the use of such procedures. These procedures were not imposed on a subsidiary, but

Table 6.11. Mean values for control mechanisms (N=76).

Control mechanisms	Mode value[1]	Mean (s.d.)
Written reports*:		
production volume [1b]**	Monthly	5.65 (1.60)
sales turnover [1a]	Monthly	5.46 (1.34)
market share development [1c]	Quarterly	3.80 (1.15)
product and process R&D [1e]	Semi-annually	3.21 (1.23)
training of personnel [1d]	Yearly	2.98 (1.24)
HQs' inquiries on submitted reports:		
sales turnover [2a]***	50% of the reports	4.49 (1.67)
production volume [2b]	50% of the reports	4.24 (1.82)
product and process R&D [2e]	50% of the reports	3.74 (1.42)
development of market share [2c]	50% of the reports	3.70 (1.74)
training of personnel [2d]	Hardly ever	2.92 (1.45)
Development of standardised polices and procedures[2] [3a]	Jointly with HQ	3.56 (1.30)

[1] The value that has the largest number of observations.

[2] This value concerns only those cases in which standardized policies and procedures were used [N=49].

* scale 1-8; 1 less than once a year, 2 yearly, 3 semi-annually, 4 quarterly, 5 monthly, 6 semi-weekly, 7 weekly, 8 daily.

** [...] question number in Appendix 1.

*** scale 1-7; 1 never, 2 hardly ever, 3 rarely, 4 in half of the cases, 5 often, 6 very often, 7 always.

in many cases (43%) developed jointly by the subsidiary and its headquarters. Interestingly, in 45% of the cases the subsidiary developed the standards independently. Only in one case were all procedures developed by headquarters. These joint actions of HQs and subsidiaries may indicate a genuine strategic change towards, for example, a transnational strategy (see Sections 3.3.5 and the results on international clusters in Section 6.9).

Communication and reports may also be formalised. For example, a report may require a signature or the stamp of a person bearing the final responsibility before it can be submitted to the headquarters. The mean value of use of formalised reporting is 3.53 (see Table 6.12), which is rather low. The high standard deviation of 2.23 shows that there were large differences between the subsidiaries in the sample, meaning that there were subsidiaries with strongly formalised reports or not formalised at all. By measuring the standardisation and formalisation of the reports and personal communication we were able to estimate the way the information between subsidiary and headquarters was exchanged. In the investigated group of subsidiaries, more than 70% applied standardised procedures and policies, but at the same time 50% did

Table 6.12. Formalisation of contacts and information exchange (N=76).

Information collection	Mean (s.d.)
Use of pre-structured formal documents in reporting [4]*	3.53 (2.23)
Formality of personal contacts	
between CEOs [6a]	4.16 (1.89)
manufacturing dep. [6d]	4.13 (1.78)
logistics dep. [6e]	4.09 (1.39)
R&D dep. [6c]	4.07 (1.22)
marketing dep. [6b]	3.88 (1.56)

All questions 7-point Likert scale anchors: 1 not formalised at all, 7 fully formalised.
* [...] question number in Appendix 1.

not use formal documents. The character of personal communication often showed formality aiming at acquiring approval from headquarters at all levels of the subsidiary organisation, from the CEOs to the manufacturing departments (in 45% of subsidiaries). However, in the majority of cases (55%) the purpose of the personal communication was to reach a joint agreement by negotiation and discussion with the HQs.

To sum up, the results show intense reporting on operational issues and less on the strategic issues, such as R&D and human resource management. Written reports and other procedures were standardised and often developed together with the headquarters. Furthermore, intensified inquiries on submitted reports showed headquarters' commitment and attention for their new businesses in Poland.

6.4.3 Coordination

While HQ control mechanisms were on average based on a monthly cycle, coordination mechanisms were used with a slightly lower intensity (compare Tables 6.12 and 6.13). Coordination through attunement showed similar intensity to the control intensity with the exception of attunement of the market share development, which was more often reported (quarterly) than attuned (yearly). HQs' coordination through personal contacts shows lower frequencies (quarterly) than both reporting as well as attuning.

Personal contacts were only frequent between CEOs and the logistic departments. Joint activities, task groups and business meetings which required personal meetings as well, took place with quarterly occurrence. In 10% of the cases, the R&D and logistics departments of the headquarters and subsidiaries had personal contacts even less than once per year.

Table 6.13. Subsidiary coordination with headquarters (N=76).

Coordination	Mode	Mean (s.d.)
Attunement:*		
production volume [7b]**	Monthly	4.27 (1.68)
sales turnover [7a]	Monthly	4.09 (1.61)
product and process R&D [7e]	Quarterly	3.38 (1.27)
development of market share [7c]	Yearly	3.11 (1.13)
training of personnel [7d]	Yearly	2.71 (1.14)
Personal contacts:		
between CEOs [6a]	Quarterly	4.87 (1.53)
logistics dept. [6e]	Quarterly	4.61 (1.77)
manufacturing dept. [6d]	Quarterly	4.34 (1.74)
marketing dept. [6b]	Quarterly	4.19 (1.50)
R&D dept. [6c]	Monthly	3.86 (1.37)
Joint task and projects groups [8]	Quarterly	4.07 (1.80)
Business meetings among subsidiaries [9]	Quarterly	3.64 (1.18)
ICT integration-speed of the information flow [10]***	At once	5.77 (0.98)

* scale 1-8; 1 less than once a year, 2 yearly, 3 semi-annually, 4 quarterly, 5 monthly, 6 semi-weekly, 7 weekly, 8 daily.

**[…] question number in Appendix 1.

*** Likert scale 1-7, 1 slowly to 7 at once (e.g. shared database).

A large geographical distance between headquarters and subsidiaries and, resulting from this, the high costs of such contacts, might have been a cause of the relatively low frequency of personal contacts. Moreover, booming developments in information technology, the use of the internet or intranet-based communication, probably contributed to the relatively infrequent personal communication as well. Indeed, as the high mean value of 5.77 in Table 6.13 shows, subsidiaries were strongly ICT-integrated with their headquarters. Almost 90% of subsidiaries were supported by integrated ICT tools which enabled fast communications with their HQs. The fastest – immediate information exchange through a shared database or other ICT-supported communication took place in 25% of the subsidiaries.

Summing up, operational issues were attuned more often than strategic issues. Personal contacts took place more often at the top management level. Generally, personal contacts were not frequent and subsidiaries were strongly ICT-integrated to ensure fast communication.

6.4.4 ICT integration

We explored the differences in governance mechanisms between highly and less ICT integrated subsidiaries. We divided the sample into two groups: highly ICT integrated (with a question score > 5) and relatively low integrated MNEs (with a score ≤ 5 on a 7-point Likert scale). As we read from Table 6.14, highly integrated subsidiaries showed more frequent personal contacts between CEOs. This result is interesting in view of the generally low frequency of personal contacts. The ICT tools replaced personal contacts at the operational level but not the contacts between CEOs. We can explain this by the fact that the strategic issues are generally more difficult to discuss using standardised ICT tools. Another interesting finding is the more frequent attunement of the production process in highly ICT-integrated subsidiaries. In view of the function of ICT in management we expected a lower attunement score for this group. But the ICT systems in those subsidiaries may have been in the development or implementation phase, therefore requiring intensified attunement between parts of the MNE. This attunement may also be product-related, if the subsidiary developed new products for which the existing standardised ICT tools were insufficient for exchanging ideas and planning activities with HQ.

Highly ICT integrated subsidiaries showed more frequent reporting and attuning on production volume. Apparently ICT did not replace these control and coordination mechanisms. The personal contacts between CEOs were more frequent in the highly ICT-integrated subsidiaries. However, we may expect that a third aspect played a role in these groups' comparison: subsidiary size.

6.4.5 The control and coordination correlations in HQ-S governance

Exploring the relationships between governance mechanisms further, we found that the reports of production volume, market share development and personnel training were positively related to the frequency of attunement on these aspects. When headquarters

Table 6.14. Significant differences between low/high ICT-integrated subsidiaries.

Governance mechanisms	Low ICT- integrated (N=21)	High ICT- integrated (N=55)
Written reports on production volume [1b]*	5.19 (1.60)	5.82 (1.59)
Personal contacts between CEOs [6a]	4.33 (1.28)	5.07 (1.57)
Attunement of production volume [7b]	3.67 (1.39)	4.49 (1.74)

*[…] question number in Appendix 1.
Kruskal-Wallis tests significant at p<.05, $p < .10$.

imposed standards of procedures, a more frequent attunement took place of sales turnover, production volume, education of the personnel, as well as product and process R&D. In international relationships between units of an MNE, standardisation can play an important role in overcoming language and cultural barriers. If standardised polices and procedures are applied throughout the whole multinational network, personal communication and arranging activities become easily accessible and understood across the network. Formalisation, on the other hand, indicated a negative relationship with personal contacts. Formalisation may create a psychological distance which hampers personal contacts inside an MNE.

To sum up, with the exception of the formalisation, our results indicated positive relationships between control mechanisms (reports and standardisation) and coordination mechanisms (attunement) on operational, strategic level and in knowledge development.

6.5 Environment

The respondents perceived their subsidiaries' environment as highly dynamic and competitive. This is in line with the general description of the Polish business environment presented in Chapter 2 of this thesis. Nearly 80% of the CEOs stated that they were operating in a highly competitive environment (see Table 6.15). However, the subsidiaries' customers seem to be more predictable than their competitors; 55% of the CEOs noticed little change in customer needs and expectations in the last three years. Environmental constraints concerning the instability of the suppliers' network and the resource scarcity were generally assured, showing relatively low mean values: 2.18 for suppliers and 3.50 for other resources, such as a qualified workforce (see Table 6.15). Finally, the general political climate did not hamper the development of a subsidiary. However, respondents indicated the negative effect of the interpretation and execution of law on the subsidiaries' operations. Comparing the responses of CEOs and non-CEOs, the results show that CEOs experienced this negative influence

Table 6.15. Descriptive statistics for environment perception (N=76).

Environmental factors*		Mean (s.d.)
Market dynamism:	market with many competitors [13]**	5.79 (1.57)
	customer needs change [14]	4.31 (1.84)
Resource constraints:	instability of suppliers network[15]	2.18 (1.23)
	insufficient qualified workforce [17]	3.50 (1.91)
	insufficient resources [16]	2.89 (1.72)
Political uncertainty:	unstable political environment [11]	4.48 (1.90)
	incoherent law interpretation [12]	4.63 (1.86)

*all 7-point Likert scale; 1 strongly disagree to 7 strongly agree.

** [...] question number in Appendix 1.

significantly stronger than other respondents (mean values 5.1 and 4.3 respectively for CEOs and non-CEOs, Kruskal Wallis, significance at p <0.1, N=35 for CEOs; N=22 non-CEOs).

6.5.1 Governance and environment

When subsidiaries' CEOs perceived their environment as strongly competitive, they experienced difficulties in ensuring enough resources and acquiring a sufficiently qualified workforce. Strong competition in the market was also negatively related to both control (written reports) and attunement concerning human resource management (see Table 6.16). It appeared that in a dynamic environment the HRM-related issues were strongly decentralised and left entirely to the subsidiary's authority. Changing customer needs and expectations were positively associated with the reports and the attunement concerning the development of market share. In such an environment, headquarters often questioned these reports (see control in Section 6.4.2).

Table 6.16. Relationship between environmental dynamism and governance (N=76).

	Competitive Environment [13]
Attunement of training of personnel [7d]*	-.27
Reports on training of personnel [1d]	-.28

Spearman rank correlations are significant at p < .05 (two-tailed).
* [...] question number in Appendix 1.

6.6 Cultural distance

Cultural distance is the sum of the distances between headquarters and its Polish subsidiary on power distance and uncertainty avoidance indexes. Figure 6.6 shows the distances on both dimensions and their sum – the overall cultural distance. As we can read from the figure, two countries showed a particularly small cultural distance; Belgium had a zero power distance and France zero uncertainty avoidance distance to Poland. At the same time, the culturally-close countries were under-represented in our sample but this can probably be explained by their large geographical distance from Poland. We see that the largest group of investors (see Table 6.9) originated from Germany and the Netherlands, which have a medium cultural distance to Poland. During the interviews with Polish CEOs, we learned that the cooperation with the HQs from culturally-close countries caused more difficulties in general than with culturally distant countries, e.g. cooperation with Scandinavian investors (with the largest cultural distance to Poland – see Figure 6.6) enjoyed a very positive opinion among the directors of the Polish subsidiaries.

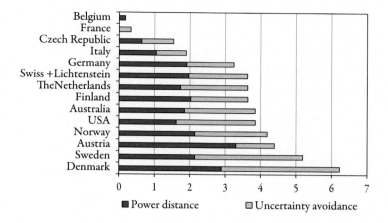

Figure 6.6. Cultural distance of headquarters to their subsidiaries (N=76).

6.7 Performance

As could be expected, performance evaluation was piled up on the positive side of the scale; more than 75% of CEOs expressed their satisfaction with the general performance of their subsidiaries. However, the evaluation of the short-term operational performance presented a slightly different picture; more than 30% of the subsidiaries did not reach the goals for the last year. The mean score on this question is 4.66, which is only slightly lower than performance satisfaction in general. However, the CEOs' opinions were quite diverse, as the high standard deviation shows (see Table 6.17).

Table 6.17. Descriptive statistics of performance (N=76).

Performance indicators	Mean (s.d.)
General performance satisfaction [23]*	4.89 (1.65)
Achieving operational goals last year [24]	4.66 (2.02)
Outperforming competitors [25]	5.05 (1.51)
Performance in multinational network [26]**	5.06 (1.26)
Dealing with customer claims [27]	5.90 (1.11)
Response to changes in customer needs [28]	5.51 (1.30)

All questions on a 7-point Likert scale; 1 strongly disagree to 7 strongly agree.

** N = 48 for this variable, as 48 subsidiaries were part of a multinational with more subsidiaries.

* [...] question number in Appendix 1.

Generally, subsidiaries increased their market share. Out of 39 subsidiaries that filled out the data for 2002 and 2004, 21 subsidiaries increased their market share by 59%, on average. The market share in 8 subsidiaries decreased between 2002 and 2004 by 17%. Another 11 companies sustained their market share. Table 6.18 exhibits the market share percentages for the three consecutive years.

Subsidiaries which experienced more competition in the environment reported a lower market share, but the difference slightly missed the $p < 0.1$ significance level in the Kruskal-Wallis test.

Table 6.18. Subsidiaries' market share in % in 2002-2006.

Year	Mean	Median	Std. deviation	N
2002*	16%	9%	20.66	42
2004	19%	10%	23.48	40
2006 (projected)	20%	14%	20.94	32

*Question number 30 for all three years

6.7.1 Governance and performance

We expected excellent performing subsidiaries to have different HQ-S governance mechanisms than subsidiaries that showed average performance. To investigate these differences we divided the sample in two clusters: average (N=27) and excellent (N=49) performing subsidiaries. We observed that the excellent performing subsidiaries were established as Greenfield investments and sold a higher percentage of their production in the international markets. Not surprisingly, this group expressed more trust in the relationship with their headquarters. Excellent subsidiaries showed differences in the HQ-S governance mechanisms, e.g. high ICT integration, frequent attunement of production volume and regular business meetings with other subsidiaries. In general, excellent subsidiaries were less intensively controlled by their headquarters. However, the governance mechanisms in excellent performing subsidiaries were strongly formalised, especially between the logistics departments. Although formalisation may create a psychological distance as mentioned in Section 6.4.5, together with the ICT integration it may create transparency in information exchange and show clear-cut responsibilities. This effect may even be stronger in combination with a high power distance culture (as is the case in Poland) and eventually improve performance. Table 6.19 shows the significant differences between excellent and average performing subsidiaries.

Table 6.19. Differences between average and high-performing subsidiaries.

Governance mechanisms	Performance	
	Average Mean (s.d.)	**Excellent** Mean (s.d.)
ICT integration [10]*	5.42 (1.13)	5.96 (0.84)
Attunement production volume [7b]	3.74 (1.41)	4.55 (1.77)
Business meetings among subsidiaries [9]	3.34 (1.08)	3.81 (1.21)
Inquiries on submitted reports on sales turnover [2a]	4.90 (1.50)	4.28 (1.73)
Inquiries on reports development of market share [2c]	4.31 (1.73)	3.37 (1.68)
Formality of personal contacts logistics dep. [6e]	3.67 (1.58)	4.32 (1.23)
N	27	49

Kruskal-Wallis tests significant at p < .05, p < .10.

* [...] question number in Appendix 1.

6.8 Partial least squares model for HQ-S governance

The research model presented in Figure 4.1 was developed using Partial Least Squares (PLS), a structural equation modelling technique that is well suited to highly complex predictive models (Jöreskog and Wold, 1982). The test of the measurement model included the estimation of the internal consistency and the convergent and discriminant validity of the instrument items – reflective constructs. The variables with loadings below the generally accepted level .5 were excluded from the estimations of the inner model. Formative constructs were treated differently. All measures included for measuring formative constructed were retained in the PLS modelling. The reason being that unlike the reflective measures, of which reliability and validity can be assessed by examining the loadings, cross loadings, and internal consistency, the reliability of formative measures cannot be examined using the measures in PLS modelling (Chin and Newsted, 1999).

Evaluation of the measurement (outer) model

Reflective constructs used for the PLS model estimation show high-composite reliability estimates – α (see Table 6.20). Higher than the recommended level .7 for Cronbach alpha indicating adequate internal consistency of the constructs (Nunnally, 1978). The PLS alpha measure of internal consistency is similar to Cronbach α, however it does not assume equal weights (as Cronbach α does) of its indicators and as a result shows even closer approximations (Chin, 1998).

Table 6.20. Outer model estimation.

Construct	Items – manifest variables	Loading
Strategic control	written reports market share development [32c]	.748
α = .858	written reports product and process r&d [32e]	.755
	written reports on training of personnel [32d]	.683
	HQ inquiries on market share [33c]	.736
	HQ inquiries on sales turnover [33a]	.613
	HQ inquiries on production volume [33b]	.683
	HQ inquiries on training of personnel [33d]	.537
Operational control	written reports on sales turnover [32a]	.859
α = .854	written reports on production volume [32b]	.867
Coordination	attunement of sales turnover [40a]	.703
α = .876	attunement of production volume [40b]	.802
	attunement of training of personnel [40d]	.690
	attunement of product and process development [40e]	.762
	personal contacts between CEOs [38a]	.629
	personal contacts between logistics dept. [38e]	.697
	personal contacts between marketing dept. [38b]	.537
	personal contacts between manufacturing dept. [38d]	.637
Performance	general performance [9]	.887
α = .901	achievement of operational goals [10]	.828
	performance as compared to competitors [11]	.885
Prospector strategy	new products development and introduction [5a]	.668
α = .851	new operations being 'first in' [5b]	.878
	new market segments access [5c]	.872

Concepts used in PLS are considered to have an adequate discriminant validity, if the square root of the average variance extracted (AVE) for each construct is larger than the correlation between the construct and any other construct in the model (Chin, 1998). All constructs in the estimated model fulfilled this condition (see Table 6.21).

Evaluation of the structural (inner) model

Consistent with the distribution-free, predictive approach of PLS, the structural model was evaluated using the R-square for the dependent (indogene) constructs as well as t-statistics and significance levels of structural path coefficients. The t-statistics were estimated with a bootstrapping re-sampling procedure. According to the suggestions of Chin (1998), the number of re-samples was set at 200. The modelling process was repeated until stable results

Table 6.21. Discriminant validity (correlation coefficients between constructs and Average Variance Extracted).

AVE in diagonal	Correlation				
	1	**2**	**3**	**4**	**5**
1. Strategic control	**.467**				
2. Operational control	.245	**.745**			
3. Coordination	.205	.247	**.472**		
4. Performance	-.052	.032	.227	**.752**	
5. Prospector strategy	.214	-.136	.029	.224	**.659**

were achieved. The significant results of the structural model are presented in Table 6.22 and visualised in Figure 6.12. The results show that the model explains 44% of coordination, 14% of control, and 12% of performance.

The total effect of indirect impacts can be calculated by multiplying the coefficients of the indirect effects (Birkinshaw *et al.*, 1995; Chin, 1998). In the final significant model, operational control is a function of subsidiary size, whereas strategic control is dependent on the duration of the HQ-S relationship, headquarters size and cultural distance between headquarters and subsidiary.

Operational Control = .21[SSize]
Strategic Control = .26[HQSize] + .24[CultDist] – .27[RelDur]

Coordination mechanisms are a function of the external environment, international sales and strategic and operational control. Rather unexpectedly, only two of three dimensions of the environment show a significant effect on coordination. Environmental Dynamics had no significant effect on the governance mechanisms in the PLS model despite the fact that it was negatively correlated with two governance variables (see section 6.5.1 Table 6.14). The amount of international sales shows the strongest positive relationship with coordination (path coefficient 0.37).

Coordination = .21[SSize] x .26[OControl] + .28[ECon] + .25[EUncer] + .37 [IntSales] +
            .21[SControl] (-.27[RelDur] + .26[HQSize] + .24[CultDist])

Performance was directly affected by the coordination activities and prospector strategy of subsidiary. Indirectly, operational and strategic control positively influenced the performance.

Strategic control influence was mediated by coordination and by prospector strategy, although the latter at lower significance.

Performance = .25[Coord](.21[SSize] x .26[OControl] + .28[Econ] + .25[EUncer] + .37[IntSales] − .27[RelDur] x .21[SControl] + .26[HQSize] x .21[SControl] + .24[CultDist] x .21[SControl]) + .21[SControl] x .21[PStrat](-.27[RelDur] + .26[HQSize] + .24[CultDist])

The overview of all significant relationships and path coefficients is presented in Table 6.22.

In the final model the influence of the international strategy did not show any significant relationship either with coordination or control. For that reason, we decided to explore possible relationships between the international strategy and the control and coordination variables applying a clustering method and searching for a significant difference between clusters. These results are presented in the next section.

Table 6.22. Inner (structural) model estimations.

Constructs	Path coefficient	Observed t-value	Sig. level
Effects on coordination (R^2 = .436)			
Environmental uncertainty	+ .253	1.490	*
Environmental constraints	+ .275	2.489	***
Subsidiary international sales	+ .371	3.536	***
Operational reports	+ .257	1.782	**
Strategic control	+ .210	1.528	*
Effects on strategic control (R^2 = .142)			
Relationship duration	- .271	2.048	**
Cultural distance	+ .239	1.983	**
Headquarters size	+ .260	1.731	**
Effects on operational control (R^2 = .082)			
Subsidiary's size	+ .209	1.485	*
Effects on prospector strategy (R^2 = .046)			
Strategic control	+ .214	1.456	*
Effects on performance (R^2 = .121)			
Coordination	+ .251	2.414	***
Prospector strategy	+ .250	2.571	***

Significance levels: *** p < .010; **p < .050; *p < .100.

6.9 International strategy clusters

The international strategy of subsidiaries was estimated based on the scores in four statements. These scores were then used in a hierarchical Ward cluster analysis with the resulting three strategy groups among subsidiaries: global, transnational and multidomestic (see Table 6.23).

The centres from the hierarchical solution were subjected to a non-hierarchical analysis for validation. Both solutions were placed in a cross-table (see Table 6.24). The convergence in the cluster membership between both methods showed that clusters were stable and valid (cluster 2 was perfectly stable, the other two clusters showed some small discrepancies but at a generally accepted level), therefore the 3-cluster-solution could be accepted.

Obtained clusters were labelled according to the expected scores of the focus of a subsidiary's strategy for three clusters (see Table 6.23). Global strategies concentrated on selling standard products internationally and supplying worldwide markets. Subsidiaries did not control the marketing of export products and seldom provided ideas for new products for international markets. In global companies, these activities usually stay centralised at the headquarters level. This first strategy cluster was labelled as *global* and included 33 cases. Transnational strategy combined the advantages of local market focus with the ability to compete in global markets. The second cluster showed a combination, in which companies focused on the competition in the global market, but at the same time they actively competed in the local market. In

Table 6.23. Expected and actual scores on the strategy variables.

Variable	Global cluster	Transnational cluster	Multidomestic cluster
Concentration on local market [19]*			
Actual	Low	High	Medium
Expected	Low	High	High
Concentration on worldwide market [20]			
Actual	High	High	Medium
Expected	High	High	Low
Provide ideas for international products [21]			
Actual	High	High	Low
Expected	Low	High	Low
Subsidiary export [22]			
Actual	Medium	Medium/high	Low
Expected	Medium	High	Low

* [...] question number in Appendix I.

Table 6.24. Validation of hierarchical cluster with non-hierarchical solution.

		K-means cluster			Total
		1 Global	**2 Transnational**	**3 Multidomestic transitional**	
Ward cluster	1	29	0	1	30
	2	1	16	1	18
	3	3	0	25	28
Total subsidiaries		33	16	27	76

this group, subsidiaries contributed to the development of the products for international markets and controlled their export sales. Comparing the actual scores and the expected scores from Table 6.23, we labelled this strategy cluster as *transnational*. This cluster included 16 subsidiaries. The third cluster – *multidomestic* was created by companies concentrating mostly on local markets and developing products tailored to local tastes and local customer expectations. These subsidiaries were hardly involved in the development or marketing of products internationally. There were 27 subsidiaries included in the multidomestic cluster.

Subsidiaries in each international strategy cluster showed different international sales. As Figure 6.7 shows, global companies sold the majority of their products (82%) in the international market. Furthermore, as predicted, nearly 70% of their production was sold via headquarters. This meant in practice almost full dependency of the subsidiary on its headquarters. Quite unexpectedly, multidomestic companies showed a relatively strong international activity, selling almost 50% of their products to the international markets (see Figure 6.7). These high international sales together with a strong sales-dependency on the headquarters show a very specific multidomestic strategy for the Polish subsidiaries. It may show changes in the strategy and being in transition to other types of strategy, e.g. transnational. For that reason we adjust the label of this group to *multidomestic –transitional*. The sales of transnational companies reflected their strategy choice on combining competition on the local and international markets; they sold 60% of their products on the domestic market and 40% on the international market. Combining sales on both international and domestic markets distinguished these companies from the other two groups. Concurrently, this group showed the lowest dependency on the headquarters in organising their sales.

The decision-making process in the transnational companies showed decentralisation of important decisions, such as concerning R&D and advertising and promotion to the subsidiary authority. In contrast, the global cluster centralised those decisions at the headquarters' level (mind the low values in Figure 6.8).

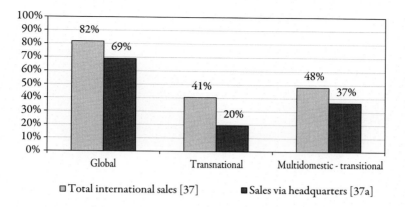

Figure 6.7. Dependent and independent international sales of subsidiaries.

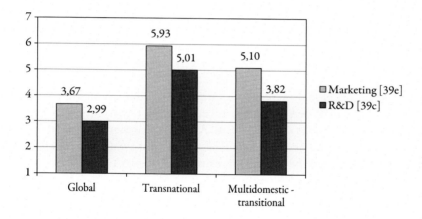

Figure 6.8. Locus of decision making (N=76).
7-point Likert scale: 1 decision-making centralized at HQ; 7 fully autonomous at subsidiary.

Looking at the link between the generic (described in Section 6.3.2) and the international strategy, the results show that the transnational strategy cluster was the most innovative concerning new areas of operations (prospector strategy) (see Figure 6.9). This result is in line with the expectations of Bartlett and Goshal (1987) who claim that pursuing a transnational strategy will enhance worldwide learning and improve information flows which allow for the creation of new opportunities for MNE development.

An international strategy orientation of an MNE is associated with a different HQ-S governance mechanism. As Figure 6.10 shows, the transnational strategy was characterised by the lowest level of formalisation, both in terms of reporting and in terms of personal contacts.

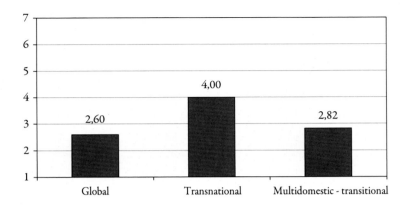

Figure 6.9. Being 'first-in' in new areas of activities (N=76).
Scale: x ≤ 2 defenders; 2 < x ≤ 5 analysers; 5 < x ≤ 7 prospectors.

Although we expected that the transnational strategy would require intensive coordination between headquarters and subsidiaries, only the frequency of business meetings showed a significantly higher frequency for this cluster (quarterly meetings see Figure 6.10).

Subsidiaries focusing on global markets and transferring almost all their production to headquarters most often set up personal contacts between logistics departments, probably with the goal of assuring a continuous output stream. A similar situation held for the operational aspects of coordination, such as attunement of production volume; here again globally-oriented subsidiaries indicated the highest intensity (see Figure 6.11).

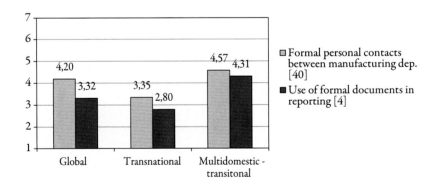

Figure 6.10. Formalisation levels in the three strategy clusters (N=76).
Scale: 7-point Likert scale: 1 informal, 7 entirely formal.

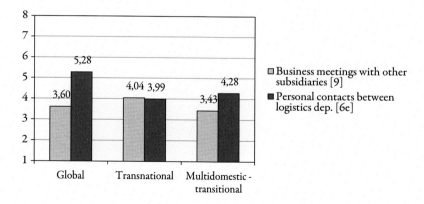

Figure 6.11. Business meetings and personal contacts in three clusters (N=76).
Scale 1-8: 1 less than once a year, 2 yearly, 3 semi-annually, 4 quarterly, 5 monthly, 6 semi-weekly, 7 weekly, 8 daily.

6.10 Concluding remarks

This chapter described the results of the survey and analysed the possible reasons for non-response. The findings from the sample of 76 subsidiaries in Poland presented the general characteristics of their organisation structure as well as the HQ-S governance mechanisms. The PLS modelling approach was used for testing the proposed relationships between the dimensions of the external environment, strategy and organisational factors. It revealed significant influences on the HQ-S governance mechanisms of contingency factors. Figure 6.12 cultural differences and the size of the MNE (headquarters and subsidiary) are related to control. Cultural distance and headquarters' size are positively associated with strategic control while the subsidiary's size is positively associated with operational control. The duration of the relationship between headquarters and a subsidiary is negatively associated with strategic control. External business environment, especially political uncertainty and resource constraints, are positively related to the intensity of coordination. Also international sales have a strong relationship with the coordination. Although we expected both coordination and control to be positively related to performance, the model shows a direct relationship between coordination and performance and no significant direct relationship between control and performance. Both strategic and operational control are mediated by coordination in the relationship with performance. It seems also that prospector subsidiaries perform better, which is shown in the relationship between prospector strategy and performance. Strategic control shows a positive relationship with the prospector's strategy. Contrary to our expectations, we did not find any significant path between international strategy and the HQ-S governance mechanisms. However, the in-between-groups comparison showed that transnational strategy is positively associated with coordination and network-oriented (such as business meetings) mechanisms.

In the next chapter, we present the results from the qualitative part of the study, the in-depth interviews with headquarters.

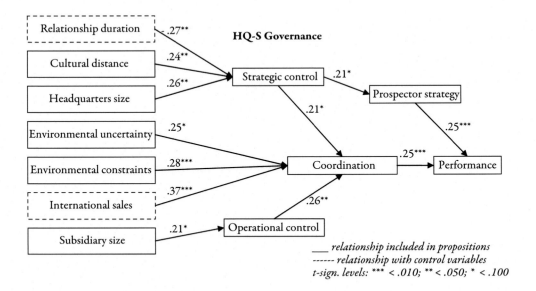

Figure 6.12. PLS model for HQ-S governance (N=76).

Chapter 7. In-depth interviews with headquarters

In this chapter we describe the results of the in-depth interviews performed with the representatives of French and Dutch headquarters. The representatives were managers of international affairs directly responsible for the management of Polish and other Central and East European subsidiaries. For the in-depth interviews with the headquarters, we used the same concepts as developed in the survey part of the study. The ideal situation would be to include all the headquarters of subsidiaries participating in the survey. Unfortunately it was not feasible within the time frame and with the resources available for this study (see Figure 5.1). The results presented in this chapter have been gathered from 14 French and 10 Dutch headquarters with single or multiple subsidiaries in Poland and/or another CEE country, and were collected through extended interviews with the company representatives. The choice of headquarters from France and the Netherlands formed a convenience sample[26]. The interviews took place at the end of 2004 in France and in 2005 the Netherlands. In both countries similar data collection procedures were applied. The potential respondents were first contacted by telephone to check the correctness of the address data, to ensure they (still) had subsidiaries in Poland and to introduce the research project in general. During these conversations the date, place and the character of the interview was planned. Some managers, for example, preferred to be interviewed by telephone or asked to send the interview guide first so they could prepare for the conversation. The telephone calls were followed by the official letter which described the goals of the project and listed potential benefits such as benchmarking for the participating companies. All the headquarters that participated in the interviews received an extended executive summary of the results, with a special focus on the situation in their company.

7.1 Baseline description of the headquarters

Table 7.1 presents an overview of the baseline information for the Dutch and French headquarters. Generally, wholly-owned Greenfield investments (see explanation in Section 2.1) were chosen for the entry in Poland. However, several acquisitions took place as well, more often by French than by Dutch HQs. Interestingly, one Dutch acquisition was characterised by a stepwise entry process over a period of ten years, which means that the investor first acquired a minority stake in a Polish company by establishing a joint venture, and then in a second step increased its stake to full ownership. Most of the investigated headquarters were manufacturing companies; Dutch HQs operated in non-food industries, such as textile or

---

[26] Convenience sampling is used in exploratory research where the researcher is interested in getting an approximation of the truth. This non-probability method is often used during preliminary research efforts to get a gross estimate of the results, without incurring the cost or time required to select a random sample. Source: http://www.statpac.com.

Table 7.1. Overview of general information for Dutch and French headquarters.

	French HQ	Dutch HQ
Number of participating companies	14	10
Industry	Manufacturing and retailers in the food branch	Manufacturing companies and one retail company
Size – range (s.d.)	Mean 4000 ftes (2700) Range 80 – 8000 ftes	Mean 186 ftes (182) Range 10 – 600 ftes
Date of investment in Poland (s.d.)	Mean 1996 (2.52) Range 1992-2001	1995 (2.5) Range 1989-1998
Entry mode in Poland	62% Acquisitions 31% Greenfield investments 7% Joint Ventures	60% Greenfield investments 20% Acquisitions 20% Joint Ventures
HQs capital share in subsidiary	99% – 100%	100%
Motivations for investment in Poland – most often mentioned	1. Market size and market growth opportunities (5 cases) 2. Stagnating local markets (5 cases)	1. Resource and production cost reductions (5 cases) 2. Stagnating local markets (2 cases)
CEO expatriate	In 6 cases	In 5 cases In the set-up phase all were managed by expatriates
Number of subsidiaries in Poland per headquarters	1	1
Number of subsidiaries in CEEC (s.d.)	Mean 4 (2.5) Range 1-10	Mean 1.4 (1.3) Range 1-5

chemical, whereas French HQs operated mostly in food processing. The size of the subsidiaries in Poland varied from 10 full-time equivalents (ftes) up to 600 ftes for the Dutch production subsidiaries. In the French subsidiaries, the range of measured size was even larger, from 80 ftes to over 8000 ftes.

All companies considered investment in Poland as a first step in the expansion into other CEECs and further to the East (Russia, Ukraine, etc.). Interestingly, many of the investigated HQs invested in Poland a relatively long time after the transformation process started in 1989. As shown in Table 7.1, Dutch headquarters invested on average in 1995 whereas the French headquarters did so a year later. Despite this rather late entry, French headquarters showed pro-activeness in developing their business abroad; e.g., 11 out of the 14 headquarters set up at least 2 subsidiaries in CEECs (except Poland) during the last 10 years. Additionally, many French headquarters developed a broad network of subsidiaries, holding on average 4 subsidiaries in the CEE region. In contrast to the French HQs, Dutch HQs mostly had one relatively small subsidiary in CEEC.

Dutch and French headquarters expressed different motives for establishing a subsidiary in Poland. For the Dutch headquarters, the low costs of resources, i.e. labour and raw materials, were the most often mentioned motives for expansion into Poland. French HQs were primarily motivated to enter the Polish market to benefit from the large growth opportunities as compared to the saturated 'old' EU members' markets. Among all the CEE countries, Poland was considered to hold a strategic position because of its central geographical location. Other motives mentioned by the headquarters' managers included the large market size, 'passion-for-pioneering', and following their key customers especially in B2B deliveries, who had entered Poland earlier. The director of a Dutch headquarters said he had been pushed to internationalise by a stagnating Dutch market, and so perceived the internationalisation step as a major possibility for the continuation of the operations of his enterprise.

Although Poland is generally considered rich in resources (Hitt *et al.*, 2000), French headquarters stressed the difficulties in developing and sustaining stable supplier networks. So they tended to vertically integrate suppliers and distributors in their company's value chain to assure current operations. As a foreign operations manager of a food processing company said: *as headquarters we reorganised our supply chain in France in order to provide the raw materials for our subsidiaries in the CEECs.*

7.2 Characteristics of Dutch and French HQ-S governance

Expatriates performed an important role in the control of foreign subsidiaries, both for French and Dutch headquarters. In the French headquarters, the HQ-S governance (in terms of intensity of control and coordination) was clearly related to the nationality of the CEO and to the entry mode. In nearly 60% of the cases French headquarters appointed a local person as the director of a subsidiary and in 30% the subsidiary's director was an expatriate from France. In 9% of the cases (three companies) directors were expatriates from a third country, originating from other – often regional sub-headquarters; for example, one company had a sub-headquarters in Austria, responsible for the operations of all CEEC-subsidiaries.

French subsidiaries established through acquisitions were most often managed by local Polish CEOs. In these subsidiaries, HQs more intensively controlled operations (monthly reporting as compared to quarterly or semi-annually in subsidiaries with an expatriate – French CEOs). In contrast to this, subsidiaries established through a Greenfield investment more often had a French CEO and HQs control and coordination were less intensive.

In the Dutch firms, the expatriates' presence usually changed over time. Just after the investment, all headquarters staffed the subsidiaries with their own HQ's employees but then half of them gradually replaced the expatriates. Expatriates also played an important role when a subsidiary showed disappointing results. Then Polish CEOs were replaced with expatriates from the HQs' country. In such cases an expatriate from the headquarters replaced the local manager '*to get the subsidiary on track*'.

Table 7.2 exhibits the mean values for different governance mechanisms in French and Dutch headquarters. For presenting the results, we applied the same concepts as developed in the survey part of the study (see the model in Section 6.9).

Table 7.2. Mean values and (s.d.) for HQ-S governance, the headquarters' point of view.

Governance	Item*	French HQ (N=14)	Dutch HQ (N=10)
Strategic control		3.5 (0.69)	4.2 (1.13)
Written reports on:	market share development [1c]	4.1 (1.03)	3.7 (1.43)
	products and process R&D [1e]	3.8 (0.83)	4.1 (1.29)
	training of personnel [1d]	2.6 (0.65)	5.2 (1.30)
Operational control		5.3 (0.51)	5.8 (1.34)
Written reports on:	sales turnover [1a]	5.0 (0.00)	5.6 (1.27)
	production volume [1b]	5.6 (1.12)	6.1 (1.62)
Coordination – attunement		3.7 (0.33)	4.1 (0.93)
Attunement of:	sales turnover [7a]	4.6 (0.51)	4.5 (1.35)
	Investments	2.8 (0.80)	4.1 (0.99)
	financing and debts	3.0 (0.88)	3.7 (1.34)
	Results	4.7 (0.47)	4.7 (1.49)
	training of personnel [7d]	3.3 (1.06)	3.6 (1.17)
Coordination – personal contacts		4.8 (1.24)	6.2 (1.28)
Personal contacts of:	CEOs [6a]	5.9 (1.75)	6.6 (1.26)
	marketing dept. [6b]	4.6 (1.56)	5.9 (1.85)
	manufacturing dept. [6d]	5.0 (1.67)	6.1 (2.13)
	logistics dept. [6e]	4.2 (1.53)	6.3 (2.00)

* all items measured on the scale 1-8; 1 less than yearly, 2 yearly, 3 semi-annually, 4 quarterly, 5 monthly, 6 bi-weekly, 7 weekly, 8 daily.
** [...] question number in Appendix 1.

7.2.1 Strategic control

Strategic control includes the reports on market share development, human resource management (HRM) and product and process R&D. Generally, French HQ required a low frequency of reports on the strategic issues (semi-annually or quarterly). Among the three elements of strategic control, the market share development was checked upon the most intensively – on a quarterly basis and training of personnel the least intensively – once to twice a year. Strategic control of Dutch headquarters and their Polish subsidiaries showed a slightly different picture. The HRM issues were important to the headquarters and were intensively controlled with monthly reports. This might be a way of coping with the consequences of the different working habits and different organisational behaviour between Poland and Western (with market economies) countries, inherited from the communist period when job efficiency was of minor importance in measuring the organisation's output (Fabry and Zeghni, 2003).

Contrary to French HQs control, Dutch HQs controlled the market share development less intensively with quarterly reports. In Dutch headquarters, the control frequencies varied greatly between companies, as the high standard deviation values show (see Table 7.2).

7.2.2 Operational control

Operational control regards reports on the production volume and sales turnover. For the French headquarters the sales turnover was particularly important and checked upon by monthly reports from their subsidiaries. The reports on the production volume showed some divergent pattern. Eight out of 14 subsidiaries reported to the headquarters monthly and the other with a bi-weekly or daily frequency. The companies showing the highest frequency of operational reports (on a daily or two-weekly basis) were joint ventures and acquisitions.

Dutch headquarters required slightly higher frequencies for operational reporting: on average bi-weekly for reports on production volume and sales turnover. From the recently founded subsidiaries, headquarters required daily reporting on production volume.

7.2.3 Coordination

Coordination includes the frequency of personal contacts and joint planning as well as attunement of subsidiary operations. French headquarters engaged subsidiaries in joint project groups and task forces and encouraged business meetings among subsidiaries. French headquarters also organised quarterly business meetings with their subsidiaries, especially with those that were focusing on the international market. Personal contacts, by phone or face-to-face, between HQ and S-employees took place on a monthly basis, whereas the HQ-S CEOs had personal contacts on a weekly or bi-weekly basis. The logistics managers seldom had personal contacts (on average on a quarterly basis).

The six subsidiaries with a French CEO (an expatriate) showed a lower frequency of personal contacts with the headquarters: mostly semi-annually at each functional level. In contrast, the eight subsidiaries with a local CEO (Polish) showed a relatively high frequency of contacts: at least quarterly at each functional level.

Dutch headquarters showed higher frequency of personal contacts, namely on a bi-weekly basis (see Table 7.2). There were almost no differences in the frequencies of personal contacts among the different departments of HQ and subsidiaries. Only CEO contacts were slightly more often – with a weekly frequency – in the Dutch headquarters.

Attunement, which includes discussion and exchange of opinions between French headquarters and their Polish subsidiaries, took place four times a year on average, with strong emphasis on performance, sales turnover and general results of the subsidiary (the latter on average with a monthly frequency). Subsidiary's investments and financing issues received little attention from the HQs and were attuned only twice a year.

In contrast, Dutch headquarters showed higher attunement of investments and financing issues, with a monthly frequency (compare frequencies in Table 7.2). The attunement of sales turnover, subsidiary results and HRM issues showed similar frequencies in Dutch and French headquarters (see Table 7.2).

7.2.4 Performance

Interestingly, both French and Dutch headquarters were very satisfied with the performance of their subsidiaries (both 5.6 on a 7-point scale). Looking at the headquarters' evaluation of the achievement of the original investment motivation, we found that French headquarters were slightly more satisfied than Dutch headquarters (5.6 versus 5.3 respectively). In a closer investigation we observed that the mean score for Dutch HQs was influenced by one HQ that indicated a strong dissatisfaction with the results of its Polish subsidiary. This Dutch headquarters founded a subsidiary in Poland, motivated by a stagnating Dutch market. The subsidiary was managed autonomously by a Dutch HQ expatriate and showed a relatively low intensity of HQ-S governance mechanisms. This was the only HQ that showed disappointing results, other companies that we contacted and which had unsatisfying results withdrew from the market by closing down their subsidiaries and declined participation in the interview, probably unwilling to share negative experiences.

French HQs of Polish subsidiaries that were established as Greenfield investments managed by an expatriate from the HQ with relatively low intensity of control and coordination were the most satisfied with their subsidiaries' performance. In contrast, headquarters which acquired subsidiaries in Poland appeared to benefit from intensified governance mechanisms, especially in the form of many personal contacts as these contacts were associated with high-performance satisfaction. *Personal contacts contribute to an intensive information exchange and learning between the HQs and our subsidiaries which allows for a good understanding of the underlying reasons for differences in the perceptions of certain management issues,* as one respondent stated.

7.3 Comparison of the HQ and S governance mechanisms

Although the subsidiary groups and headquarters do not overlap, meaning that we did not interview the headquarters of the subsidiaries from the survey sample, some interesting comparisons can be made between the headquarters' and subsidiaries' perceptions. For the purpose of this comparison we combined Dutch and French HQs in one group and used the subsidiary sample for the comparison. This resulted in a group of 24 headquarters and 76 subsidiaries.

In the comparisons, two control and several coordination aspects show significant differences between the HQ and subsidiaries (see Table 7.3). Also two performance indicators encountered slightly different perceptions by the headquarters compared to the subsidiaries. Interestingly, all the means for the two groups show higher values for the HQs' compared to the subsidiaries. The intensity of control showed hardly any differences, with the exception of the reports on R&D, on which the participating HQs required quarterly information and the participating subsidiaries reported semi-annually. Also the formalisation level was different; it appeared to be much higher at the HQs compared to the subsidiaries. Other aspects of control, such as reports on manufacturing, training of personnel and market share development as well as the HQ's sensitivity to the information in these reports [questions 2a-e], did not show significant differences between headquarters and subsidiaries.

In the concept of coordination more differences appeared, for example in attunement, personal contacts but also joint task groups and business meetings frequency (see Table 7.3). According to HQs, joint task groups and meetings were organised bi-weekly whereas according to subsidiaries it was quarterly. Also personal contacts between manufacturing departments show a large discrepancy between the views, again bi-weekly according to headquarters and quarterly according to subsidiaries. Personal contacts between marketing and R&D departments show a one-point difference between HQs and subsidiaries, with a monthly frequency of contacts for the HQs and quarterly for the subsidiaries. Business meetings, the attunement of market share development and attunement of personnel training show the smallest differences between the HQs and subsidiaries (less than one point on the frequency scale (see Table 7.3)).

Interestingly, the subsidiaries' performance was evaluated more positively by the headquarters than by the subsidiaries themselves (see Table 7.4).

Table 7.3. Different HQ and S perceptions on the governance mechanisms.

Governance mechanisms	HQ Mean (s.d.) (N = 24)	Subsidiary Mean (s.d.) (N = 76)
Control		
Use of pre-structured formal documents in reporting [4]*	5.17 (1.63)	3.53 (2.23)
Written reports on product and process R&D [1e]**	3.91 (1.04)	3.21 (1.23)
Coordination**		
Joint task and projects groups [8]	5.54 (1.22)	4.07 (1.80)
Personal contacts between manufacturing dept. [6d]	5.52 (1.94)	4.34 (1.74)
Personal contacts between marketing dept. [6b]	5.08 (1.86)	4.19 (1.50)
Personal contacts between R&D dept. [6c]	4.92 (1.67)	3.86 (1.37)
Business meetings among subsidiaries [9]	4.58 (1.25)	3.64 (1.18)
Attunement of development of market share [7c]	3.86 (1.10)	3.11 (1.13)
Attunement of training of personnel [7d]	3.48 (0.90)	2.71 (1.14)

Kruskal-Wallis tests significant at p < .05, p < .10.

* 7-point Likert scale, scale anchors 1 informal, 7 formal.

** scale 1-8; 1 less than once a year, 2 yearly, 3 semi-annually, 4 quarterly, 5 monthly, 6 bi-weekly, 7 weekly, 8 daily.

Table 7.4. Different HQ and S perceptions on performance.

Performance	HQ Mean (s.d.) (N = 24)	Subsidiary Mean (s.d.) (N = 76)
General performance satisfaction [23]*	5.60 (1.19)	4.89 (1.65)
Outperforming competitors [25]*	5.90 (0.57)	5.05 (1.51)

Kruskal-Wallis tests significant at p < .05, p < .10.

* 7-point Likert scale; 1 strongly disagree to 7 strongly agree.

7.4 Concluding remarks

The in-depth interviews allowed for complementing the views of subsidiaries on the HQ-S governance mechanisms with the views of the headquarters. In general, Dutch and French headquarters report a similar intensity of control and coordination with their subsidiaries. Strategic control takes place less often (on a quarterly basis) than operational control (monthly, bi-weekly) and coordination (quarterly). The personal contacts took place slightly more often in the Dutch than French subsidiaries. The higher intensity of coordination and control for Dutch HQs may be explained by the difference in size between the groups or may be an effect of the cultural distance as described by Hofstede (1997), which predicts more complex management of culturally distant subsidiaries (see earlier Section 4.3.2).

Moreover, the in-depth interviews showed an important role for the headquarters' expatriates in the management of the subsidiaries. The coordination dimension of the HQ-S governance showed a divergent intensity, depending on whether the expatriate or local CEO was appointed to manage the Polish subsidiary. In view of the absence of geographical proximity, we expected that the headquarters would have difficulties in directly supervising subsidiary management behaviour and would therefore use other mechanisms than direct supervision to monitor the subsidiary management. But headquarters emphasised the role their expatriates played in developing and restructuring especially acquired subsidiaries (as compared to Greenfield investments). This effect was mentioned earlier by Egelhoff (1984). The entry mode in the Polish market has an effect on the HQ-S governance mechanisms as well; headquarters more intensively controlled and coordinated acquired subsidiaries with a Polish CEO, than Greenfield-established subsidiaries with an expatriate CEO.

The results show that headquarters have a slightly different vision of HQ-S governance compared with subsidiaries. Interestingly, all aspects with significant differences show a higher intensity of HQ-S governance mechanisms in the perception of the HQs than in the subsidiaries', especially with respect to the coordination mechanisms (i.e. joint task groups and business meetings as well as the intensity of personal contacts and attunement).

Finally, despite the difficulties headquarters face in the external business environment in Poland, such as political interference and the (un)predictability of the business environment in Poland, the headquarters were highly satisfied with the results of their subsidiaries' operations. They emphasised the importance of a long-term vision in this country, both for the development of subsidiaries but also for the evaluation of their performance. Commenting on growing market opportunities a manager of a company processing fresh fruit for the food industry was quoted as saying: The *Polish market was only a local business 3 to 4 years ago.*

Chapter 8. Discussion and conclusions

In this final chapter, we discuss the results in view of the propositions, the research model and its theoretical foundation. We provide answers to the research questions and assess whether the propositions we formulated are confirmed or falsified. Both the quantitative as well as the qualitative results of the study are reviewed, and linked to the current stream of international business literature. Finally, the theoretical and practical contributions of the study are described, and suggestions for further research are made. In section 8.1 the characteristics of the HQ-S governance mechanisms highlighted. Sections 8.2 and 8.3 pay attention to the influence of the environment and cultural distance. Section 8.4 is devoted to the influence of strategy on HQ-S governance, while the effects on performance are summarized in Sections 8.5. Section 8.6 presents some additional conclusions and the in-depth interviews are evaluated in Section 8.7. Finally, Section 8.8 gives an evaluation of this study and Section 8.9 provides an outlook on future research. In Section 8.10 the managerial implications for potential investors in CEE countries are presented. The last Section 8.11 presents some final conclusions of the study.

8.1 The HQ-S governance mechanisms

This study has attempted to create a sound theoretical foundation for explaining the characteristics of governance mechanisms in the relations between MNE headquarters and their subsidiaries.

Research question (1) was stated as follows:

What are the characteristics of the different HQ-S governance mechanisms used by international headquarters in relation to their Polish subsidiaries?

We proposed that the characteristics of HQ-S governance mechanisms could be linked to agency theory (with the 'classical' principal-agent relationship as a core) and to stewardship theory (implying relations between partners based on equality and mutual interdependence). Although the predictions of these two theoretical foundations on the governance mechanisms may seem contradictory at first sight, our research shows that the agency and stewardship mechanisms tend to be mutually supportive and reinforcing and may appear subsequently, rather than exclusively. This is in line with the organisational design literature, which proposes that organisations face extreme pressures that will initially tighten control (as such pressure is likely to threaten the survival in the short run), and then adopt organic (such as stewardship-based) governance modes (Khandawalla, 1977; Chenhall, 2003). The results of the present study indeed show that the agency and stewardship mechanisms are used alongside and complementary to each other. As shown in Section 6.8, the PLS model for HQ-S governance explains the relationship between these two kinds of mechanisms. Control (agency mechanisms) provides a solid platform on which stewardship mechanisms can be built. The complementarities of these two mechanisms may be linked to earlier studies which show that successful organisations combine tight control with more open, informal and flexible information and communication systems (Chapman, 1998, Chenhall and Morris, 1995, Simons, 1987). A recent article by Henri (2006) described flexible and dominant types of control and showed that a more flexible attitude from top managers supports strategic decision-making and organisational design. A focus which bends too much towards control or too much towards coordination (cooperation and organic control) may threaten a company's existence, as was also shown by Sundaramurthy and Lewis (2003). Our research provides a theoretical explanation for such findings, as we state that the agency theory and the stewardship theory are not opposing standpoints but complementary dimensions of HQ-S governance.

8.2 The influence of the business environment on HQ-S governance

Research question (2) was stated as follows:

What is the impact of the Polish business environment on the HQ-S governance mechanisms?

We have investigated the influence of environmental factors on the HQ-S governance: the transitional environment of a CEE country, the task environment and the impact of cultural distance between the home-countries of headquarters and subsidiaries. We adopted the contingency theory, and included contingent elements of the environment as well as elements of organisational design in the model. The survey data provided an input for an explorative study which tested the proposed relationships by applying a PLS-modelling technique. In Section 3.4.2, we proposed including three dimensions of the external environment: (1) environmental uncertainty which accounted for the transitional character of the Polish economy, (2) environmental dynamism which referred to the predictability and variability of the external environment, and (3) environmental constraints, which referred to the limitations of the resources availability such as the labour force or the quality of the suppliers. Although we decided to measure three different dimensions of the environment, we proposed that they all have a similar effect on the HQ-S governance mechanism deployment. Therefore, one general proposition was formulated:

> *Proposition 1*
>
> *In turbulent (transition) environments, HQ-S governance mechanisms that primarily rely on coordination (in terms of attunement and personal contacts) will be positively associated with performance.*

The results show that the environment represents an important explanatory factor for the HQ-S governance-characteristics. The survey participants perceived the Polish environment as dynamic, highly competitive and rich in labour resources. The perceived uncertainties were related to the interpretation and execution of law, rather than to political interference and the instability of the economy. PLS-modelling showed that, in congruence with proposition 1, the turbulence in the environment was associated with the occurrence of stewardship mechanisms (extensive coordination between Headquarters and Subsidiary). These stewardship mechanisms have proven to affect performance positively.

The second dimension of the environment, dynamism, may be dealt with by an MNE by exploiting the experience and the knowledge acquired from earlier market entries in other countries. Previous research on the internationalisation processes of MNEs showed that this knowledge is further developed and used on an incremental basis when new operations abroad are established. The basic assumption behind our empirical model was therefore, that a lack of such knowledge is an important obstacle to the development of international operations (Johanson and Vahlne, 1977). When markets are moderately dynamic, i.e. change occurs in the context of a stable industry structure, it may be sufficient for HQ-S governance to rely on existing routines of which a linear execution of plans produces a predictable outcome (Nelson and Winter, 1982). In highly dynamic markets where industry structure is blurred, the HQ-S governance has a different character. It is characterised by experiential, unstable processes that rely on quickly created new knowledge and iterative execution to produce adaptive, but often unpredictable outcomes (Cui *et al.*, 2005). This is only possible with intensified personal interactions (stewardship) between parts of the MNE organisation (as opposed to a control-centred approach in a principal-agent relationship). In dynamic environments, interactive control systems, i.e. those that force a dialogue among all organisational participants about the data coming out of the system and about what to do with these data, lead to organisational learning and an improved emergent strategy (Simons, 1987). However, earlier studies showed little use of interactive, also called high-involvement, control systems in European and Japanese multinationals. A positive effect on organisational learning and outcomes was found in Korean firms (Bae and Lawler, 2000). Our study provides some initial results showing that interactive – in our study combining control and coordination – mechanisms in the HQ-S governance enhance company performance.

In contrast to our expectations, no significant relationship was found between environmental dynamism and HQ-S governance mechanisms.

An exception is the negative bi-variate relationship we found between the dynamism of the environment and coordination and control of HRM issues (see Table 6.19). This negative relationship may be explained by the specific character of human resource management (Lepak *et al.*, 2003). In turbulent and dynamic environments, companies often differentiate their products to spread the risk of failure (e.g. while pursuing an analyser strategy – see more in Section 3.4.4). Such strategies are linked to flexible working systems with a strong focus on education, training and employee involvement. Environmental dynamism and cultural distance will induce a departure from a centrally-governed and global human resource strategy, even if in all other managerial aspects a global strategy is fostered. Locally-based HR practices are possibly regarded as more effective than uniform guidelines for personnel. Therefore, developing MNE-wide HRM policies may be difficult to implement in turbulent environments, and in effect HRM is strongly decentralised – that is: locally sourced and organised. This was also the case in western MNEs in China, as the results of the study of Braun and Warner (2002) show. In our study, a focus on local education sources and in-house training was predominantly observed, supplemented by HQs' ad-hoc short-term assistance to regional operations.

The third dimension of the environment, the resource constraints, was supposed to be predominantly positively associated with stewardship mechanisms in the HQ-S governance mechanisms. That is because in the case of scarcity or constraints in non-human resources, headquarters' knowledge, experience and network may contribute to solving shortage problems. Therefore, a subsidiary would search for intense personal contacts and welcome attuning with the headquarters to assure new resource opportunities. The model developed for the HQ-S governance showed a positive, highly significant relationship between environmental constraints and coordination. A similar result was found in the study by Luo (2003) in which headquarters-subsidiary linkages and interactions with HQs helped to mitigate the problems of the emerging markets by reducing external dependence and contribute to capitalising emerging market opportunities.

In summary, two of the three dimensions of the external environment (uncertainty and resource constraints) were positively associated with the coordination dimensions of the HQ-S governance mechanisms. Environmental dynamism had no significant effect on coordination and none of the environmental factors seemed to have a relationship with the control dimension of HQ-S governance.

8.3 The cultural distance influence on HQ-S governance

Cultural distance has been added to the contingency model as it may complicate managing foreign subsidiaries, in general. The HQs governance mechanisms often appear to be ineffective and sometimes even counterproductive when applied to the management of foreign subsidiaries. We suggested that agency-based mechanisms enable transparency and provide culturally compromised instruments for data exchange, while at the same time reducing uncertainty related to unknown aspects of the subsidiary country. The following proposition was therefore formulated:

Proposition 2

In case of a large cultural distance, HQ-S governance mechanisms that primarily rely on operational and strategic control will be positively associated with performance.

To evaluate the proposition, we calculated cultural distance from the scores on the country level. Applying such a cultural distance measure to a sample is meaningful, provided there is similarity among respondents from country samples with respect to their individual value rankings (Schaffer and Riordan, 2003). Collecting data at subsidiary level and mostly from local CEOs (see Section 6.4.1) assured a relative homogeneity of the respondents.

The model we built (Section 6.8) showed a positive relationship between cultural distance and strategic control, but no relationship with operational control. Therefore the proposition is confirmed, but with respect to strategic control only. The division in strategic and operational control emerged during the PLS model estimation, which showed two clearly separate dimensions (remark the loadings in the outer model estimation in Section 6.8). Strategic control is related to policy building and there the difference in perceptions and value sets appeared to be the most disturbing for the MNE operations. Control system objectives aim at maximizing the predictability through the use of input and output measures (Hamilton *et al.*, 1996). Cultural differences may have caused barriers in communication as they influence interpretations and thereby affect perceptions of appropriate behaviour. In addition, subsidiary managers have to act according to local social constraints, which may sometimes inhibit application of the HQ procedures (Hamilton *et al.*, 1996).

In conclusion, the PLS model shows that cultural distance is positively associated with strategic control and has no direct significant links with either operational control or coordination.

8.4 The influence of strategy on HQ-S governance

The third research question considered the influence of two groups of strategies: generic and international on the HQ-S governance. Research question (3) was formulated as follows:

What is the influence of the strategic choices of MNE on the HQ-S governance mechanisms?

The way an MNE deals with its external environment and the kind of governance mechanisms it applies with respect to its subsidiaries depends on the strategy an MNE chooses to implement. Two sets of propositions were developed; one concerning a relationship between a generic strategy and HQ-S governance mechanisms and the other between an international strategy and governance mechanisms.

A generic strategy concerns the extent to which a company is willing and able to explore new opportunities in the market and develop new products. It can be divided into prospector, analyser and defender strategy (see Miles and Snow, 1978). Prospectors pursue an offensive strategy, aggressively seizing new market opportunities, no matter what the risk. Defenders are less pro-active, and are 'protection-oriented', seeking stability by maintaining current market positions and defending against encroachment of their market share by other firms. Analysers are located between prospectors and defenders, balancing the opportunity-seeking nature of prospectors against the risk aversion of defenders. We therefore posed that for a prospector strategy flexibility and agility are necessary, which are more related to stewardship than to agency mechanisms. The following proposition was put forward:

Proposition 3

For subsidiaries pursuing a prospector strategy, the HQ-S governance mechanisms that primarily rely on coordination (in terms of attunement and personal contacts) will be associated with better performance.

With respect to the generic strategy, in general, the results show that the majority of the subsidiaries (53%) regard themselves as defenders and focus their activities on serving current markets with existing products and operations. Looking at the generic strategy we notice that the more innovative the subsidiary (or otherwise stated: the more it pursues a prospector strategy), the more autonomy it receives from the HQs and the less agency-focused their HQ-S governance mechanisms are. Prospectors, however, with the exception of business meetings within the MNE network, do not show intense coordination as could be expected from a stewardship theory perspective. With this result, proposition 3 is not supported.

The international strategy concerns the markets and the competition-mode an MNE chooses for its international operations. MNEs pursuing a global international strategy treat the whole world as one homogeneous market. In contrast, multidomestic companies recognize the national differences in multiple national markets and try to respond to different customer needs. A global strategy assures economies of scale and achieves that by spreading the value chain of activities over a number of countries. Compared to a global strategy this multidomestic orientation is less focused at cost efficiency. Cost levels play a subordinate role since local responsiveness and tailoring products to local needs are its main focus. In extreme cases, for optimal responsiveness a complete new value chain is established in each (domestic) market. Finally, there is a group of MNEs that address both requirements and implement a strategy that comes up to these contradictory requirements, by adopting a transnational strategy (Bartlett and Goshal, 1987). We formulated the following propositions:

Proposition 4

For subsidiaries pursuing a global strategy, the HQ-S governance mechanisms that primarily rely on control (operational and strategic) will be associated with better performance.

Proposition 4a

For subsidiaries pursuing a transnational strategy, the HQ-S governance mechanisms that primarily rely on coordination (in terms of attunement and personal contacts) will be associated with better performance

Incorporating the generic and international strategy variables in the multivariate model for HQ-S governance shows no significant relationships, either with stewardship or with the agency mechanisms. So we have not found support for the above propositions 4 and 4a.

This result does not mean that there was no relationship between strategy and governance mechanisms at all. The influence may have been absorbed by other variables such as the external environment in the multivariate model.

In a closer investigation, we compared three international strategy clusters. Interestingly, then the results showed significant differences between the different international strategy clusters (see Section 6.9). The subsidiaries of MNEs pursuing a global strategy have little autonomy in decision making on the marketing and R&D decisions, but show frequent attuning of production processes and frequent personal contacts with HQ managers of logistics and R&D departments. As was expected in the global strategy cluster, governance mechanisms which rely heavily on control of output and efficiency are revealed. A pure multidomestic cluster could not be discerned. We decided to put another label on this cluster: 'multidomestic-transitional', as the companies probably are in a transitional stage due to a strong international activity; this would not be expected in a classical multidomestic strategy.

The transnational strategy cluster shows significantly more frequent business meetings within the MNE network with other subsidiaries and the lowest level of formalisation in reporting. A high frequency of personal contacts and much inter-unit attuning is also observed.

Although neither the international nor the generic strategy variables are significantly associated with HQ-S governance in the multivariate model, this study provides additional evidence for the validity of the Miles and Snow typology applied as an instrument to examine MNE subsidiaries in transition markets. In the multivariate model, the positive relationship between strategic control and performance is mediated[27] by the prospector strategy. Prospectors showed better performance and stronger satisfaction on all measured dimensions: general short term,

---

[27] With a moderator variable being one that influences the strength of the relationship, and a mediator variable being one that explains the relationship between the two other variables (Baron and Kenny, 1986).

long term and compared to competitors. For many firms, creating new products, ideas or processes is a central path by which they adapt and sometimes even transform themselves in changing environments (Verdu-Jover *et al.,* 2005). Our findings indicate that the strategic orientations in the Miles and Snow typology differ in type and intensity of performance, as shown earlier by Luo and Parker (2001) in the emerging market of China.

8.5 HQ-S governance and performance

This brings us to the last research question of this study. Research question (4) was:

What is the impact of the different governance mechanisms on MNE performance?

In exploring the composition as well as the influence of the external and internal factors, based on the contingency theory we predict that there is an optimal fit between these factors and companies showing this fit will show enhanced performance (Burton *et al.,* 2000). In fact all our propositions indicate an effect on performance, proposing that if subsidiaries recognise the influences included in the propositions, they will show enhanced performance. This PLS model for HQ-S governance incorporates this assumption, as the model shows a direct relationship between coordination and performance, so all positive direct relationships with coordination are also positively related to performance. In our study, performance is related to the long-term continuity of the company in areas such as market share, strategic position, and consumer satisfaction. In general, subsidiary managers are satisfied with their short- and long-term goal achievement. The group of excellent-performing subsidiaries has closer (coordination-) links with their HQ. They cooperate more intensively, attend joint meetings more often and show a high level of ICT integration (Section 6.7.1). The multivariate model for the HQ-S governance shows a significant positive relationship between coordination mechanisms and performance. As mentioned in the previous paragraph, agency mechanisms, such as strategic control, showed an indirect path to performance through a prospector strategy, and also through coordination. Operational control is indirectly related to performance through coordination mechanisms. In that sense coordination appears to be the central mediating variable in the association of control and performance.

8.6 The role of expatriates, international sales and relationship duration

In the PLS model, the expatriates do not show any direct or indirect significant relationship with the external environment or with performance. Generally speaking there were few expatriates in the subsidiaries. In the recently founded subsidiaries (2000 or later), hardly any expatriates were present. At the top of marketing, manufacturing and financial departments there were no expatriates at all. Furthermore, there were no headquarters' representatives in CEO positions. A few foreign CEOs originated from a third country. This in line with insights from current international management literature which suggest that expatriates are less intensively used as a result of acculturation and expatriate family problems (Werner, 2002; Paik and Sohn, 2004). On the other hand, however, in the interviews the expatriates were mentioned as an important instrument for governing foreign subsidiaries. For example, all Dutch headquarters used expatriates in the initial phase of setting up a foreign subsidiary.

In the multivariate model for the HQ-S governance a number of control variables derived from the contingency theory were included, such as the size of headquarters and subsidiary, the international activity of the subsidiary and the age of the relationship with headquarters. In line with the theory of organisational control (Hedlund, 1984; Flamholtz *et al.,* 1985; Wijbenga, 2004), the size of the organisation had a significant effect on the control intensity. Interestingly however, headquarters' size was positively associated with strategic control while subsidiary's size was related to operational control. So, the larger headquarters used more intensive strategic control over their subsidiaries. Larger headquarters probably have a more explicit strategy and better developed instruments to monitor its implementation (for example, reporting on market share development). Moreover, large headquarters usually had larger subsidiaries, which means that their subsidiaries have gained a strong position in the local and/or international market or even aim at leadership in the market. Then the strategic control plays an important role in reaching this goal. However, in the time following the headquarters' investment, subsidiaries are granted more strategic freedom. Larger subsidiaries play a more important role in the MNE network, and it may be the case that the whole production takes place in these subsidiaries and headquarters only sell the product in different markets, which may explain the positive relationship with operational control which includes sales turnover and manufacturing reports (see Table 6.19).

It is interesting to note that the amount of international sales of the subsidiaries showed the highest path-coefficient of all relationships in the PLS multivariate model. Strong international activity of the subsidiary is associated with intense coordination, and indirectly with enhanced performance. International sales are positively associated with a global strategy and negatively with multidomestic strategy. This is in line with the earlier publications on international strategy (Martinez and Jarillo, 1991; Roth *et al.,* 1991; Buckley and Ghauri, 2004). If international sales are related to coordination and to international strategy, the question arises: why there was no significant relationship between international strategy and coordination, as we have not found support for proposition 4 and 4a (see Section 8.4). The possible explanation might be that it does not matter which strategy HQ wants its subsidiary to pursue, rather it matters which strategy a subsidiary actually carries out. So the difference may be vested in a gap between intended and emergent strategy (Mintzberg and Waters, 1985.; Liedtka and Rosenblum, 1996). For example, high international sales clearly indicate that a subsidiary has an international orientation, not local as would be expected in the case of a multidomestic strategy. The intention of a subsidiary might be a more international orientation and its strategy may emerge in the direction of global or transnational.

8.7 In-depth interviews with headquarters

Looking at the headquarters' evaluation of the subsidiaries' achievements (see Table 7.1), we found that French headquarters were slightly more satisfied with their subsidiaries than the Dutch (mean values 5.6 and 5.3 respectively). It may seem that the opportunities of the size of Polish market, which were the most often mentioned motives for investment in Poland by the French HQs, bring better organisational outcomes than the cost-reduction motive, which was more often mentioned by the Dutch HQs. The cost-reduction motive for investment or internationalisation of a company has only a short-term positive effect on MNEs' performance (Luo, 2004). The investment must be based on a long-term strategy to be able to achieve a lasting above-average performance.

The interviews shed some light on the in-between country differences in the governance mechanisms, as was suggested by Bhimani (1999). Dutch headquarters put a strong emphasis on people management, developing training programs and creating opportunities for personal interaction. In contrast to this, French headquarters preferred to send expatriates to the subsidiaries. The effect is that the cultural gap is less noticeable between HQs and subsidiary, but more between expatriate and subsidiary. Subsidiaries that were set up from scratch in a form of Greenfield investment and with an expatriate from the HQ showed the highest performance satisfaction and at the same the lowest intensity of control and coordination. This result of our empirical research should be viewed with caution as the respondent was the manager responsible for the foreign operations and in some cases he/she was engaged in the foundation of the subsidiary him/herself; therefore actually he/she was evaluating his/her own performance.

The results show that headquarters have a slightly different vision of the HQ-S governance compared with subsidiaries. All significant outcomes show a higher intensity of HQ-S governance in the perception of the HQs compared with the subsidiaries. Especially, the intensity coordination, i.e. joint task groups and business meetings, as well as the intensity of personal contacts and attunement differ between HQ and subsidiaries. This result is interesting as it shows no contradictory discrepancies between HQ and subsidiaries opinions. It would be problematic, if for example HQ evaluated performance lower than the subsidiary, but at the same showed higher intensity for governance mechanisms. In such a case, the relationships we find between contingent factors and governance mechanisms as developed in the PLS model would be questionable.

8.8 Study evaluation

This study provides important theoretical and methodological contributions to the international management literature. Theoretically, based on the concepts from organisational control, strategy and international management, the study develops a model of the relationship between HQ-S governance mechanisms and performance in multinational enterprises. Using a cross-disciplinary integrative approach incorporating strategy, organization and contingency theory and measuring the impact of multiple factors on the governance mechanisms, the study contributes to creating interdependent linkages between different perspectives on MNE research. In doing so, the study fills an important gap in the literature, which used either strategy influence or environmental forces to explain the MNE organisation.

The theoretical contributions of this study are four-fold:

1. It has integrated theoretical streams, which at first glance might look contradictory and mutually exclusive, in one comprehensive framework. Extensive effort has been put into developing a conceptual framework that integrates agency-, stewardship- and contingency-based insights in one overall model. We have gathered strong indications, both theoretical and based on empirical evidence, that such an integrative approach is necessary to grasp the complexity of the HQ-S governance relationship. Complementing the agency theory with the stewardship dimension creates a framework for exploring the interdependences between HQ-S governance mechanisms, providing deeper explanations than one dimension or a sum of dimensions. This is in line with the recent development and strategic and accounting literature calling for a broader and multidimensional approach to governance issues in multinational corporations (Busco *et al.*, 2007).

2. A second contribution is the fact that we applied insights with respect to HQ-S governance to subsidiaries located in transition markets in one of the former planned economies of Central Eastern Europe. Poland is special in the sense that it has a Western cultural origin and was dominated for decades by culturally alien occupants. The special mindset which resulted even obstructed our research, since Polish managers (at the time we sent out our survey) were in general reluctant to provide information. Despite all barriers to our research we were able to propose a theory-based model which explains performance via governance mechanisms, and which may be used for longitudinal studies and comparison (see Section 8.8.3). The present study takes an important step in enlarging the body of knowledge on the HQ-S governance mechanisms in transition and emerging markets (Meyer and Peng, 2005).

3. We combined data from the local subsidiaries' level with the data from headquarters. Such an approach, although challenging in implementation, is in our view more beneficial than building conclusions on one side of the relationship only, as has been done in earlier studies, e.g. Harzing (1999).

4. Our methodological contribution refers to the application of the partial least squares technique (PLS). By using PLS we avoided distributional problems of the variables in the sample. Our research has proven that PLS is especially suitable for structural equation modelling with small samples. Unlike the covariance methodology developed by Jöreskog (1969), which is based on maximum likelihood estimation and has special restrictions attached to it (sample size and scale, parametric assumptions of normality and independency of observations, and use of reflective variables), the requirements of PLS with respect to sample size, scale of variables and their distribution are minimal (Chin, 1998; Chin and Newsted, 1999, p. 309-312; Fornell and Bookstein, 1982). In this way we contributed to

its adoption in social research. Especially in business administration small data sets are quite common, since it is difficult to acquire information from companies because of the 'competition' arguments.

8.9 Suggestions for further research

As stated, the HQ-S relationship is not static, but evolves over time. Above all, cultural distance evolves and is constantly changing, especially between Western countries and the nations that were isolated earlier and are now undergoing major transformations, such as Poland. In the cross-cultural psychological research, it is referred to as (periodic) changeability of culture (Mikułowski-Pomorski, 2001). We found strong indications, both theoretical as well as empirical, that a dynamic approach towards explaining the occurrence and appropriateness of a governance form is mandatory. And, surprisingly, it has been hardly present in the research on the subject until now. Research on the dynamic aspects of HQ-S development is therefore badly needed. We suggest a more dynamic approach in which the evolvement of the HQ-S governance mechanisms of subsidiaries in culturally different environments is followed in time. This could deepen our insights into the appropriate management of subsidiaries as well as suggested, from a theoretical perspective, 'typical' paths of development.

A second suggestion is related to the fact that cultural differences can also be formed at the regional level and that a 'generic' country-level approach, as we performed, should be supplemented with a more differentiated focus. Moreover, despite the fact that the explanatory power of the Hofstede´s cultural dimensions has been recently proven (Drogendijk and Slangen, 2006), the complexity of the concept may require that it is further split up into three important elements: ethnicity, race and national difference. More dimensions in cultural distance than country-level differences may present a more complete view of the impact on governance and performance. The research by Brewer (2007) presents a sound and comprehensive starting-point for exploring differences in psychic distance, of which cultural distance is only a part.

Thirdly, the results are based on data from Polish subsidiaries in the manufacturing industries. Therefore, the findings might not necessarily reflect the general pattern of all companies across industries or across countries. Future research might use cross-industry data as well as data from other countries to investigate the composition of the HQ-S governance mechanisms, their influencing factors and effect on performance. Moreover, our study of Polish subsidiaries should be repeated to get insight into the validity and reliability of our findings in a more 'generic' way and capture the time effect of the developments.

Fourthly, further exploration of the views of HQ-S governance is needed. The PLS model for HQ-S governance may also be tested on the HQs of the subsidiaries. It would be preferable if both sides, HQ and S, in the same companies were investigated. We were not able to accomplish this because of time and financial constraints. Additional countries should be included to expand the database. Also the difference in the perceptions between HQs and subsidiaries may be further explored: are they an effect of presenting the reality in a more favourable light (as described in e.g. Harzing, 1999) or are they the results of the influence of other factors?

Finally, some interesting results may be investigated in-depth by applying case study methodology to the HQ-S governance mechanisms: for instance, to explore the effects of the less intensive strategy control in subsidiaries which are part of a larger MNE network on a longer time scale. For example, in our sample the group of 49 subsidiaries which were part of a larger MNE network would serve as a population for further research.

8.10 Managerial implications

Below we try to provide managerial suggestions based on our research to answer the following question:

If an investor wants to develop and succeed in operations in transition/emerging CEEC market, what factors should he/she take into account? What are the pitfalls and what are the opportunities?

First, choose the entry mode carefully. Our data suggest that for a transition type of economy, Greenfield investment may be the most beneficiary entry mode.

As extensively elaborated on in Section 2.1 of this thesis, each investment mode has its particular advantages and disadvantages, and the investment decision is a difficult one. For example, a Greenfield investment entry mode including full ownership of the newly established foreign operations enables full exploitation of local resources and market advantages and gives full control of the production process. However, at the same time it requires a large capital investment and extensive management involvement. As Greenfield investments provide relatively strong control over the operations of subsidiaries, it is often the preferred entry mode in highly uncertain transition environments (Meyer, 1998). In the case where an investor-company chooses for an acquisition-mode, it gets immediate access to the market and local knowledge, but at the same time it should be aware of the additional managerial effort and time needed to restructure the acquired subsidiary into the existing governance structure. This is probably the most important reason why acquisitions in transition economies often fail. Also, in our study the Greenfield investments prevailed. In comparison with other entry modes and/or different types of acquisitions (see Section 6.2), Greenfield entries were extremely active internationally and included the best performing subsidiaries. Despite the fact that acquisitions may offer some immediate advantages, they often bring many reorganisational side-effects.

Second, especially in the post-entry period, building a well-functioning strategic and operational control platform for the subsidiary is essential.

This study has shown that an effective HQ-S relationship is based on a sound platform of strategic and operational control. When a large cultural distance between the HQ and the subsidiary exists, an intensive strategic control is required. The intensity of strategic control may decrease in the years after the initial investment. The data further indicates that especially if the subsidiary is large, operational control may have to be intensive. However, strong control will not assure better performance, not directly at least, therefore ...

Third, build a coordination system on this control platform for flexibility and agility needed in uncertain and constrained transition-type of environments.

Coordination, meaning attunement and personal contact with a subsidiary is positively associated with enhanced performance. But this effect occurs only when coordination takes place on a sound base of strategic control. In uncertain and resource-constrained environments, intensive coordination with the headquarters may reduce uncertainties or provide ideas for solving resource shortage problems. In both situations, this will lead to better organisational outcomes.

Fourth, use ICT tools not only for fast information exchange but also to bridge cultural distance and to create transparency of operations.

ICT integration between headquarters and subsidiary enables a smooth flow of information but may also serve as a basis for intensified information exchange. Excellent subsidiaries showed extensive ICT integration with their headquarters. Our results show also that CEOs of highly-integrated subsidiaries, in terms of information technology, also have more personal contacts with the CEOs from HQs. Also the information exchange concerning the production process is more intensive in this group of subsidiaries. In geographically and culturally distant relations ICT creates a platform for personal communication. The positive effects of overcoming cultural differences with ICT solutions in developing new products on a global basis were recently described in Lefebvre *et al.* (2006).

Fifth, a prospector strategy, exploring new products, operations, and markets is clearly a successful strategy for entering transition economies.

Our results show that prospector subsidiaries were clearly more successful than other subsidiaries. Enhanced strategic control applied by prospectors was related to significant better performance. One would think that is better to introduce existing products in new markets in order to avoid the 'suicide square' of innovation – new products, new market and new technology combination (Wheelwright and Clark, 1992), especially in entries in transition environments, but our results show exactly the opposite.

Finally, start with expatriates to build a sound control platform but quickly switch to subsidiary's home-countries CEOs to create coordination systems that ensure flexibility and agility of operations.

In the past, HQs' regulatory stringency has been the dominant instrument for managing Eastern European countries. Such a 'hierarchical enforcement' policy is very much related to agency-based instruments. It may be inefficient, stifling innovation, as well as inviting enforcement difficulties in the long run (compare: Fairman and Yapp, 2005 from a different perspective). In this context, the position of the expatriate is problematic. Equipped with home-country capabilities, an expatriate is the focal point of two cultures. On the one hand, the expatriate has to satisfy the strategic demands of the headquarters, which in many cases are imposed uniformly throughout an MNE. On the other hand, the expatriate is confronted with a different set of values, habits and skills which, especially in human resource management, requires flexibility. Headquarters' expatriates should be aware of the dual set of norms and values an expatriate is confronted with and provide him with space to manoeuvre. Moreover, taking into account the acculturation and family problems as a result of life in a foreign social environment (Werner, 2002; Paik and Sohn, 2004), the idea of using expatriates as controlling agents may even be abandoned. In our sample, especially in younger subsidiaries, hardly any expatriates were present, and only sporadically in the CEO position. At the top of marketing, manufacturing and financial departments there were no expatriates at all.

8.11 Final remarks

The findings of the present study indicate the importance of MNE subsidiaries' strategic flexibility at the operations level, which requires capabilities which are not the same in (1) time and in (2) place. Matching an organisation to its external environment is constantly under challenge as environments do not stand still for organisations to catch up, and organisations themselves, as organic entities, are in a continuous state of change. In due time, subsidiaries, just like the transition countries in which they are located, evolve from initial dependent and immature production or service facilities to mature, strategically contributing and capable business partners. This implicates that managing subsidiaries in transition markets is not a static process, in which the choice for governance mechanisms is made in the initial phase and then implemented and left unchanged, but should be adjusted to the evolving asset/base (knowledge and skills of labour, force for instance) and environmental conditions. Actually, management should be aware that both HQ and subsidiary take part in a continuous, bilateral learning process. The political and institutional environment in countries like Poland evolves from 'command and control' to 'cooperation and self-regulation', especially now that Poland is a member of the European Community.

Our explorative empirical research has shown that the road from governance to performance is not a one-way street, but alternative routes are available which accelerate performance more than sticking to past-made agency-based choices. Our research has shown that there is no simple and uniform recipe for managing subsidiaries, especially if environmental change is strong. Under such circumstances, it is advisable to create flexibility and learning capabilities at the subsidiary level, rather than maintaining a subsidiary in a state of dependence.

We hope that this thesis has provided the insights and instruments needed not just to maintain static fit but to arrive at a dynamic fit between headquarters and subsidiary, which is essential for lasting success in dynamic transition environments.

References

Agarwal, S. and S.N. Ramaswami, 1992. Choice of Foreign Market Entry Mode: Impact of Ownership, Location and Internationalization Factors. Journal of International Business Studies 23(1): 1-28.

Agthe, K.E., 1990. Managing the mixed marriage - multinational corporations. Business Horizons Retrieved 14-11-2006, 2006, from http://www.findarticles.com/p/articles/mi_m1038/is_n1_v33/ai_8867791.

Aldrich, H.E., 1979. Organizations and Environments. Englewood Cliffs, Prentice-Hall.

Anderberg, M.R., 1973. Cluster analysis for applications. New York [etc.], Academic press.

Andersen, O., 1993. On the Internationalization Process of Firms: A Critical Analysis. Journal of International Business Studies 24(2): 209-232.

Anderson, E. and H. Gatignon, 1986. Modes of Foreign Entry: A Transaction Cost Analysis and Propositions. Journal of International Business Studies 17(3): 1-26.

Andersson, U., I. Bjorkman and M. Forsgren, 2005. Managing subsidiary knowledge creation: The effect of control mechanisms on subsidiary local embeddedness. International Business Review 14(5): 521-538.

Anthony, R.N. and V. Govindarajan, 2001. Management Control Systems. New York, Mc Graw-Hill.

Aoki, M., 2004. Comparative Institutional Analysis of Corporate Governance. Corporate Governance and Firm Organization: Microfundations and Structural Forms. A. Grandori. New York, Oxford University Press.

Armstrong, J.S. and T.S. Overton, 1977. Estimating Nonresponse Bias in Mail Surveys. Journal of Marketing Research 14: 396-402.

Ashby, W.R., 1956. An introduction to cybernetics. London, Chapman and Hall.

ATKearney, 2003. FDI Confidence Index. Global Business Policy Council. Alexandria, Virginia, A.T.Kearney Inc.

ATKearney, 2004. FDI Confidence Index. Global Business Policy Council. Alexandria, Virginia, A.T.Kearney Inc.

Bae, J. and J.J. Lawler, 2000. Organizational and HRM strategies in Korea: Impact on firm performance in an emerging economy. Academy Of Management Journal 43(3): 502-517.

Bagozzi, R.P., Y. Yi and L.W. Phillips, 1991. Assessing Construct Validity in Organizational Research. Administrative Science Quarterly 36(3): 421-458.

Barnard, C., 1938. The functions of the executive. Cambridge, Harvard University Press.

Barney, J., 1991. Firm Resources and Sustained Competitive Advantage. Journal of Management 17(1): 99-120.

Barney, J.B. and M.H. Hansen, 1994. Trustworthiness As A Source Of Competitive Advantage. Strategic Management Journal 15: 175-190.

Baron, R.M. and D.A. Kenny, 1986. The moderator-mediator variable distinction in social psychological research: Conceptual, strategic, and statistical considerations. Journal of Personality and Social Psychology 51: 1173-1182.

Bartlett, C.A. and S. Ghoshal, 1987. Managing Across Borders - New Organizational Responses. Sloan Management Review 29(1): 43-53.

References

Bartlett, C.A. and S. Ghoshal, 1987. Managing Across Borders - New Strategic Requirements. Sloan Management Review 28(4): 7-17.

Bartlett, C.A. and S. Ghoshal, 1998. Managing across borders: the transnational solution. Boston, MA, Harvard Business School Press.

Bartlett, C.A. and S. Goshal, 1987. Managing Across Borders: New Organizational Responses. Sloan Management Review Fall: 43-52.

Bell, J., 1996. Joint or Single Venturing? An Eclectic approach to foreign entry mode choice. Tilburg, Katholieke Universiteit Brabant: 191.

Bhimani, A., 1999. Mapping methodological frontiers in cross-national management control research. Accounting Organizations And Society 24(5-6): 413-440.

Birkinshaw, J., 2001. Strategy and Management in MNE Subsidiaries. Oxford Handbook of International Business. A.M. Rugman and T.L. Brewer. Oxford, Oxford Univeristy Press. chapter 14: 381-399.

Birkinshaw, J. and A. Morrison, 1995. Configurations of Strategy and Structure in Subsidiares of Multinational Structure. Journal of International Business Studies 26(4): 729-754.

Birkinshaw, J., A. Morrison and J. Hulland, 1995. Structural and Competitive Determinants of a Global Integration Strategy. Strategic Management Journal 16(8): 637-655.

Borgatti, S.P. and P.C. Foster, 2003. The Network Paradigm in Organizational Research: A Review and Typology. Journal of Management 29(6): 991-1013.

Borsos-Torstila, J., 1997. Foreign direct investment and technology transfer: results of a survey in selected branches in Estonia. CIS Middle European Centre Discussion Paper Series 48.

Boyd, B.K., G.G. Dess and A.M.A. Rasheed, 1993. Divergence Between Archival And Perceptual Measures Of The Environment - Causes And Consequences. Academy Of Management Review 18(2): 204-226.

Braun, W.H. and M. Warner, 2002. Strategic human resource management in western multinationals in China - The differentiation of practices across different ownership forms. Personnel Review 31(5-6): 553-579.

Bremmers, H.J., S. W. F. Omta and M. Smit, 2003. Managing environmental information flows in food and agribusiness chains: a study on the relationship between ICT development and environmental performance. Wageningen, Wageningen University.

Brewer, P.A., 2007. Operationalizing psychic distance: A revised approach. Journal of International Marketing 15(1): 44-66.

Bruggeman, W. and W. Stede, 1993. Fitting Management Control Systems to Competitive Advantage. British Journal of Management 4(3): 205-218.

Bruton, G.D., F.T. Lohrke and J.W. Lu, 2004. The evolving definition of what comprises international strategic managament research. Journal of International Management 10: 413-429.

Buchko, A.A., 1994. Conceptualization and Measurement of Environmental Uncertainty: An Assessment of the Miles and Snow Perceived Environmental Uncertainty Scale. Academy of Management Journal 37(2): 410-425.

Buckley, P.J. and P.N. Ghauri, 2004. Globalisation, economic geography and the strategy of multinational enterprises. Journal of International Business Studies 35(2): 81-98.

Burt, R.S., M. Guilarte, H.J. Raider and Y. Yasuda, 2002. Competition, contingency, and the external structure of markets. Advances in Strategic Management, JAI. Volume 19: 167.

Burton, R.M., J. Lauridsen and B. Obel, 2000. Fit and Misfits in the Multi-Dimensional Contingency Model: An Organizational Change Perspective. Retrieved June, 2006, from http://www.lok.cbs.dk/images/publ/Burton%20og%20Obel%20og%20Lauridsen%202000.pdf.

Burton, R.M. and B. Obel, 2004. Strategic Organizational Diagnosis and Design: Developing Theory for Application. Boston, Kluwer Publishers.

Busco, C., E. Giovannoni and A. Riccaboni, 2007. Globalisation and the international convergence of management accounting. Issues in Management Accounting. T. Hopper, D. Northcott and R. Scapens, Prentice Hall: 65-92.

Calantone, R.J., D. Kim, J.B. Schmidt and S.T. Cavusgil, 2006. The influence of internal and external firm factors on international product adaptation strategy and export performance: A three-country comparison. Journal of Business Research 59(2): 176-185.

Calori, R., L. Melin, T. Atamer and P. Gustavsson, 2000. Innovative international strategies. Journal of World Business 35(4): 333.

Cantwell, J. and R. Mudambi, 2005. MNE competence-creating subsidiary mandates. Strategic Management Journal 26(12): 1109-1128.

Carpenter, M.A., T.G. Pollock and M.M. Leary, 2003. Testing a Model of Reasoned Risk-Taking: Governance, the Experience of Principals And Agents, and Global Strategy in High-Technology IPO Firms. Strategic Management Journal 24: 803-820.

Castrogiovanni, G.J., 1991. Environmental Munificence - A Theoretical Assessment. Academy of Management Review 16(3): 542-565.

Chakravarthy, B.S., 1986. Measuring Strategic Performance. Strategic Management Journal 7: 437-458.

Chandler, A.D. and B. Mazlish (eds.), 2005. Leviathans: Multinational Corporations and the New Global History. USA Edition, Cambridge University Press.

Chandler, G.N. and S.H. Hanks, 1993. Measuring performance of emerging businesses. Journal of Business Venturing 8: 3-40.

Chang, E. and M.S. Taylor, 1999. Control in multinational corporations (MNCS): the case of Korean manufacturing subsidiaries. Journal of Management 25(4): 541-565.

Chatelin, Y.M., V.E. Vinzi and M. Tenenhaus, 2002. State-of-art on PLS Path Modeling through the available software.

Chen, T.J., 2006. Liability of foreignness and entry mode choice: Taiwanese firms in Europe. Journal of Business Research 59(2): 288-294.

Chenhall, R.H., 2003. Management control systems design within its organizational context: findings from contingency-based research and directions for the future. Accounting, Organizations and Society 28(2-3): 127-168.

Child, D., 1970. The essentials of factor analysis. London [etc.], Holt, Rinehart and Winston.

Child, J., 1984. Organization: a guide to problems and practice. London [etc.], Harper & Row.

Chin, W.W., 1998. Commentary: Issues and Opinion on Structural Equation Modeling. MIS Quarterly 22(1): vii-xvi.

Chin, W.W., 1998. The Partial Least Squares Approach to Structural Equation Modeling. Modern Methods for Business Research. G.A. Marcoulides. Mahwa, New Jersey, London, Lawrence Erlbaum Associates: 295-335.

References

Chin, W.W. and P.R. Newsted, 1999. Structural Equation Modeling Analysis with Small Samples Using Partial Least Squares. Statistical Strategies for Small Sample Research. R.H. Hoyle. Thousand Oaks etc., Sage.

Choi, F.D.S. and I.J. Czechowicz, 1983. Assessing Foreign Subsidiary Performance: A Multinational Comparison. Management International Review 4: 14-25.

Chojna, J., 2005. The role of foreign-owned companies in Poland's economy. Foreign Investments in Poland. Annual Report. J. Chojna. Warsaw, Foreign Trade Research Institute: 100-120.

Coase, R.H., 1937. The firm, the market and the law. Chicago [etc.], University of Chicago Press.

Cool, K., I. Dierickx and D. Jemison, 1989. Business Strategy, Market Structure and Risk-Return Relationships: A Structural Approach. Strategic Management Journal 10(6): 507-522.

Cortina, J.M., 1993. What is coefficient alpha? An examination of theory and applications. Journal of Applied Psychology 78: 98-104.

Covaleski, M.A., M.W. Dirsmith and S. Samuel, 2003. Changes in the institutional environment and the institutions of governance: extending the contributions of transaction cost economics within the management control literature. Accounting, Organizations and Society 28(5): 417.

Cray, D., 1984. Control and Coordination in Multinational Corporations. Journal of International Business Studies 15(2): 85-98.

Croft, G.W., 1996. Glossary of Systems Theory and Practice for the Applied Behavioral Sciences. Freeland, WA, Syntropy Incorporate.

Cui, A.S., D.A. Griffith and S.T. Cavusgil, 2005. The influence of competitive intensity and market dynamism on knowledge management capabilities of multinational corporation subsidiaries. Journal of International Marketing 13(3): 32-53.

Daft, R., 1989. Organizational Theory and Design. St. Paul, West Publishing.

Daft, R., J. Sormunen and D. Parks, 1988. Chief executive scanning, environmental characteristics, and company performance: An empirical study. Strategic Management Journal 9: 123-139.

Daily, C.M., D.R. Dalton and A.A. Cannella, 2003. Introduction to special topic forum corporate governance: Decades of dialogue and data. Academy of Management Review 28(3): 371-382.

Davis, I. and E. Stephenson, 2006. An executive take on the top business trends: A McKinsey Global Survey. The McKinsey Quarterly.

Davis, J.H., F.D. Schoorman and L. Donaldson, 1997. Toward a Stewardship Theory of Management. The Academy of Management Review 22(1): 20-47.

Davis, J.H., F.D. Schoorman, R.C. Mayer and H.H. Tan, 2000. The trusted general manager and business unit performance: Empirical evidence of a competitive advantage. Strategic Management Journal 21(5): 563-576.

Delios, A. and S. Makino, 2003. Timing of entry and the foreign subsidiary performance of Japanese firms. Journal of International Marketing 11(3): 83-105.

Desai, A., M. Kroll and P. Wright, 2003. CEO duality, board monitoring, and acquisition performance: A test of competing theories. Journal of Business Strategies 20.

Dess, G.G. and D.W. Beard, 1984. Dimensions of Organizational Task Environments. Administrative Science Quarterly 29(1): 52-73.

Dess, G.G. and R.B. Robinson Jr., 1984. Measuring Organizational Performance in the Absence of Objective Measures: The Case of Privately-held Firm and Conglomerate Business Unit. Strategic Management Journal 5(3): 265-73.

Diamantopoulos, A. and H.M. Winklhofer, 2001. Index Construction with Formative Indicators: An Alternative to Scale Development. Journal of Marketing Research 38(May): 269-277.

Dickinson, G.M., 1971. Classification of Foreign Capital Flows of Insurance Companies. The Journal of Risk and Insurance 38(1): 93-98.

Ditillo, A., 2004. Dealing with uncertainty in knowledge-intensive firms: the role of management control systems as knowledge integration mechanisms. Accounting Organizations And Society 29(3-4): 401-421.

Donaldson, L., 1990. The ethereal hand: organizational economics and management theory. Academy of Management Review 15: 369-81.

Donaldson, L., 2005. Following the scientific method: How I became a committed functionalist and positivist. Organization Studies 26(7): 1071-1088.

Donaldson, L., 2005. For positive management theories while retaining science: Reply to Ghoshal. Academy of Management Learning & Education 4(1): 109-113.

Douma, S., R. George and R. Kabir, 2006. Foreign and Domestic Ownership, Business Groups, and Firm Performance: Evidence from a Large Emerging Market. Strategic Management Journal 27: 637-657.

Doz, Y., C.A. Bartlett and C.K. Prahalad, 1981. Global Competitive Pressures vs. Host Country Demands: Managing Tensions in Multinational Corporations. California Management Review 23(3): 63-74.

Doz, Y. and C.K. Prahalad, 1984. Patterns of Strategic Control within Multinational Corporations. Journal of International Business Studies 15(2): 55-72.

Doz, Y. and C.K. Prahalad, 1991. Managing DMNCs: A Search for a New Paradigm. Strategic Management Journal 12(Special Issue: Global Strategy): 145-164.

Drogendijk, R. and A. Slangen, 2006. Hofstede, Schwartz, or Managerial perceptions: The Effects of Various Cultural Distance Measures on Establishment Mode Choices by Multinational Enterprises. International Business Review 15(361-380).

Durka, B., 2004. Podnoszenie Konkurencyjnosci Polskiej Gospodarki. Nowe Zycie Gospodarcze 8(370).

Durka, B., J. Chojna, J. Przystupa, I. Zagozdzinska, W. Karpinska-Mizielinska, T. Smuga, K. Marczewski, R. Pac, J. Osinski, U. Kopec and P. Wazniewski, 2003. Foreign Investments in Poland. Annual Report. B. Durka. Warsaw, Foreign Trade Research Institute: 209.

Egelhoff, W.G., 1984. Patterns of Control in U.S, U.K and European Multinational Corporations. Journal of International Business Studies 15(2): 73-84.

Egelhoff, W.G., 1988. Strategy and Structure in Multinational Corporations: A Revision of the Stopford and Wells Model. Strategic Management Journal 9(1): 1-14.

Eisenhardt, K.M., 1989. Agency Theory: An Assessment and Review. Academy of Management Review 14(1): 57-74.

Epstein, M.J. and J.F. Manzoni (eds.), 2002. Performance Measurement and Management Control: A compendium of Research. Studies in Managerial and Financial Accounting. Amsterdam, JAI.

References

Eurostat, 2005. Eurostat Yearbook 2005. Europe in Figures. Eurostat. Luxembourg, European Commission: 288.

Everitt, B.S., 1993. Cluster Analysis. London, Edward Arnold.

Fabry, N.H. and S.H. Zeghni, 2003. FDI in CEECs: How do Western investors survive? Thunderbird International Business Review 45(2): 133-147.

Fama, E. and M. Jensen, 1983. Separation of ownership and control. Journal of Law and Economics 26.

Flamholtz, E.G., T.K. Das and A.S. Tsui, 1985. Toward an integrative framework of organizational control. Accounting, Organizations and Society 10(1): 35-50.

Flinders, M., 2002. Governance in Whitehall. Public Administration 80(1): 51.

Fornell, C. and F. Bookstein, 1982. Two Structural Equation Models: Lisrel and PLS Applied to Consumer Exit-Voice Theory. Journal of Marketing Research 19: 440-452.

Fornell, C., P. Lorange and J. Roos, 1990. The Cooperative Venture Formation Process: A Latent Variable Structural Modeling Approach. Management Science 36(10, Focussed Issue on the State of the Art in Theory and Method in Strategy Research): 1246-1255.

Galbraith, J.R., 1976. Designing Complex Organizarions, Addison Wesley.

Gates, S.R. and W.G. Egelhoff, 1986. Centralization in Headquarters-Subsidiary Relationship. Journal of International Business Studies 17(2): 71-92.

Geringer, J.M.B., Paul W.; daCosta, Richard C., 1989. Diversification Strategy and Internationalization: Implications for MNE Performance. Strategic Management Journal 10(2): 109-119.

Geyskens, I., J.-B.E.M. Steenkamp and N. Kumar, 2006. Make, Buy, or Ally: a Transaction Cost Theory Meta-Analysis. The Academy of Management Journal 49(3): 519-543.

Ghoshal, S. and P. Moran, 1996. Bad for Practice: A Critique of the Transaction Cost Theory. Academy of Management Review 21(1): 13-47.

Goll, I. and A.M.A. Rasheed, 1997. Rational decision-making and firm performance: The moderating role of environment. Strategic Management Journal 18(7): 583-591.

Gomez, C. and S. Werner, 2004. The effect of institutional and strategic forces on management style in subsidiaries of US MNCs in Mexico. Journal of Business Research 57(10): 1135-1144.

Gonzalez-Benito, O. and J. Gonzalez-Benito, 2005. Cultural vs. operational market orientation and objective vs. subjective performance: Perspective of production and operations. Industrial Marketing Management 34(8): 797-829.

Govindarajan, V. and A.K. Gupta, 1985. Linking control systems to business unit strategy: impact on performance. Accounting, Organizations and Society 10(1): 51-66.

Granovetter, M., 1985. Economic Action and Social Structure: The Problem of Embeddedness. American Journal of Sociology 91(3): 481-510.

Grossman, S.J. and O.D. Hart, 1986. The Cost and Benefit of Ownership: A Theory of Lateral and Vertical Integration. Journal of Political Economy 94: 691-719.

Gupta, A.K. and V. Govindarajan, 1991. Knowledge flows and the structure of control within multinational corporations. Academy of Management Review 16(4): 768-792.

GUS, 2004. Wyniki finansowe podmiotow gospodarczych 2003. (Financial Results of enterprises in 2003) Warszawa, GUS Glowny Urzad Statystyczny: 90.

Hair, J.F.J., R.E. Anderson, R.L. Tatham and W.C. Black, 1998. Multivariate Data Analysis. New Jersey, Prentice-Hall.

Haley, G.T., 2000. Intellectual property rights and foreign direct investment in emerging markets. Marketing Intelligence & Planning 18/5 [2000]: 273-280.

Hamilton, R.D., V.A. Taylor and R.J. Kashlak, 1996. Designing a control system for a multinational subsidiary. Long Range Planning 29(6): 857-868.

Harzing, A.W., 1997. Response rates in the international mail surveys. Results from a 22-country study. International Business Review 6(6): 641-665.

Harzing, A.W., 2000a. Cross-national mail surveys: Why do response rates differ between the countries? Industrial Marketing Management 29(3): 243-254.

Harzing, A.W., 2000b. An Empirical Analysis and Extension of the Bartlett and Ghoshal Typology of Multinational Companies. Journal of International Business Studies 31(1): 101-120.

Harzing, A.W., 2002. Acquisitions versus greenfield investments: international strategy and management of entry modes. Strategic Management Journal 23(3): 211-227.

Harzing, A.W., A. Sorge and J. Paauwe., 2001. HQ-Subsidiary Relationship in Multinational Companies: a British-German Comparison. A revised version of this paper is accepted for: M. Geppert, D. Matten and K. Wiliams (eds.) Challenges for European Management in a Global Context - Experiences from Britain and Germany. Retrieved 18-02-2003, 2003.

Harzing, A.-W.K., 1999. Managing the multinationals: an international study of control mechanisms. Cheltenham, UK, Edward Elgar Publishing Limited.

Hedlund, G., 1984. Organization in-Between: The Evolution of the Mother Daughter Structure of Managing Foreign Subsidiaries in Swedish Multinational Corporations. Journal of International Business Studies 15(2): 109-124.

Henisz, W.J., 2000. The institutional influence on the investment entry mode. Working Papers of Reginald H. Jones Centre Retrieved 28 Oct., 2005, from http://www-management.wharton.upenn.edu/henisz/papers/wiib.pdf.

Hennart, J.F. and Y.-R. Park, 1994. Location, Governance, and Strategic Determinants of Japanese Manufacturing Investment in the United States. Strategic Management Journal 15(6): 419-436.

Hennart, J.F. and J. Larimo, 1998. The impact of culture on the strategy of multinational enterprises: Does national origin affect ownership decisions? Journal of International Business Studies 29(3): 515-538.

Hennart, J.F., 1999. What is Internalization? Corporate governance. Volume 3. Governance mechanisms, Part 2. Elgar Reference Collection. International Library of Critical Writings in Economics, vol. 106. Cheltenham, U.K. K. Keasey, S. Thompson and -.M. Wright. and Northampton, Mass., Elgar; distributed by American International Distribution Corporation Williston: 523-36.

Henri, J.F., 2006. Organizational culture and performance measurement systems. Accounting Organizations And Society 31(1): 77-103.

Hitt, M.A., M.T. Dacin, E. Levitas, J.L. Arregle and A. Borza, 2000. Partner selection in emerging and developed market contexts: Resource-based and organizational learning perspectives. Academy Of Management Journal 43(3): 449-467.

Hofstede, G., 1980. Culture's consequences: international differences in work-related values. Beverly Hills London New Dehli, Sage.

Hofstede, G., 1997. Cultures and Organizations. Software of the Mind. New York, McGraw-Hill.

Hofstede, G., 2001. Culture's consequences: comparing values, behaviors, institutions, and organizations across nations, Sage.

Hoskisson, R.E., L. Eden, C.M. Lau and M. Wright, 2000. Strategy in emerging economies. Academy Of Management Journal 43(3): 249-267.

Hoskisson, R.E., L. Eden, C.M. Lau and M. Wright, 2000. Strategy in emerging economies. Academy of Management Journal 43: 249-267.

Howell, J.M., D.J. Neufeld and B.J. Avolio, 2005. Examining the relationship of leadership and physical distance with business unit performance. Leadership Quarterly 16(2): 273-285.

Hulland, J., 1999. Use of Partial Least Squares (PLS) in Strategic Management Research: A Review of Four Recent Studies. Strategic Management Journal 20(2): 195-204.

Jackson, J.H., R.L. Miller and S.G. Miller, 1997. Chapter 8: Strategy in the Global Environment. Business and Society Today: Managing Social Issues, Dame Publishing: 776.

Jensen, M.C. and W.H. Meckling, 1976. Theory of the firm: Managerial behavior, agency costs and ownership structures. Journal of Financial Economics 3(4): 305-360.

Jobber, D., 2001. Principles & Practice of Marketing, McGraw HIll.

Johanson, J. and J.E. Vahlne, 1977. The Internationalization Process of the Firm-A Model of Knowledge Development and Increasing Foreign Market Commitments. 8(1): 23-32.

Johansson, J.K. and G.S. Yip, 1994. Exploiting Globalization Potential: U.S. and Japanese Strategies. Strategic Management Journal 15(8): 579-601.

Jöreskog, K.G. and H. Wold, 1982. The ML and PLS techniques for modeling with latent variables: Historical and comparative aspects. Systems under indirect observation: Causality, structure, prediction. K.G. Jöreskog and H. Wold. Amsterdam, North Holland: 263-270.

Kahler, M., 2003, November 13-14. Global Governance Redefined. Proceedings of The Globalization, the State, and Society Conference Retrieved 30-08, 2006, from http://law.wustl.edu/centeris/index.asp?id=1821.

Kaplan, R.S. and D.P. Norton, 1996. The Balanced Scorecard: translating strategy into action. Boston, Harvard Business School Press.

Kaufmann, D., A. Kraay and M. Mastruzzi., 2005. Governance Indicators for 1996-2004. World Bank Governance Matters Series Retrieved 29-08, 2006.

Kim, B., J.E. Prescott and S.M. Kim, 2005. Differentiated governance of foreign subsidiaries in transnational corporations: an agency theory perspective. Journal of International Management 11(1): 43.

Kobrin, S.J., 1991. An Empirical Analysis of the Determinants of Global Integration. Strategic Management Journal 12(Special Issue: Global Strategy): 17-31.

Kogut, B., 1984. Normative Observations on the International Value-Added Chain and Strategic Groups. Journal of International Business Studies 15(2): 151-168.

Kogut, B. and H. Singh, 1988. The Effect of National Culture on the Choice of Entry Mode. Journal of International Business Studies 19(3): 411-423.

Kruskal, W.H. and W.A. Wallis, 1952. Use of Ranks in One-Criterion Variance Analysis. Journal of the American Statistical Association 47(260): 583.

Kumar, N. and J.P. Pradhan, 2002. FDI, Externalities and Economic Growth in Developing Countries. RIS: 38.

Kumar, N. and P.J. Prakash, 2002. Foreign Direct Investment in Asia. How to Maximise its Benefits? Views of a Civil Society Organisation. Global Forum on International Investment. Attracting Foreign Investment For Development, Shanghai, OECD.

Lascu, D.N., L.A. Manrai, A.K. Manrai and R. Kleczek, 2006. Interfunctional dynamics and firm performance: A comparison between firms in Poland and the United States. International Business Review 15(6): 641-659.

Lawrence, P.R., 1981. Organization and Environment Perspective. Perspectives on Organization Design adn Behevior. A.H. Van de Ven and W.F. Joyce. Boston, Harvard Business Press.

Lawrence, P.R., 1981. Organization and Environment Perspective. Perspectives on Organization Design and Behevior. A.H.V.d. Ven and W.F. Joyce. Boston, Harvard Business Press.

Lawrence, P.R. and J.W. Lorsch, 1967. Organization and environment: managing differentiation and integration. Boston, Harvard Univ.

Lebas, M. and J. Weigenstein, 1986. Management Control: The roles of Rules, Markets and Culture. Journal of Management Studies 23(3): 259-271.

Lefebvre, E., L.A. Lefebvre, G.L. Hen and R. Mendgen, 2006. Cross-Border E-Collaboration for New Product Development in the Automotive Industry. Interntional Conference on System Sciences, Hawaii.

Leiblein, M.J., 2003. The Choice of Organizational Governance Form and Performance: Predictions from Transaction Cost, Resource-based, and Real Options Theories. Journal of Management 29(6): 937-961.

Lepak, D.P., R. Takeuchi and S.A. Snell, 2003. Employment flexibility and firm performance: Examining the interaction effects of employment mode, environmental dynamism, and technological intensity. Journal of Management 29(5): 681-703.

Levitt, T., 1983. The Globalization of Markets. Harvard Business Review(May-June): 92-102.

Liedtka, J.M. and J.W. Rosenblum, 1996. Shaping conversations: Making strategy, managing change. California Management Review 39(1): 141-&.

Lipsey, R.E., 2000. Inward FDI and economic growth in developing countries. Transnational Corporation 9(1): 67-95.

Little, R.J.A. and D.B. Rubin, 1987. Statistical analysis with missing data. New York [etc.], Wiley.

Lorr, M., 1983. Cluster analysis for social scientists. San Francisco [etc.], Jossey-Bass.

Luo, Y., 2003. Market-seeking MNEs in an emerging market: How parent-subsidiary links shape overseas success. Journal of International Business Studies 34(3): 290-309.

Luo, Y. and M.W. Peng, 1999. Learning to Compete in a Transition Economy: Experience, Environment, and Performance. Journal of International Business Studies 30(2): 269-95.

Luo, Y. and H. Zhao, 2004. Corporate link and competitive strategy in multinational enterprises: a perspective from subsidiaries seeking host market penetration. Journal of International Management 10(1): 77.

Luo, Y.D., 2002. Capability exploitation and building in a foreign market: Implications for multinational enterprises. Organization Science 13(1): 48-63.

References

Luo, Y.D., 2004. Building a strong foothold in an emerging market: A link between resource commitment and environment conditions. Journal of Management Studies 41(5): 748-773.

Luo, Y.D. and S.H. Park, 2001. Strategic alignment and performance of market-seeking MNCs in China. Strategic Management Journal 22(2): 141-155.

Lyles, M.A., T. Saxton and K. Watson, 2004. Venture survival in a transitional economy. Journal of Management 30(3): 351-375.

Maffry, A., 1954. Direct Versus Portfolio Investment in the Balance of Payments, in Corporate International Investment Policies and Programs. The American Economic Review 44(2): 614-623.

Makadok, R., 2003. Doing the right thing and knowing the right thing to do: why the whole is greater than the sum of the parts. Strategic Management Journal 24(10): 1043-1055.

March, J. and H. Simon, 1958. Organizations. New York, Willey.

Marcoulides, G.A. (ed.), 1998. Modern Methods for Business Research. Quantitative Methodology Series. Mahwah, New Jersey, London, Lawrence Erlbaum Associates.

Martinez, J.I. and C. Jarillo, 1991. Coordination Demands of International Strategies. Journal of International Business Studies 22(3): 429-444.

Martinez, J.I. and J.C. Jarillo, 1989. The Evolution of Research on Coordination Mechanisms in Multinational Corporations. Journal of International Business Studies 20(3): 489 - 514.

Mayer, R.C., J.H. Davis and F.D. Schoorman, 1995. An Integrative Model of Organizational Trust. Academy of Management Review 20(3): 709-734.

Mayntz, R. (ed.), 2003. New Challenges to Governance Theory. Governance as Social and Political Communication. Manchester, Manchester University Press.

McCarthy, Daniel J., S.M. Puffer and P.J. Simmonds, 1993. Riding the Russian Roller Coaster: U.S. Firms Recent Experience and Future Plans in the Former USSR. California Management Review 36(1): 99-115.

Mears, P.E. and C.M. Sánchez, 2001. Going global: How do law firms do it and what does it change? Business Law Today 10(4).

Meehl, P.E., 1990. Why Summaries of Research on Psychological Theories are often Uninterpretable? Psychological Reports 66: 195-244.

Merchant, K.A. and W.A. v.d. Stede, 2003. Management Control Systems: performance Measurement, Evaluation and Incentives. Harlow, England, Prentice Hall.

Meyer, K., 1998. Entry into Transition Economies: Beyond Markets and Hierarchies. Kopenhagen: 31.

Meyer, K. and S. Estrin, 1998. Entry Mode Choice in Emerging Markets: Greenfield, Acquisition, and Brownfield. CEES Working Paper: 1-27.

Meyer, K. and M.W. Peng, 2005. Probing theoretically into Central and Eastern Europe: transactions, resources, and institutions. Journal of International Business Studies 36(6): 600-621.

Mikułowski-Pomorski, J., 2001. Poles and Hofstede's Dimensions of Culture: Directions of Change. Retrieved 20-08-2006, 2006, from http://janek.ae.krakow.pl/%7Eekse/htm/change.htm.

Miles, R.E. and C.C. Snow, 1978. Organizational strategy, structure, and process. New York, McGraw-Hill Book Co.

Miller, D. and P.H. Friesen, 1983. Strategy making and environment: The third link. Strategic Management Journal 4(3): 221-235.

Mintzberg, H., 1979. The structuring of organizations: a synthesis of the research, Englewood Cliffs: Prentice-Hall.

Mintzberg, H., 1983. Structure in Fives. Designing Effective Organizations. Englewood Cliffs NJ, Prentice Hall.

Mintzberg, H. and J.A. Waters, 1985. Of Strategies: Deliberate and Emergent. Strategic Management Journal 6: 257-272.

Morck, R., A. Shleifer and R.W. Vishny, 1989. Alternative Mechanisms For Corporate-Control. American Economic Review 79(4): 842-852.

Morgan, G., 1980. Paradigms, metaphors, and puzzle solving in organisation theory. Administrative Science Quarterly 9(4): 605-20.

Mortimore, M., 1998. Getting a lift: modernizing industry by way of Latin American integration schemes. The example of automobiles. Transnational Corporations 7(2): 97-137.

Myers, M., 2000. Qualitative research and the generalizability question: Standing firm with Proteus. The Qualitative Report [On-line serial] Retrieved November, 2005, from http://www.nova.edu/ssss/QR/QR4-1/myers.html.

Nahapiet, J. and S. Ghoshal, 1998. Social capital, intellectual capital, and organisational advantage. Academy of Management Review 23(2): 242-266.

Nelson, R. and Winter, S., 1982. An Evolutionary Theory of Economic Change. Cambridge, MA., Belknap Press.

Nobel, R. and J. Birkinshaw, 1998. Innovation in Multinational Coroporations: Control and Communication Patterns in International R&D Operations. Strategic Management Journal 19: 479-496.

Nohria, N. and S. Ghoshal, 1994. Differentiated Fit and Shared Values: Alternatives for Managing Headquarters-Subsidiary Relations. Strategic Management Journal 15(6): 491-502.

Nunnally, J.C., 1978. Psychometric theory. - 2nd ed., New York [etc.]: McGraw-Hill.

O'Donnell, S.W., 2000. Managing foreign subsidiaries: agents of headquarters, or an interdependent network? Strategic Management Journal 21(5): 525-548.

OECD, 1996. OECD Benchmark Definition of Foreign Direct Investment. Paris, Organization For Economic Co-operation and Developement: 51.

Omta, S.W.F., 1995. Critical Success Factors in Biomedical Research and Pharmaceutical Innovation. Dordrecht, Kluwer Academic Publishers.

Ouchi, W.G., 1979. A Conceptual Framework for the Design of Organizational Control Mechanisms. Management Science 25(9): 833-848.

Paik, Y. and J.D. Sohn, 2004. Expatriate managers and MNC's ability to control international subsidiaries: the case of Japanese MNCS. Journal of World Business 39(1): 61-71.

PAIZ., 2003, 03-07-2003. PAIZ Report on FDI in Poland. Retrieved 03-03-2003, http://www.paiz.pl/facts2_3.html, from http://www.paiz.pl/.

PAIZ, 2005. Rocznik 2004 (Yearbook 2004). Warsaw, Polska Agencja Informacji i Inwestycji Zagranicznych S.A. (Polish Institution of Foreign Direct Investment): 85.

References

Pease, S., S. Paliwoda and J. Slater, 2006. The erosion of stable shareholder practice in Japan ("Anteikabunushi Kosaku"). International Business Review 15(6): 618-640.

Peng, M.W., 2003. Institutional transitions and strategic choices. Academy of Management Review 28(2): 275-296.

Peng, M.W. and P.S. Heath, 1996. The Growth of the Firm in Planned Economies in Transition: Institutions, Organizations, and Strategic Choice. The Academy of Management Review 21(2): 492-528.

Peng, M.W. and A.S. York, 2001. Behind Intermediary Performance in Export Trade: Transactions, Agents, and Resources. Journal of International Business Studies 32(2): 327-46.

Perrow, C., 1970. Organisational analysis: a sociological view. California, Wadsworth Publishing Company.

Perrow, C., 1986. Complex Organizations. New York, Random House.

Pfeffer, J. and G.R. Salancik, 1978. The external control of organizations: a resource dependence perspective. New York [etc.], Harper & Row.

Porter, M.E., 1985. Competitive advantage: Creating and sustaining superior performance. New York, Free Press.

Porter, M.E., 1986. Competition in global industries. Boston, Harvard Business School Press.

Porter, M.E. and M.R. Kramer, 2006. Strategy and society. Harvard Business Review 84(12): 78-+.

Powell, W.W., 1990. Neither Market Nor Hierarchy - Network Forms of Organization. Research in Organizational Behavior 12: 295-336.

Prachowska, A., 2005. FDI in Poland. List of Major Foreign Investors. Investment Reports Retrieved April 2006, 2006, from http://paiz.gov.pl/files/?id_plik=885.

Prahalad, C.K. and Y.L. Doz, 1987. The Multinational Mission: Balancing Local Demands and Global Vision. New York, Free Press.

Preble, J.F., 1992. Towards a Comprehensive System of Strategic Control. Journal of Management Studies 29(4): 391-409.

Robinson, K.C. and P.P. McDougall, 2001. Entry Barriers and New Venture Performance: a Comparison of Universal and Contingency Approaches. Strategic Management Journal 22: 659-685.

Rodrigues, C.A., 1995. Headquarters-foreign subsidiary control relationships:three conceptual frameworks. Empowerment in Organizations 3(3): 25-34.

Romeneyi, D., B. Williams, A. Money and E. Swartz, 1998. Doing Research in Business and Management. London etc., Sage.

Root, F.R., 1998. Entry Strategies for International Markets. San Francisco, Jossey-Bass A Wiley Company.

Rosenthal, R. and R.L. Rosnow, 1991. Essentials of Behavioral Research Methods and Data Analysis. New York, McGraw-Hill.

Roth, K. and A.J. Morrison, 1992. Implementing Global Strategy: Characteristics of Global Subsidiary Mandates. Journal of International Business Studies 23(4): 715-736.

Roth, K., D.M. Schweiger and A.J. Morrison, 1991. Global Strategy Implementation at the Business Unit Level: Operational Capabilities and Administrative Mechanism. Journal of International Business Studies 22(3): 369-402.

Rugman, A.M. and A. Verbeke, 1992. A Note on the Transnational Solution and the Transaction Cost Theory of Multinational Strategic Management. Journal of International Business Studies 23(4): 761-771.

Schaffer, B.S. and C.M. Riordan, 2003. A review of cross-cultural methodologies for organizational research: A best-practices approach. Organizational Research Methods 6(2): 169-215.

Scott, W.R., 1987. Organizations: rational, natural, and open systems. Englewood Cliffs, Prentice-Hall.

Segev, E., 1989. A Systematic Comparative Analysis and Synthesis of Two Business-Level Strategic Typologies. Strategic Management Journal 10(5): 487.

Shleifer, A. and R.W. Vishny, 1997. A Survey of Corporate Governance (in Review Article. The Journal of Finance 52(2): 737-783.

Shortell, S.M. and E.J. Zajac, 1990. Perceptual and Archival Measures of Miles and Snow's Strategic Types: A Comprehensive Assessment of Reliability and Validity. Academy of Management Journal 33(4): 817-832.

Simons, R., 1987. Accounting control systems and business strategy: An empirical analysis. Accounting, Organizations and Society 12(4): 357.

Slangen, A.H.L., 2005. Studies on the Determinants of Foreign Entry Mode Choices and Performance. Department of Organisation and Strategy. Tilburg, Tilburg University. Ph.D. thesis: 110.

Slangen, L.H.G., 2000. Framework for analyzing institutions of sustainability. Wageningen: 33.

Snow, C.C., R.E. Miles and H.J. Coleman, 1992. Managing 21st-Century Network Organizations. Organizational Dynamics 20(3): 5-19.

Solomon, J. and A. Solomon, 2004. Corporate governance and accountability. Chichester, John Wiley & Sons.

Starbuck, W.H., 1976. Organizations and their environments. Handbook of Industrial and Organizational Psychology. M.D. Dunnette. Chicago, Rand McNally Starbuck: 1067-1123.

Steenkamp, J.-B.E.M. and H.C.M.v. Trijp, 1996. Quality guidance: A consumer-based approach to food quality improvement using partial least squares. European Review of Agricultural Economics 23: 195-215.

Steensma, H.K., L. Tihanyi, M.A. Lyles and C. Dhanaraj, 2005. The evolving value of foreign partnerships in transitioning economies. Academy Of Management Journal 48(2): 213-235.

Stoever, W., 2001. Liberalizing developing country policy toward foreign investment: a framework for analysis. American Asian Review 19(3): 121-153.

Stonehouse, G., D. Campbell, J. Hamill and T. Purdie, 2004. Global and Transnational Business: Strategy and Management, Wiley.

Stonehouse, G., J. Hamill, D. Campbell and T. Purdie, 2000. Global and Transnational Business. Strategy and Management, John Wiley & Sons.

Sullivan, D., 1994. Measuring the Degree of Internationalization of a Firm. Journal Of International Business Studies 25(2): 325-342.

Sundaramurthy, C. and M. Lewis, 2003. Control and collaboration: Paradoxes of governance. Academy of Management Review 28(3): 397-415.

Sutcliffe, K.M., 1994. What Executives Notice - Accurate Perceptions In Top Management Teams. Academy of Management Journal 37(5): 1360-1378.

Thompson, J.D., 1967. Organisation in Action. Chicago, McGraw-Hill.

Todeva, E., 2005. Governance, control and coordination in network context: the cases of Japanese Keiretsu and Sogo Shosha. Journal of International Management 11(1): 87.

Tosi, H.L., A.L. Brownlee, P. Silva and J.P. Katz, 2003. An empirical exploration of decision-making under agency controls and stewardship structure. Journal of Management Studies 40(8): 2053-2071.

Turnbull, S., 1997. Corporate Governance: Its scope, concerns and theories. Corporate Governance: An International Review 5(4): 180-205.

UNCTAD, 1999. World Investment Report. Geneva, United Nations Conference on Trade and Development: 172.

UNCTAD, 2003. World Investment Report. FDI Policies for Development and International Perspectives. Geneva, United Nations Conference on Trade and Development: 172.

UNCTAD, 2004. World Investment Report. The Shift Towards Services. New York and Geneva, United Nations.

UNCTAD, 2005. World Investment Report. End of the Downturn. Transnational Corporations and Internationalisation of R&D. New York and Geneva, United Nations.

UNCTAD, 2006. World Investment Report, UNCTAD.

Ven, A.H.v.d., A.L.Delbecq and R. Koening, 1976. Determinants of Coordination Modes within Organizations. American Sociological Review 41(2): 332-338.

Venaik, S., D.F. Midgley and T.M. Devinney, 2005. Dual paths to performance: the impact of global pressures on MNC subsidiary conduct and performance. Journal of International Business Studies 36(6): 655-675.

Venkatraman, N. and J.E. Prescott, 1990. Environment-Strategy Coalignment: An Empirical Test of Its Performance Implications. Strategic Management Journal 11(1): 1-23.

Venkatraman, N. and V. Ramanujam, 1987. Measurement of business economic performance: An examination of method convergence. Journal of Management 13: 109-122.

Verdu-Jover, A.J., J.F. Llorens-Montes and V.J. Garcia-Morales, 2005. Flexibility, fit and innovative capacity: an empirical examination. International Journal of Technology Management 30(1-2): 131-146.

Verschuren, P. and H. Doorewaard, 1999. Designing a research project. Utrecht, LEMMA.

Volberda, H.W., 1992. Organizational Flexibility: Change and Preservation. Groningen, Wolters-Noordhoff.

Watty, K. and B. Terzioglu, 1999. Performance Measures Employed by Australian Subsidiaries of US Service Multinational Companies: an Empirical Survey. RMIT Business.

Weber, M., 1968. Economics and Society. New York, Bedminster Press.

Werner, S., 2002. Recent Developments in International Management Research: A Review of 20 Top Management Journals. Journal of Management 28(3): 277-305.

Wheelwright, S.C. and K.B. Clark, 1992. Revolutionizing Product Development: Quantum Leaps in Speed, Efficiency, and Quality. New York, Free Press.

Wijbenga, F., 2004. Strategy and performan[c]e of venture capital-backed SMEs: entrepreneurial locus of control, and the role and influence of the venture capitalist. Capelle aan den IJssel, Labirynt publication.

Wikipedia., 2005. governance def. Retrieved 20 Sep. 2005, from http://www.answers.com/topic/governance.

Wilcox, R.R., 1998. How Many Discoveries Have Been Lost by Ignoring Modern Statistical Methods? American Psychologist 53(3): 300.

Williamson, O.E., 1979. Transaction-Cost Economics: the Governance of Contractual Relations. Journal of Law Economics 22(233-261).

Williamson, O.E., 1999. The Mechanisms of Governance. Oxford, New York, Oxford University Press.

Wold, H., 1985. Partial Least Squares. Encyclopedia of Statistical Sciences. S. Kotz and N.L. Johnson. New York, Wiley. 6: 581-591.

Wolf, J. and W.G. Egelhoff, 2002. A reexamination and extension of international strategy- structure theory. Strategic Management Journal 23(2): 181-189.

WorldBank, 2002. Ten years of transition, World Bank.

Wright, R.W. and D.A. Ricks, 1994. Trends in International Business Research: Twenty Five Years Later. Journal of International Business Studies 25(4 Special Issue 25 Year Index): 687-701.

Yeniyurt, S., S.T. Cavusgil, G. Tomas and M. Hult, 2005. A global market advantage framework: the role of global market knowledge competencies. International Business Review 14(1): 1-19.

Yin, R.K., 1984. Case Study Research. Design and Methods. Beverly Hills London New Delhi, Sage Publications.

Yin, X. and E.J. Zajac, 2004. The strategy/governance structure fit relationship: theory and evidence in franchising arrangements. Strategic Management Journal 25(4): 365-383.

Zagozdzinska, I., S. Czeczko and E. Szefler, 2005. Dzialalnosc Gospodarcza Spolek z Udzialem Kapitalu Zagranicznego (Economic Activity of Companies with Foreign Capital Share, Glowny Urzad Statystyczny (Polish Central Statistical Office).

Zaheer, S. and E. Mosakowski, 1997. The Dynamics of the Liability of Foreignness: A Global Study of Survival in Financial Services. Strategic Management Journal 18(6): 439-463.

Zajac, E.J. and J.D. Westphal, 1994. The costs and benefits of managerial incentives and monitoring in large U.S. corporations: when is more not better? Strategic Management Journal 15: 121-142.

Zingales, L., 1997. Corporate Governance. NBER Working Paper No. W6309 Retrieved 20 September 2005, from http://ssrn.com/abstract=226064.

Zou, S.M. and S.T. Cavusgil, 2002. The GMS: A broad conceptualization of global marketing strategy and its effect on firm performance. Journal of Marketing 66(4): 40-56.

Appendices

Appendix 1. Questionnaire

Control

1. How frequently does your subsidiary report to the headquarters(HQ) on the following items:
   a) sales turnover
   b) production volume
   c) development of market share
   d) education and motivation of personnel
   e) product and/or process development

Scale 1-8; 1 less than once a year, 2 yearly, 3 semi-annually, 4 quarterly, 5 monthly, 6 bi-weekly, 7 weekly, 8 daily.

2. How often do the HQs ask questions about the content of the submitted reports?
   a) sales turnover
   b) production volume
   c) development of market share
   d) education and motivation of personnel
   e) product and/or process development

Scale 7-point Likert scale; 1-not all to 7- always.

3. Are your policies and procedures standardised?
   Standardized policies and procedures mean the same form/standard is used as in the HQ and it may concern for example: hiring new employees, rewarding employees, communicating with suppliers, negotiating contracts, etc.

Not standardised at all to Fully standardised
   a) Development of standardised polices and procedures

Scale anchors: 1 – all by the subsidiary to 7 all by the HQ.

4. Your subsidiary uses pre-structured, formal documents in reporting to the HQ

Scale anchors: 1 – Strongly disagree to 7 – Strongly agree.

5. What is the nationality of the head of the following departments?
   Please tick one box for each answer!

   a) Chief Executive Office (CEO) ☐ Polish ☐ HQ's country ☐ third country ☐ NA
   b) Manufacturing and quality   ☐ Polish ☐ HQ's country ☐ third country ☐ NA
   c) Marketing   ☐ Polish ☐ HQ's country ☐ third country ☐ NA
   d) Finance   ☐ Polish ☐ HQ's country ☐ third country ☐ NA
   e) R&D   ☐ Polish ☐ HQ's country ☐ third country ☐ NA

Coordination

6. What is the frequency of the personal contacts between employees at different functional levels of the subsidiary and HQ's personnel?
   a) CEOs
   b) Marketing departments
   c) R&D
   d) Manufacturing departments
   e) Logistics Departments

Scale 1-8; 1 less than once a year, 2 yearly, 3 semi-annually, 4 quarterly, 5 monthly, 6 bi-weekly, 7 weekly, 8 daily.

7. How often do you attune any of the following activities with the HQ?
   a) sales turnover
   b) production volume
   c) development of market share
   d) education and motivation of personnel
   e) product and/or process development

Scale 1-8; 1 less than once a year, 2 yearly, 3 semi-annually, 4 quarterly, 5 monthly, 6 bi-weekly, 7 weekly, 8 daily.

8. The subsidiaries' employees participate in committees or project groups, both temporary and permanent with managers from different subsidiaries and the HQs.

Scale 1-8; 1 less than once a year, 2 yearly, 3 semi-annually, 4 quarterly, 5 monthly, 6 bi-weekly, 7 weekly, 8 daily.

9. The subsidiaries' employees have business meetings with other subsidiaries and HQ.

Scale 1-8; 1 less than once a year, 2 yearly, 3 semi-annually, 4 quarterly, 5 monthly, 6 bi-weekly, 7 weekly, 8 daily.

10. Suppose you would like to know, what is the inventory level of a certain raw-material/ product at the central (HQ's) stock. How fast can you get such information?

External environment

All 7-point Likert scale; 1-strongly disagree to 7- strongly agree.

11. Unexpected and frequent political changes impede the development of our subsidiary.
12. Incoherent law interpretation and inconsistent execution influenced our performance negatively.
13. We operate in a market with many competitors.
14. Customer tastes and expectations changed very often in the last three years.
15. We cooperate with a stable group of suppliers.
16. There are enough resources available.
17. There is enough qualified workforce available.

Generic strategy

18. How would you describe the overall strategic orientation of your subsidiary?
    Take a position by putting a circle around one number on each of the following scales!

    Example: in the first case, if your subsidiary is very innovative and introduces many new products instead of concentrating on one set of products, you should put a circle around the number on the right side of the scale.

Our subsidiary offers **a solid set of products** /services concentrating on superior quality	1 2 3 4 5 6 7	Our subsidiary introduces many **new products**, responds rapidly to early signals of a market
Our subsidiary tends to concentrate on the **current areas of operations** and ignores those that have no direct impact on these operations	3 2 1 0 1 2 3	Our subsidiary tries to pioneer by being 'first in' in **new areas of service or market activity**
Our subsidiary concentrates on doing the best job possible in **its present market** segments	3 2 1 0 1 2 3	Our subsidiary tries to enter **new market segments**

International strategy

All 7-point Likert scale; 1-strongly disagree to 7- strongly agree.

19. Our subsidiary tries to meet local tastes and preferences and exploit the potential of local market specifics.
20. Our subsidiary tries to meet worldwide consumer demand and exploit scale economies.
21. Our subsidiary provides ideas to develop and market products internationally.
22. Our subsidiary controls the marketing of export products.

Performance

All 7-point Likert scale; 1-strongly disagree to 7- strongly agree.

23. In general, we are satisfied with our performance.
24. *Short-term*: We achieved our projected operational goals last year.
25. *Market*: We outperform our competitors.
26. Compared to other subsidiaries within the MNE network, our subsidiary performs better.
27. We can satisfactorily deal with claims and inquiries from our customers.
28. We successfully respond to changes in customer needs.
29. We re-invest a major part of our profits in our subsidiary.
30. Market share was in 2002; in 2004, forecast for 2006.

Control variables – general information about MNE

HQ
31. HQ Country of origin
32. HQ capital share in our subsidiary .... %
33. The capital was acquired in .... year
34. Subsidiary's company was founded in .... year
35. HQ Employees (approx.) .... fte's (full time equivalents)
36. Number of employees in this subsidiary in 2002; 2004(present) and planned 2006
37. Our subsidiary sales products: ....% in international market
38. HQ and subsidiary key activity (e.g. EKD code) ....

Item	Scale	Q no
Headquarters and subsidiary size	Number of employees in FTE – full time equivalents	34,35
Relationship duration	2004 minus the investment date	32, 33
International sale	% export of production	37
International sale via HQ	% of int. sales that is sold to HQ-internal	37a
HQ capital share in subsidiary	%	31

Subsidiary autonomy

39. Where are the important decisions concerning this subsidiary made?
   a) strategic planning
   b) setting performance standards
   c) product and process R&D
   d) manufacturing operations and quality control
   e) marketing; product distribution and advertising

Scale 1 – decision-making centralized at HQ; 7 – fully autonomous at subsidiary.

Appendix 2. Topic list for in-depth interviews with HQ

Control

1. How frequently does your subsidiary report to the headquarters(HQ) on the following items:
   a) sales turnover
   b) production volume
   c) development of market share
   d) education and motivation of personnel
   e) product and/or process development

Scale 1-8; 1 less than once a year, 2 yearly, 3 semi-annually, 4 quarterly, 5 monthly, 6 bi-weekly, 7 weekly, 8 daily.

2. How often do the HQs ask questions about the content of the submitted reports?
   a) sales turnover
   b) production volume
   c) development of market share
   d) education and motivation of personnel
   e) product and/or process development

Scale 7-point Likert scale; 1-not all to 7- always.

4. Your subsidiary uses pre-structured, formal documents when reporting to the HQ

Scale anchors: 1 – Strongly disagree to 7 – Strongly agree.

Coordination

6. What is the frequency of the personal contacts between employees at different functional levels of the subsidiary and HQ's personnel?
   a) CEOs
   b) Marketing departments
   c) R&D
   d) Manufacturing departments
   e) Logistics Departments

Scale 1-8; 1 less than once a year, 2 yearly, 3 semi-annually, 4 quarterly, 5 monthly, 6 bi-weekly, 7 weekly, 8 daily.

7. How often do you attune any of the following activities with the HQ?
   a) sales turnover

b) investments
c) financing and debts
d) education and motivation of personnel
e) results

Scale 1-8; 1 less than once a year, 2 yearly, 3 semi-annually, 4 quarterly, 5 monthly, 6 bi-weekly, 7 weekly, 8 daily.

8. The subsidiaries' employees participate in committees or project groups, both temporary and permanent with managers from different subsidiaries and the HQs.

Scale 1-8; 1 less than once a year, 2 yearly, 3 semi-annually, 4 quarterly, 5 monthly, 6 bi-weekly, 7 weekly, 8 daily.

Performance

All 7-point Likert scale; 1-strongly disagree to 7- strongly agree.

23. In general, we are satisfied with our performance.
24. *Short-term*: We achieved our projected operational goals last year.
25. *Market*: We outperform our competitors.
26. Compared to other subsidiaries within the MNE network, our subsidiary performs better.
27. We can satisfactorily deal with claims and inquiries from our customers.
28. We successfully respond to changes in customer needs.
29. We re-invest a major part of our profits in our subsidiary.

Appendix 3. Spearman correlations

All significance levels are presented in (...) and are two-tailed.
Number in [...] indicates question number

Table 3.1. Correlations between international and generic strategy (N=76).

	[19]	[20]	[21]	[22]
Concentration on local market [19]*				
Concentration on worldwide market [20]	-0.23 (0.05)			
Provide ideas for international products [21]		0.48 (0.00)		
Subsidiary's control over export [22]		0.25 (0.03)	0.53 (0.00)	
Innovative operations [18b]				0.29 (0.01)

Scale for strategy variables: 7-point Likert scale; 1 strongly disagree to 7 strongly agree.

Table 3.2. Correlations between subsidiary's autonomy and strategy (N=76).

Subsidiary's autonomy in:	[18b]	[19]	[20]	[22]
strategic planning [39a]	0.27 (0.02)			
product and process R&D [39c]		0.37 (0.00)		0.36 (0.00)
manufacturing operations and quality control [39d]				0.23 (0.04)
marketing; product distribution and advertising [39e]	0.26 (0.02)	0.45 (0.00)	-0.23 (0.04)	0.33 (0.00)

Scale for autonomy variables: 7-point Likert scale; 1 decision-making centralized at HQ; 7 decision-making fully autonomous at subsidiary.

Table 3.3. Correlations between control and strategy (N=76).

HQs' inquiries on the reports on:	[18b]	[19]
sales turnover [2a]	0.38 (0.00)	
production volume [2b]		0.25 (0.03)
development of market share [2c]		0.24 (0.05)
education and motivation of personnel [2e]	0.31 (0.01)	

Scale for control variables: 7-point Likert scale; 1 not all to 7 always.

Table 3.4. Correlations between coordination and strategy (N=76).

Personal contacts between HQ and subsidiaries between:	[19]	[20]	[21]
marketing departments [6b]	- 0.29 (0.01)		
R&D [6c]	- 0.29 (0.01)	0.23 (0.05)	
logistics departments [6e]	- 0.46 (0.00)	0.31 (0.01)	
Attuning of production volume [7b]		0.27 (0.02)	
Attuning of education and motivation of personnel [7d]		0.26 (0.02)	
Joint task groups and project teams [8]		0.29 (0.01)	
Business meetings with other subsidiaries [9]		0.27 (0.02)	0.25 (0.03)

Scale for coordination variables: 1-8; 1 less than once a year, 2 yearly, 3 semi-annually, 4 quarterly, 5 monthly, 6 bi-weekly, 7 weekly, 8 daily.

Table 3.5. Correlations between external environment variables (N=76).

	I1	I2	I3	I4	I5	I6
Unstable political environment [I1]		0.57 (0.00)			- 0.23 (0.05)	
Incoherent law interpretation [I2]						
Market with many competitors [I3]				0.42 (0.00)		
Customers' needs change [I4]						
Instability of suppliers network [I5]						- 0.23 (0.04)
Insufficient resources [I6]			- 0.33 (0.00)			
Insufficient qualified workforce [I7]			- 0.24 (0.03)			

Scale for external environment variables: 7-point Likert scale; I strongly disagree to 7 strongly agree.

Table 3.6. Correlations between external environment and control (N=76).

	I1	I3	I4	I7
Written reports on sales turnover [1a]	- 0.23 (0.04)			- 0.24 (0.03)
Written reports on market share development [1c]			0.24 (0.04)	
Written reports on training of personnel [1d]		- 0.28 (0.01)		
HQs' inquiries on the reports on sales turnover [2a]			0.32 (0.01)	
HQs' inquiries on the reports on market share development [1c]	- 0.27 (0.02)		0.24 (0.04)	

Scale for written reports: 1-8; 1 less than once a year, 2 yearly, 3 semi-annually, 4 quarterly, 5 monthly, 6 bi-weekly, 7 weekly, 8 daily.
Scale for HQs' inquiries on the reports: 7-point Likert scale; 1 not all to 7 always

Table 3.7. Correlations between external environment and coordination (N=76).

	I1	I2	I3	I4	I6	I7
Personal contacts between CEOs [6a]						0.27 (0.02)
Personal contacts between marketing dept. [6b]	0.26 (0.02)				0.23 (0.05)	
Personal contacts between R&D dept. [6c]		0.42 (0.00)				
Personal contacts between logistics dept. [6e]	0.30 (0.01)	0.26 (0.02)				0.23 (0.04)
Attunement of production volume [7b]		0.23 (0.04)				
Attunement of development of market share [7c]				0.24 (0.04)		
Attunement of training of personnel [7d]		0.26 (0.02)	- 0.27 (0.02)			
Attunement of product and process R&D [7e]		0.27 (0.02)			0.23 (0.05)	
Business meetings with other subsidiaries [9]				- 0.23 (0.05)		

Scale for coordination variables: 1-8; 1 less than once a year, 2 yearly, 3 semi-annually, 4 quarterly, 5 monthly, 6 bi-weekly, 7 weekly, 8 daily.

Table 3.8. Correlations between performance variables (N=76).

	24	25	26	27	28
General performance satisfaction [23]	0.74 (0.00)	0.59 (0.00)	0.52 (0.00)	0.45 (0.00)	0.41 (0.00)
Achieving operational goals last year [24]		0.55 (0.00)	0.52 (0.00)	0.43 (0.00)	0.34 (0.00)
Outperforming competitors [25]			0.36 (0.01)		
Performance in multinational network [26]*					
Dealing with customers' claims [27]					0.35 (0.00)
Response to changes in customer needs [28]					
Market share					

Scale for performance variables: 7-point Likert; I strongly disagree to 7 strongly agree.
* N = 48 for this variable, as 48 subsidiaries were part of a multinational with more subsidiaries.

Table 3.9. Correlations of control and performance (N=76).

	market share 2004	27
Written reports on market share development [Ic]	- 0.39 (0.01)	
HQs' inquiries on the reports on training of personnel [2d]		- 0.26 (0.03)

Scale for written reports: I-8; I less than once a year, 2 yearly, 3 semi-annually, 4 quarterly, 5 monthly, 6 bi-weekly, 7 weekly, 8 daily.
Scale for HQs' inquiries on the reports: 7-point Likert scale; I not all to 7 always.

Table 3.10. Correlations of coordination and performance (N=76).

	23	24	25	28
Personal contacts between CEOs [6a]			0.26 (0.02)	
Personal contacts between R&D dept. [6c]		0.22 (0.05)	0.24 (0.03)	
Personal contacts between logistics dept. [6e]				
Attunement of sales turnover [7a]	0.24 (0.03)		0.34 (0.00)	
Attunement of production volume [7b]	0.35 (0.00)	0.26 (0.03)	0.23 (0.05)	0.24 (0.04)
Joint task groups and project teams [8]			0.22 (0.05)	
Business meetings with other subsidiaries [9]			0.32 (0.00)	

Scale for coordination variables: 1-8; 1 less than once a year, 2 yearly, 3 semi-annually, 4 quarterly, 5 monthly, 6 bi-weekly, 7 weekly, 8 daily.

Appendix 4. Additional tables and classifications

Table 4.1. Headquarters' key activity.

Description of manufacturing sector	Count	Percent
Food and beverages	17	31%
Textiles	2	4%
Paper and paper products and printing	4	7%
Chemicals and chemical products	3	5%
Rubber, plastic, and non-metal products	5	9%
Fabricated metal, machinery and equipment	5	9%
Electric, audio, medical equipment	4	7%
Transport equipment	6	11%
Furniture	3	5%
Wholesale trade and commission trade	6	11%
Total	55	100%

Summary

Since the expansion of the EU with ten Central Eastern European Countries (CEECs) in 2004, it has become more attractive for western multinational enterprises (MNEs) to invest in the emerging transition economies of, for example, Poland, Hungary, Slovenia and the Czech Republic. The opening of markets in these countries, cheap labour, the availability of raw materials and not forgetting a favourable geographical location are stimulating factors for multinationals to invest and expand towards Central Eastern Europe. In general, most research up till now has focused on the exploration of the incentives and factors influencing the entry-mode decision. This research aims at understanding the factors that determine successful headquarters-subsidiary (HQ-S) governance mechanisms in Poland after the entry had taken place. The governance mechanisms are defined as the provision and application of instruments to keep companies within the boundaries of a strategy. These governance mechanisms are applied to the relationship between headquarters (HQ) and their subsidiaries (S). Two elements of governance are centrally addressed in the present study, control related to 'power exertion' and coordination focused on 'joint actions' studied respectively from agency and stewardship perspective. In designing effective HQ-S governance mechanisms, MNEs aim at finding a balance implying empowering a subsidiary and at the same time controlling certain functions to gather essential information about the conditions and processes of foreign operations.

Four research questions are formulated in this study.

Research question 1: *What are the characteristics of the different HQ-S governance mechanisms used by international headquarters in their relationship with Polish subsidiaries?*

The HQ-S governance is not an independent stand-alone concept but is embedded in the specific business environment of the Polish subsidiary. The second research question considers the influence of the external transition environment on HQ-S governance mechanisms:

Research question 2: *What is the impact of the Polish business environment on the HQ-S governance mechanisms?*

The strategy choices of MNEs concerning generic and international competition may require different HQ-S governance mechanisms. Therefore, the third research question arises:

Research question 3: *What is the influence of the strategy choices of MNEs on the HQ-S relationship governance?*

Finally, the relationships between the environment and company factors are related to MNE performance and therefore the fourth research question has been formulated:

Research question 4: *What is the impact of the different (dimensions of) governance on the overall company's performance?*

In Chapter 2 of this thesis the study domain is described. The HQ-S relationship emerges via a foreign direct investment (FDI) flow from the MNE to a foreign subsidiary. Different entry modes such as an acquisition, a joint venture and Greenfield are placed along two dimensions; first, a company can engage in an existing enterprise or create a new company from scratch; second, a company can choose from different levels of involvement: from a minority stake to full ownership (Agarwal and Ramaswami, 1992; Root, 1998). Further on in this chapter, the different positive and negative effects of the FDI flows for the receiver economy in general and domestic companies in particular are reviewed. Based on the reports of UNCTAD (United Nations Conference on Trade and Development), the FDI flows worldwide, into CEECs and into Poland are described. Finally, there is an attempt to predict further developments of Polish economy and FDI flows.

Theoretical building blocks

The theoretical framework for the study is described in Chapter 3 and rests on 3 pillars:
- agency theory;
- stewardship theory;
- contingency theory.

Under the assumptions of Agency theory the HQ-S relationship governance in MNEs can be considered as a principal-agent structure, as the headquarters delegates decision-making authority and responsibility to its foreign subsidiaries (Gupta and Govindarajan, 1991; Nohria and Ghoshal, 1994). The linkage between a headquarters and a foreign subsidiary can be appropriately compared to the agency relationships between principal and agent in that the parent company invests funds and resources in the subsidiaries, and the subsidiaries, in turn, are expected to work for the benefit of the parent headquarters (Chang and Taylor, 1999). Relying on agency theory solely in explaining HQ-S governance would cause the classical 'headquarters' hierarchy syndrome', which would indicate a clear superior-subordinate relationship (Bartlett and Ghoshal, 1998). In such a relationship subsidiaries are only implementers of headquarters' decisions and are strictly controlled for their outputs. In fact such a situation hardly ever occurs in real life and such an organisation would be doomed to extinction and would disintegrate sooner or later. We postulate adding the elements from stewardship theory to explain HQ-S governance mechanisms. Stewardship theory originates from psychology and sociology and stands in contrast to the view of human behaviour that underlies agency theory (Donaldson, 1990; Davis *et al.*, 1997). It postulates that basically there is an alignment of the interests of equity holders and managers (HQ and subsidiaries). The governance mechanisms are based on social interaction and interdependence instead of relying on power or authority, and are especially important in fast-changing environments. Stewardship theory can contribute to explaining the emergence of the new cross-departmental, informal and subtle mechanisms aimed at building network relationships between the units of MNE to cope with complex environmental conditions.

The Contingency model of MNE organisation relates managerial decision making to a number of constraints. These constraints include: the size of the organisation, how it adapts to its business environment, resources and operations, managerial assumptions about employees, strategies and technologies (Burton and Obel, 2004). A major point in Contingency Theory is that different *external* conditions might require different organisational specifics and behavioural patterns *within* the organisation (Donaldson, 1990). For the management of MNEs, an integrative contingent approach was proposed by Bartlett and Goshal (1987). They observed that companies with governance mechanisms for competing on either local or global markets experience difficulties in seizing full market capacity or fail to notice emerging markets opportunities. The present study integrates the three different theoretical viewpoints in a conceptual model for explaining HQ-S relationship governance (see Figure 1).

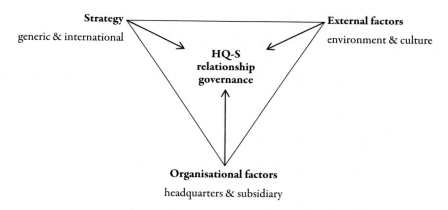

Figure 1. General research framework.

Chapter 4 of this thesis presents the operationalisation of the concepts used in the study and discuss the propositions concerning relationships between HQ-S governance mechanisms, external environment, cultural distance, HQ and S organisation factors and performance. We discern control and coordination, based on agency and stewardship theory, respectively. The following propositions are formulated:

1. In turbulent environments, HQ-S governance mechanisms that primarily rely on coordination (in terms of attunement and personal contacts) will be positively associated with performance.

2. In the case of large cultural distance, the HQ-S governance mechanisms that primarily rely on control (operational and strategic) will be positively associated with performance.
3. For subsidiaries pursuing a prospector strategy, the HQ-S governance mechanisms that primarily rely on coordination (in terms of attunement and personal contacts) will be associated with better performance.
4. For subsidiaries pursuing a global strategy, the HQ-S governance mechanisms that primarily rely on control (operational and strategic) will be associated with better performance.
4a. For subsidiaries pursuing a transnational strategy, the HQ-S governance mechanisms that primarily rely on coordination (in terms of attunement and personal contacts) will be associated with better performance.

In Chapter 5, the methods of data collection and analysis are presented. Data were collected by means of survey questionnaires at the subsidiary level and complemented with in-depth interviews at headquarters' levels. The study applies EM algorithm for dealing with missing data. Correlation and cluster analysis are used for exploring the data and a partial least squares technique (PLS) is used for developing the final model.

Results

The data collection process in 2004 provided 76 usable surveys questionnaires from manufacturing subsidiaries in Poland. The questionnaires included general information about the subsidiary and headquarters companies, control and coordination intensity, perceptions of the external environment and performance. The data analysis is described in Chapter 6 of the thesis.

The results show a higher frequency of operational compared with strategic control. In the sample, the expatriate presence was low. In the majority of subsidiaries local (Polish) managers held management and director positions. Operational issues were attuned more often than strategic issues. Personal contacts took place more often at the top management level. Generally, personal contacts were not frequent and subsidiaries were strongly ICT-integrated with their headquarters to ensure fast communication.

The most innovative prospector companies formed the smallest group of subsidiaries (11%), but at the same time were on average the most successful. Interestingly, the innovations in the operations were positively associated with international strategy variables. Subsidiaries showing high scores for operations innovativeness controlled the marketing of their export products.

The respondents perceived their subsidiaries' environment as highly dynamic and competitive. When subsidiaries' CEOs perceived their environment as strongly competitive, they experienced difficulties in ensuring enough resources and acquiring a sufficiently qualified workforce. Strong competition in the market was also negatively related to both control (written reports) and attunement concerning human resource management.

The PLS model of the HQ-S governance shows the following results.
- Environmental uncertainty and constraints (in resources) are positively associated with coordination from the headquarters.
- International sales are strongly positively associated with the coordination with HQs (attunement and personal contacts).
- The cultural distance between HQ and S countries is positively associated with strategic control.
- HQ size is positively associated with strategic control.
- The HQ-S relationship's duration is negatively associated with strategic control.
- Subsidiary's size is positively associated with operational control.
- Prospector strategy in general is positively associated with performance.
- Strategic control is a basis for prospector strategy.
- Control (strategic and operational) is positively associated with performance through coordination.

The in-depth interviews generally confirm these results and moreover provide an explanation for the limited use of expatriates in Polish subsidiaries. The results from the interviews show that expatriates are sent in the set-up phase of the subsidiary but their importance and contribution decreases in the years after entry.

Discussion and conclusions

Our research shows that the agency and stewardship mechanisms tend to be mutually supportive and reinforcing and may appear subsequently, rather than exclusively.

Research question (1): *What are the characteristics of the different HQ-S governance mechanisms used by international headquarters in relation to their Polish subsidiaries?*

As shown in Figure 2, the PLS model for HQ-S governance explains the relationship between these two kinds of mechanisms. Control (agency mechanisms) provides a solid platform on which coordination (stewardship mechanisms) can be built. Our research provides a theoretical explanation for such findings, as we state that the agency theory and the stewardship theory are not opposing standpoints but complementary dimensions of HQ-S governance.

With respect to the second research question: *What is the impact of the Polish business environment on the HQ-S governance mechanisms?*

We have investigated the influence of environmental factors on the HQ-S governance: the transitional environment of a CEE country, the task environment and the impact of cultural

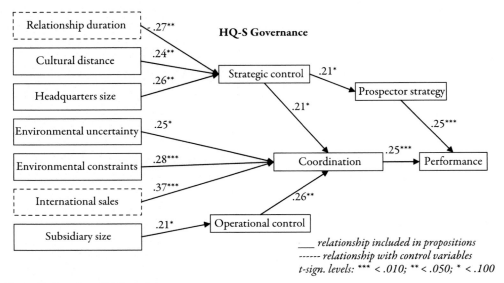

Figure 2. Results of PLS model.

distance between the home-countries of headquarters and subsidiaries. The results show that the environment represents an important explanatory factor for the HQ-S governance characteristics.

PLS modelling showed that, in congruence with proposition 1: *In turbulent environments, HQ-S governance mechanisms that primarily rely on coordination (in terms of attunement and personal contacts) will be positively associated with performance*; the turbulence in the environment was associated with the occurrence of stewardship mechanisms (extensive coordination between Headquarters and Subsidiary). These stewardship mechanisms have proven to affect performance positively. In contrast to our expectations, no significant relationship was found between environmental dynamism and HQ-S governance mechanisms. The model developed for the HQ-S governance showed a positive, highly significant relationship between environmental constraints and coordination. The model showed also a positive relationship between cultural distance and strategic control, but no relationship with operational control. Therefore, we find partial support for proposition 2: *In case of large cultural distance, the HQ-S governance mechanisms that primarily rely on control (operational and strategic) will be positively associated with performance.*

In summary, two of the three dimensions of the external environment (uncertainty and resource constraints) were positively associated with the coordination dimensions of the HQ-S governance mechanisms. Environmental dynamism had no significant effect on coordination and none of the environmental factors seemed to have a relationship with the control dimension of HQ-S governance.

In answer to the third research question in our study: *What is the influence of the strategy choices of MNEs on the HQ-S relationship governance?* and based on the results of the PLS model (see Figure 2) we can conclude that the strategy has no significant relationship with HQ-S governance mechanisms. Therefore we do not find support for two sets of propositions concerning generic and international strategy:

3. For subsidiaries pursuing a prospector strategy, the HQ-S governance mechanisms that primarily rely on coordination (in terms of attunement and personal contacts) will be associated with better performance.

4. For subsidiaries pursuing a global strategy, the HQ-S governance mechanisms that primarily rely on control (operational and strategic) will be associated with better performance.

4a. For subsidiaries pursuing a transnational strategy, the HQ-S governance mechanisms that primarily rely on coordination (in terms of attunement and personal contacts) will be associated with better performance.

In a comparison of three international strategy clusters, the results show significant differences in the use of HQ-S governance mechanisms. The subsidiaries of MNEs pursuing a global strategy have little autonomy in decision-making on the marketing and R&D decisions but show frequent attuning of production processes and frequent personal contacts with HQs' logistics managers and R&D departments. As was expected in the global strategy cluster, governance mechanisms which strongly rely on control of output and efficiency are revealed. The transnational strategy cluster shows significantly more frequent business meetings within the MNE network with other subsidiaries and the lowest level of formalisation in reporting.

Interestingly, a pure multidomestic cluster could not be discerned. We decided to put another label on this cluster: 'multidomestic-transitional', as the companies probably are in a transitional stage due to a strong international activity; this would not be expected in a classical multidomestic strategy.

Two additional variables, international sales and the size of a company, showed a strong relationship with HQ-S governance mechanisms. The size of the organisation has a significant effect on the control intensity. Strong international activity of the subsidiary is associated with intense coordination, and indirectly with enhanced performance.

The last research question, research question 4: *What is the impact of the different (dimensions of) governance on the overall company's performance?* has been answered already by analyzing the propositions. In fact all our propositions indicate an effect on performance, suggesting that if subsidiaries recognise the influences included in the propositions, they will show enhanced performance. The PLS model for HQ-S governance incorporates this assumption, as the model shows a direct relationship between coordination and performance, so all positive direct relationships with coordination are also positively related to performance. In our study, performance is related to the long-term continuity of the company in areas such as market share, strategic position, consumer satisfaction, etc. In general, subsidiary managers are satisfied with their short- and long-term goal achievement. The group of excellent-performing subsidiaries has closer (coordination-) links with their HQ. They cooperate more intensively, attend joint meetings more often and show a high level of ICT-integration. The multivariate model for the HQ-S governance shows a significant positive relationship between coordination mechanisms and performance. Agency mechanisms, such as strategic control, showed an indirect path to performance through a prospector strategy, and also through coordination. Operational control is indirectly related to performance through coordination mechanisms. In that sense coordination appears to be the central mediating variable in the association of control and performance.

The theoretical contributions

1. This thesis has integrated theoretical streams, which at first glance might look contradictory and mutually exclusive, in one comprehensive framework. Extensive effort has been put into developing a conceptual framework that integrates agency-, stewardship- and contingency-based insights in one overall model.
2. A second contribution is the fact that we applied insights with respect to HQ-S governance to subsidiaries located in transition markets in one of the former planned economies of Central Eastern Europe.
3. We combined data from the local subsidiaries' level with the data from headquarters. Such an approach, although challenging in implementation, is in our view more beneficial than building conclusions on one side of the relationship only, as has been done in earlier studies, e.g. by Harzing (1999).
4. Our methodological contribution refers to the application of the partial least squares technique (PLS). By using PLS we avoided distributional problems of the variables in the sample. Our research has proven that PLS is especially suitable for structural equation modelling with small samples.

Managerial implications

First, choose the entry mode carefully. Our data suggest that for a transition type of economy, Greenfield investment may be the most beneficiary entry mode.

Second, especially during the post-entry period, building a well-functioning strategic and operational control platform for the subsidiary is essential.

Third, build a coordination system on this control platform for the flexibility and agility needed in uncertain and constrained transition-type of environments.

Fourth, use ICT tools not only for fast information exchange but also to bridge the cultural distance and to create transparency of operations.

Fifth, a prospector strategy, exploring new products, operations and markets is clearly a successful strategy for entering transition economies.

Finally, start with expatriates to build a sound control platform but quickly switch to subsidiary's home-countries CEOs to create coordination systems that ensure flexibility and agility of operations.

Our explorative empirical research has shown that the road from governance to performance is not a one-way street, but alternative routes are available which accelerate performance more than sticking to past-made agency-based choices. Our research has shown that there is no simple and uniform recipe for managing subsidiaries, especially if the environmental change is strong. Under such circumstances, it is advisable to create flexibility and learning capabilities at the subsidiary level, rather than maintaining a subsidiary in a state of dependence.

We hope that this thesis has provided the insights and instruments needed not just to maintain static fit but to arrive at a dynamic fit between headquarters and subsidiary, which is essential for lasting success in dynamic transition environments.

Samenvatting (Nederlands)

Sinds de uitbreiding van de Europese Unie met landen uit Oost Europa is het aantrekkelijker geworden om te investeren in landen zoals Polen, Hongarije, Slovenië en Tsjechië. Nieuwe consumentenmarkten, goedkope arbeid, de beschikbaarheid van grondstoffen en een gunstige geografische ligging zijn stimulerende factoren die multinationals aanzetten in Centraal Europese transitie landen te investeren. Aan deze expansie is echter ook een besturingsprobleem verbonden, niet in de laatste plaats vanwege de culturele afstand tussen westerse landen en landen uit Centraal Europa. Met besturing bedoelen we de beschikbaarheid en inzet van instrumenten om dochterondernemingen binnen de grenzen van de strategie te houden. Besturingsinstrumenten worden onder meer toegepast in de relatie tussen hoofdkantoor (headquarters, HQ) en deelnemingen of dochterondernemingen (subsidiary, S). Tot nu toe is het meeste onderzoek verricht naar de modus die voor de investering in het buitenland wordt gekozen ('entry mode choice'); terwijl slechts beperkt onderzoek is gepleegd naar het daarmee verbonden besturingsprobleem.

Onderzoeksvragen

Dit onderzoek stelt de besturing van de relatie tussen HQ en S in Centraal Europa centraal, in het bijzonder de relatie tussen de Poolse S en het internationale HQ. Beheersing (control) en afstemming (coordination) worden beschouwd als de centrale elementen van het besturingsconcept. Het eerste hangt sterk samen met de regelgeving en uitoefening van macht (principal-agent relatie), het tweede met gelijkwaardig partnerschap, inspraak en onderlinge afstemming (stewardship relatie). Het probleem is om een balans te vinden tussen het verlenen van bevoegdheden aan een S aan de ene kant en het beheersen van de acties van die S aan de andere. De volgende onderzoeksvragen werden geformuleerd:

1. *Hoe zijn de verschillende besturingsmechanismen in de relatie tussen HQ en Poolse S te karakteriseren?*

2. *Wat is de invloed van de Poolse bedrijfsomgeving op de besturing van de relatie tussen HQ en S?*

De manier waarop bedrijven met hun omgeving interacteren is onderdeel van hun strategie. We onderscheiden een 'global strategy' (een uniforme benadering van externe markten), een 'multi-domestic strategy' (volledige aanpassing aan de locale markten) en een 'transnational strategy' (heeft kenmerken van beide). De derde onderzoeksvraag luidt daarom:

3. *Wat is de invloed van de gekozen strategie (generic en international: global, multidomestic, transnational) op de besturing van de HQ-S relatie?*

En ten slotte:

4. *Wat is de invloed van de factoren die de besturing van dochteronderneming (S) bepalen op de bedrijfsprestatie?*

Theoretische onderbouwing

De theoretische basis voor dit onderzoek wordt gevormd door drie theorieën: de 'principal-agent', de 'stewardship', en de 'contingency' theorieën. De contingency theorie bindt de besluitvorming met betrekking tot de HQ-S relatie aan een aantal (beperkende) factoren: namelijk de grootte van de organisatie, de manier waarop deze zich aan de omgeving aanpast, de beschikbare middelen en procedures, de management beslissingen en opvattingen over ondergeschikten, de strategie en de beschikbare technologie(ën). Dergelijke contingencies vragen flexibiliteit in de relatie tussen HQ en S. Het onderzoeksraamwerk ziet er in dit boek als volgt uit:

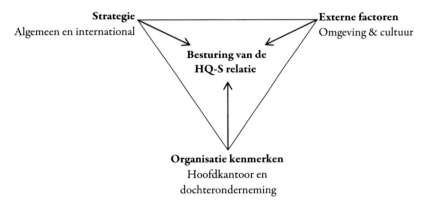

Figuur 1. Onderzoeksraamwerk.

Zoals gesteld is het onderzoeksobject de relatie, als gevolg van internationale investerings-stromen, tussen het hoofdkantoor en de vestiging in Polen. Dit proefschrift belicht de verschillende investeringsmodaliteiten alsmede hun voor en nadelen in hoofdstuk 2. Geconcludeerd is dat investeren in Polen aantrekkelijk is, mits het managementprobleem wordt opgelost. Investeringen in Polen kunnen het karakter hebben van minderheids- of meerderheidsdeelneming, van een 'Greenfield'-investering (d.w.z. het opzetten van een geheel nieuwe onderneming), of een acquisitie. Vervolgens is de omvang en de oorzaken van de verandering in omvang van investeringsstromen bestudeerd.

Hoofdstuk 3 is gewijd aan het verder uitbouwen van het theoretisch raamwerk. Dit gebeurt door een structuur en een processtroming in bestuursystemen te onderscheiden. Het processtroming heeft betrekking op beheersing mechanismen en wordt toegepast op de HQ-S relatie. In ons onderzoek, situeren we besturing ('governance') op een continuüm dat reikt van principal-agent (agency theory) aan de ene kant, tot steward (stewardship theory) aan de andere kant. Besturing definiëren we als het proces dat als doel heeft het afstemmen van de doelstellingen van HQ en S en dat tevens richting geeft aan het opereren van vestigingen van multinationals, waarbij de terugkoppeling van de vestiging wordt ondersteund door middel van (ICT- gebaseerde) informatiestromen gekoppeld aan persoonlijke interactie. De agency-benadering gaat uit van divergente doelstellingen en hanteert beheersinstrumenten zoals monitoring, beloningen en beperkingen van gedragsalternatieven. De stewardship-benadering, daarentegen, is geënt op wederzijds afstemming, vertrouwen en gelijkwaardigheid in de relatie. De plaats op het continuüm waar het besturingssysteem van een multinational terecht komt, hangt af van contingency factoren, zoals grootte, omgevingsvariabelen, cultuur en strategie. Met betrekking tot de omgeving worden de vijandigheid van de omgeving, de dynamiek en de complexiteit in de beschouwing betrokken. Culturele verschillen tussen de HQ en S landen worden betrokken aan de hand van Hofstede's (2001) classificatie. Ten aanzien van de generieke strategie die het hoofdkantoor hanteert, wordt de classificatie van Miles & Snow (1978) gehanteerd. Deze auteurs maken een onderscheid in prospectors, defenders, analyzers en reactors. Tenslotte wordt de classificatie van Harzing (1999) gebruikt om de multinationale strategie te karakteriseren: zoals reeds aangeduid, wordt er onderscheid gemaakt in een 'global', 'multi-domestic' en een 'transnational strategie'.

In hoofdstuk 4 de volgende proposities werden geformuleerd en de operationalisatie van concepten is gepresenteerd:
1. In turbulente omgevingen zullen besturingsmechanismen die gebaseerd zijn op coördinatie (afstemming en persoonlijke contacten), positief samenhangen met de bedrijfsprestatie.
2. Als de culturele verschillen groot zijn zullen de besturingsmechanismen die gebaseerd zijn op beheersing (strategisch en operationeel), positief samenhangen met de bedrijfsprestatie.
3. In vestigingen die een prospectorstrategie volgen, zullen de besturingsmechanismen die voornamelijk zijn gebaseerd op coördinatie (in termen van afstemming en persoonlijke contacten) positief samenhangen met de bedrijfsprestatie.
4. In vestigingen die een 'global' strategie volgen, zullen de besturingsmechanismen die voornamelijk berusten op beheersing (strategisch en operationeel) positief samenhangen met de bedrijfsprestatie.
4a. In vestigingen die een 'transnational' strategie volgen, zullen de besturingsmechanismen die voornamelijk gebaseerd zijn op coördinatie (in termen van afstemming en persoonlijke contacten) positief samenhangen met de bedrijfsprestatie.

Onderzoeksopzet

Nadat we het theoretische raamwerk verder hebben uitgebouwd, zijn de data verzameld door middel van een gestructureerde vragenlijsten bij productie bedrijven, dochterondernemingen (S) in Polen. De empirische data zijn aangevuld met de interviews met managers van de hoofdkantoren van Franse en Nederlandse multinationals met vestigingen in Polen.

In 2004 werden in 76 vragenlijsten ontvangen van productievestigingen in Polen. De vragenlijsten bevatte de volgende onderwerpen: algemene informatie over dochteronderneming en het hoofdkantoor, soort en tijdstip van de investering, aard en intensiteit van besturing ('control'), aard en intensiteit van coördinatie, en de bedrijfsprestatie. Bovendien werd er geïnformeerd naar de nationaliteit van de directeur and van de managers verantwoordelijk voor prestaties van de dochteronderneming.

Ontbrekende gegevens in de vragenlijsten werden ingevuld door middel van een EM-algoritme. Vervolgens werden de data geanalyseerd. De belangrijkste technieken die hierbij werden toegepast zijn: beschrijvende statistiek, correlatie-analyse, PLS-modellering en cluster-analyse.

Resultaten

Bij de analyse van de gegevens bleek, dat de vestigingen met een prospectorstrategie een minderheid vormden, maar wel het beste presteerden. Innovaties in het productie proces bleken positief samen te hangen met de aard van de internationale strategie. Naast de aard en locatie van de betreffende hoofdkantoren, leverde de data gegevens op over buitenlandse directeuren. Het aantal directeuren met een niet-Poolse nationaliteit ('expatriates') bleek laag te zijn. Ze bleken een ingewikkelde positie in te nemen om de band met het hoofdkantoor tevreden houden tegelijkertijd en een cultureel afwijkende vestiging te moeten besturen. Ons onderzoek bevestigt de vraagtekens die in toenemende mate worden gezet bij het uitzenden van directeuren vanuit het hoofdkantoor (expatriates). De resultaten tonen een grotere mate van operationele, dan strategische beheersing aan. Dit komt onder meer tot uitdrukking in de grote mate van standaardisatie van procedures die multinationals toepassen. Ten aanzien van de onderlinge afstemming bleek dat operationele zaken meer worden afgestemd dan strategische. Persoonlijke contacten vinden voornamelijk op top-management niveau plaats. Persoonlijke contacten op andere management niveaus hebben een lage frequentie, mede vanwege de sterke ICT-integratie met het hoofdkantoor. De respondenten ervaren hun omgeving als dynamisch en competitief, met een instabiel aanbod van geschoold personeel en een instabiliteit in het aanleveren van grondstoffen. De directeuren van prospector dochterondernemingen hebben de bedrijfsprestatie in het algemeen positief beoordeeld.

De belangrijkste verbanden die zijn voortgekomen uit het PLS-onderzoek staan vermeld in Figuur 2.

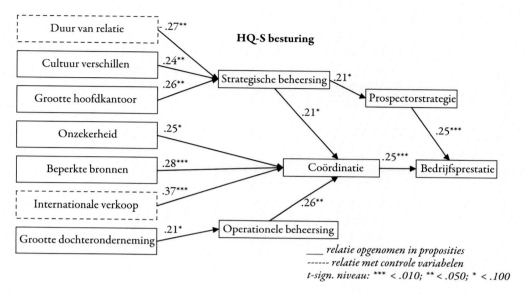

Figuur 2. PLS-resultaten.

Het onderzoek toont aan:

- Omgevingsfactoren zoals onzekerheid en beperkte bronnen (arbeid en grondstoffen) zijn positief gerelateerd met coördinatie met de hoofdkantoor.
- De internationale verkoop van producten is in sterke mate gerelateerd aan coördinatie dat is HQ-S afstemming en persoonlijke contacten.
- Cultuur verschillen tussen HQ en S landen hebben betrekking tot strategische beheersing.
- De grootte van hoofdkantoor (HQ) is positief gerelateerd aan strategische beheersing.
- De tijdsduur van de relatie HQ-S is negatief gerelateerd aan strategische beheersing.
- De grootte van dochteronderneming is positief gerelateerd aan operationele beheersing.
- Een prospectorstrategie in het algemeen is positief gerelateerd met bedrijfsprestatie.
- Strategische beheersing ligt aan de basis van een prospectorstrategie.
- Beheersing (strategisch en operationeel) is via coördinatie gerelateerd met de betere bedrijfsprestatie.

De interviews met de managers van hoofdkantoren, bevestigen bovenstaande beeld en bovendien tonen beperkte rol van het gebruik van hoofdkantoor expatriates in HQ-S besturing. Expatriates zijn belangrijk in opstartfase van een buitenlandse vestiging maar hun positieve bijdrage neemt af met een duur van de HQ-S relatie.

Discussie en conclusies

Ten aanzien van de onderzoeksvraag 1: *Hoe zijn de verschillende besturingsmechanismen in de relatie tussen HQ en Poolse S te karakteriseren,* heeft ons onderzoek aangetoond (1), dat beide typen besturingsmechanismen – 'strategic and operational control' en 'coordination' complementair zijn en in samenhang met elkaar voorkomen. Een zeer interessante vinding is dat 'control' de regels van de samenwerking tussen HQ en S bepaald en daarmee een platform creëert waarop meer geavanceerde interactie kan zich ontwikkelen – 'coordination' met afstemming en persoonlijke contacten.

In het antwoord op onderzoeksvraag 2. *Wat is de invloed van de Poolse bedrijfsomgeving op de besturing van de relatie tussen HQ en S*, kunnen wij op basis van de PLS-modellering concluderen dat de transitie omgeving zoals in Polen, een belangrijke bepalende factor is voor de HQ-S besturing mechanismen.

Ten aanzien van propositie 1. *In turbulente omgevingen zullen besturingsmechanismen die gebaseerd zijn op coördinatie (afstemming en persoonlijke contacten), positief samenhangen met de bedrijfsprestatie,* kan worden gesteld, dat grote turbulentie in de transitie omgeving de ontwikkeling van 'stewardship' mechanismen voortbrengt, en indirect een positief effect heeft op de bedrijfsprestatie. In tegenstelling tot wat we vooraf verwachtten heeft het onderzoek geen relatie kunnen leggen tussen de omgevingsdynamiek en HQ-S besturingsmechanismen. Wel constateerden we een positieve significante relatie tussen schaarste in de omgeving en coördinatie mechanismen. De verklaring is dat het netwerk van de moedermaatschappij kan bijdragen aan het verminderen van een dergelijke schaarste door bv. het organisatie van de aanvoer van de grondstoffen of integratie van leveranciers.

Propositie 2, *Als de culturele verschillen groot zijn zullen de besturingsmechanismen die gebaseerd zijn op beheersing (strategisch en operationeel), positief samenhangen met de bedrijfsprestatie,* kunnen we concluderen dat de culturele afstand toonde in ons model toonde positieve relatie aan tussen culturele afstand en strategische beheersing, maar geen relatie met operationele beheersing. Het belangrijk dat de algemene (strategische) regels van de samenwerking tussen HQ en S duidelijk gesteld en geïmplementeerd worden als de culturele verschillen groot zijn tussen de HQ en S landen. Op de operationele beheersing speelt daarin geen significante rol.

In antwoord op derde onderzoeksvraag: *Wat is de invloed van de gekozen strategie (generic en international: global, multidomestic, transnational) op de besturing van de HQ-S relatie,* kunnen we in het algemeen concluderen dat strategie geen invloed heeft op de HQ-S besturing mechanismen. Met betrekking tot het verband tussen generieke strategie en beheersingsmechanismen, Propositie 3, *In vestigingen die een prospectorstrategie volgen, zullen de besturingsmechanismen die voornamelijk zijn gebaseerd op coördinatie (in termen van afstemming en persoonlijke contacten) positief samenhangen met de bedrijfsprestatie,* is er geen significant verband aangetoond tussen het al dan niet uitvoeren van prospectorstrategie en een bepaald coördinatiemechanismen. Ook de relaties tussen international strategie en HQ-S besturingsmechanismen voorgesteld in Proposities 4 en 4a, *In vestigingen die een 'global' strategie volgen, zullen de besturingsmechanismen die voornamelijk berusten op beheersing (strategisch en operationeel) positief samenhangen met de bedrijfsprestatie* en *In vestigingen die een 'transnational' strategie volgen, zullen de besturingsmechanismen die voornamelijk gebaseerd zijn op coördinatie (in termen van afstemming en persoonlijke contacten) positief samenhangen met de bedrijfsprestatie* werden in ons onderzoek ook niet bevestigd.

Uit de resultaten van de clusteranalyse en clustervergelijking zijn er significante verschillen tussen de drie internationale strategieën voortgekomen: dochterondernemingen in de transnational cluster voeren uit prospectorstrategie en hebben een grotere autonomie in besluitvorming met een lage formalisatie niveau. Ook is uit de resultaten van de cluster analyse gebleken dat er geen multidomestic strategie in zijn zuivere vorm voorkomt in dochterondernemingen in Polen. Het cluster dat we hebben kunnen onderscheiden (naast het 'global' en het 'transnational', overigens) kan het beste gekarakteriseerd worden als een 'multidomestic-transitional' en had veel hogere international verkoop van goederen dan zou verwacht kunnen worden in de zuivere multidomestic strategie.

Ten aanzien van de controlevariabelen bleek de grootte van de bedrijf positief samen te hangen met de inzet van beheersingsinstrumenten. Een sterke internationale activiteit van de dochteronderneming bleek direct samen te hangen met meer intensieve coördinatie, en indirect met de bedrijfsprestatie. Internationale verkopen hangen positief samen met een globale strategie en negatief met een multidomestic strategie. De significante relaties met performance, zoals geformuleerd in onderzoeksvraag 4 – *Wat is de invloed van de factoren die de besturing van dochteronderneming (S) bepalen op de bedrijfsprestatie*, hebben betrekking op de relaties tussen omgevingsfactoren, controle variabelen en zijn opgenomen in alle onze proposities. De significante verbanden in het model zijn afgebeeld in Figuur 2.

De theoretische bijdragen van ons onderzoek zijn: de integratie van – eerst – contradictoire theoretische stromingen; agency en stewardship theorieën, de studie van HQ-S relaties in economieën in transitie, gecombineerde dataverzameling op dochteronderneming en hoofdkantoorniveau, en de toepassing van het relatief onbekende partial least squares (PLS) modellering binnen de management wetenschappen.

Vervolgonderzoek kan zich kunnen concentreren op het longitudinale aspect in de HQ-S relatie, het effect van (regionale) culturele verschillen, de veralgemening van het onderzoek door andere landen in de beschouwing te betrekken, en het in het onderzoek betrekken van een vestiging met bijbehorend hoofdkantoor. In ons onderzoek kwamen de vestigingen en hoofdkantoren vanuit verschillende bedrijfstakken, hetgeen minder zeggingskracht heeft.

Aanbevelingen voor het management

Aan de hand van de resultaten van ons onderzoek kunnen we volgende aanbevelingen voor het management van nieuwe opgerichte buitenlandse vestigingen in transitie landen formuleren:

- Kies de wijze van toetreding met zorg; in het algemeen lijkt een 'Greenfield'-investering effectiever te zijn dan een acquisitie in een transitie omgeving zoals in Polen.
- Na een vestiging van een dochteronderneming (S) is het zorgvuldig opbouwen van een systeem van strategische en operationele bedrijfsbeheersing van doorslaggevend belang.
- Bouw een platvorm voor coördinatie en bedrijfsbeheersing (control); coördinatie is de sleutel tot succes, maar dit om transparantie te creëren vereist het opzetten van een goede beheersingsplatform (control).
- Gebruik ICT voor het overbruggen van culturele afstand.
- Een prospector strategie lijkt meer succesvol dan een defender strategie om een markt in een transitie omgeving te betreden.

Tenslotte: het bereiken van afstemming is geen statisch maar een dynamisch proces, dat continue aandacht van het management van multinationals behoeft.

About the author

Joanna (08.07.1975, Poznan, Poland) studied Business Administration at the Institute of Law and Business Administration at Adam Mickiewicz University Poznań, Poland. She graduated in 1999 with an MSc thesis entitled: 'Cultural Constraints in Management Theories'.

In 2001, having worked for a few years in management positions, she entered a Ph.D research program at Management Studies group of Wageningen Unversity. During her Ph.D. research, Joanna gave lectures in Wageningen MSc program, in a course 'Innovation in the international markets' and in international MBA programs in Wageningen and in Prague. She supervised several MSc theses on the management control and governance aspects in multinational enterprises.

At Wageningen University, Joanna coordinated the development of International MBA and chaired the Ph.D. Council at Mansholt Graduate School for Social Sciences at Wageningen University for two years.

Since February 2007, Joanna is an assistant professor at the Department of Accounting at the Faculty of Economics and Business, University of Groningen. Her research program focuses on international intra-firm and inter-firm relationships.

List of publications

Bremmers, H. and **J. Guść** (2002). Entrance strategies Eastern Europe: a chain management approach. 5th International Conference on Chain and Network Management in Agribusiness and the Food Industry. Paradoxes in Food Chains and Networks, Noordwijk, The Netherlands.

Guść, J., H.J. Bremmers, J. Zuraw. (2003). Strategy and culture in international co-ordination mechanisms. Vienna, Austria.

Guść, J. and S. Jarka (2004). Rola Inicjatyw Gospodarczych w Upowszechnianiu Wiedzy i Doradztwa (Farmers' Entrepreneurship in Knowledge Transfer), Krakow, Poland.

Guść, J., H. J. Bremmers, S.W.F Omta (2005). Comparison of Management Control Systems in new entries in the emerging markets of Asia and Central Eastern Europe. Proceedings of International Trade and Logistics, Corporate Strategies and the Global Economy Conference, Le Havre, France.

Guść, J., H. J. Bremmers, S.W.F. Omta. (2005). Management Control Systems in new entries in the emerging market of Central Eastern Europe. Journal of Comparative International Management 8(2): 57-77.

Complete training and supervision plan

J.S. Hendriks-Guść

of Social Sciences
MANSHOLT GRADUATE SCHOOL

Description	Institute / Department	Year	ECTS*
Courses:			
Mansholt Introduction course	Mansholt Graduate School of Social Sciences (MG3S)	2001	1
Writing and presenting a Scientific Paper	MG3S	2001	1.4
Social Science Research Methods	MG3S	2001	1.4
Methodology of Research and Design	NOBEM Netherlands Organisation for Research in Business Economics & Management	2002	7
Case Research Methodology	Groningen University	2002	1.8
English for Ph.D.'s	CENTA Wageningen	2003	2.2
Behavioural Economics	MG3S	2003	4.2
Intercultural Business Management in Central and Eastern Europe	IDM and Vienna University	2003	2.8
Authorware Computerised Data	MG3S	2003	0.7
New Institutional Economics: Property Rights, Contracts and Transaction Costs	MG3S	2004	2.8
Quantitative Methods of Data Analyses	NOBEM	2005	7
Career Perspectives	Wageningen Graduate Schools	2005	1.5
Presentations at conferences and workshops:			**3**
Mansholt Multidisciplinary seminar – 2nd Mansholt PhD Day Wageningen 2005		2005	1
Supply Chain Conference, Noordwijk aan Zee		2002	1
International Conference of Business, Economics and Management Disciplines, New Brunswick Canada		2005	1
Total (minimum 30 ECTS)			**36.8**

Printed in the United States
by Baker & Taylor Publisher Services